Ma, I'm Gettin Meself a New Mammy

Ma, I'm Gettin Meself a New Mammy

The heartbreaking true story of a little girl
who just wanted to be loved

MARTHA LONG

**MAINSTREAM
PUBLISHING**

EDINBURGH AND LONDON

This edition, 2009

First published in Great Britain in 2008 by
MAINSTREAM PUBLISHING COMPANY
(EDINBURGH) LTD
7 Albany Street
Edinburgh EH1 3UG

ISBN 9781845964443

This book is a work of non-fiction based on the life, experiences and
recollections of the author. In some cases, names of people, places,
dates, sequences or the detail of events have been changed to protect
the privacy of others. The author has stated to the publishers that,
except in such respects, not affecting the substantial accuracy of
the work, the contents of this book are true

A catalogue record for this book is available
from the British Library

Typeset in Caslon and Granjon

Printed in Great Britain by
CPI Cox and Wyman, Reading, Berkshire RG1 8EX

As always, to my children, Tina, Fabian and MarieClaire.
Just being your mother has been my greatest achievement.
All else pales into dust.

To the memory of the girls who shared the last days of my
childhood. Though it was brief, and gave me a glimpse of being
a child, even as it vanished, I still treasure it. There is, in a little
corner of my heart specially reserved, a place where you sit, and in
my mind's eye you will always be young.

To Sister Eleanor,
I salute you for your goodness.

To Mary Dunne, my friend.
Thank you, Mary, for your friendship.

To Gerry (Ger) Keegan and Seamus (Shea) Reid, the last of
the great Irish wits. Thanks, fellas, for all the laughs.

ACKNOWLEDGEMENTS

I was bemused and overwhelmed by the amount of goodness, love and well wishes from readers of my first book. I simply shared my childhood, for those of you who knew what life was like back then, to be poor, or a bastard. So you could give voice like me to your children and say, 'This was me. I was like that little child.'

Not many of us learned to read and write. So we could not tell it in our own words on paper. I had taught myself to read and write, and had a natural love of books, so without knowing, the document I wrote intended for my children when I am gone, became, after some time, a realisation that it is the property of the many, many millions of you all spread out across the world who once shared the 'Little Martha's' history. And for those of you who did not know, now you have some insight. So now, my way of saying thank you for all your warm loving wishes is to continue my story.

A special word of thanks to Bill, my publisher, he is only one of a kind.

My editor – who had the misfortune of having me thrust on her! – she is a master of her craft.

PART I

*

CHAPTER I

I sat starin at me hands sittin in me lap, thinkin about nothin. The Maria rocked along the road, movin over the bumps bouncin us against each other, our heads rockin wit it, gently noddin left te right. Then we lifted, goin up inta the air, an me belly jerked an sank goin over a hill. We couldn't see out, but I felt the distance an was lost inside meself listenin te the hum of the engine.

We were all very quiet, nobody movin. I listened te someone shudder in a big breath, then hold it an let it out through his nose, an felt him shiftin, rockin himself backwards an forwards then droppin his shoulders an squeezin his hands together, pushin them inta his lap. Me head was lyin in his direction an me eyes half opened, an I knew he was feelin the same as me. More afraid than I ever felt in me life. Them poor young fellas will get it worse than me. Stuck miles away in the arsehole of nowhere an the brothers killin them night an day, cos that's wha Jackser always said they did te him. An their mammies won't be able te come down an see them.

I dropped me shoulders, lettin out me breath, an closed me eyes again, thinkin nothin lasts for ever an this will come te an end, too. I just have te be patient. It can't be any worse than bein wit tha bandy aul bastard. No! Only bein locked up is the worry.

The Maria suddenly slowed down then swung inta a bend an kept movin slowly. The detective let out a big sigh an stirred himself, half standin up. I lifted me head, comin te me senses, wonderin wha was goin te happen.

'First drop off, Mick!' the detective muttered te the policeman, then rubbed his nose an shoved his finger up, twistin it an pulled it out, lookin te see wha he had on his finger. An rolled it up, flingin it at the door. Me stomach was turnin, but now I felt sick watchin him. The Maria stopped an the detective made fer the door, waitin fer it te open.

'OK! First dispatch!' an aul fella roared happily, swingin the door open an scratchin his arse an hikin up his trousers, then tryin te button the jacket of his policeman's uniform. It wouldn't close cos his belly was too fat an the trousers was halfway up his legs.

'Right! That's you, Long!' the detective roared te me, jumpin down an snappin his fingers at me. I leapt up wit the fright an jumped down after him without thinkin, landin on the ground next te him an looked back at the others all leanin out te get a look at me, but not movin too much in case the aul fellas roared at them. I looked at the little fella, his legs shakin like mad an rockin himself backwards an forwards tryin te ease his worry, wit his hands jammed between his knees. They all stared at me, wit the fear of God in them, an their eyes gaped outa their skulls, an I could see they were wonderin how I was takin it, an Emmet's mouth was clamped shut hangin aroun his jaw lookin like he wanted te cry. I looked back at the little fella, an he was keenin in a quiet whisper. Then his head turned, an his eyes locked on me. Fer a split second we stared at each other, like he wanted me te help him.

I stared at the red rims aroun his eyes sittin inside his grey little face. He's only eight! Tha's wha his granny screamed when she tried te hide him in her shawl, te stop the policemen gettin their hands on him. I suddenly wanted te grab him an say, 'Run!' Gettin them all runnin in different directions, an him an me can run like hell an make our escape. I'll bring him back te his granny, an rush off te catch the ship te England. I could sneak on, takin meself off te London, where I could get lost in the crowd an keep me head down. I wouldn't be stupid enough te get meself caught this time, because this is different. I know me way there, an nobody would ever find me again. I could eat meself aroun the supermarkets – they have them there, too! Then find somewhere safe te sleep. I could wait until I'm big enough te get meself started an find a job, an nobody would ever be able te touch me again. I'd be me own person. Oh, dear God! If only.

'Get a move on, Long!'

I came te me senses, lookin up te see the detective takin a big gollop of phlegm an sendin it flyin in the air, te land in the grass over be the black iron fence.

'Come on!' he roared, throwin his big head at me then aimin it at the convent. 'Move yourself! We haven't all day for the love a God!' Then he spat again. The veins stuck out on his big red neck an his eyes bulged wit annoyance, fixin them on me, cos I was standin still lost inside meself, an waitin fer him te finish wha he was doin. He bounced over te grab me an held on te me tight, wit his hand under me arm as if he could read wha I was thinkin, an headed me over te high steps leadin up te a big green door. Then he let me go an rushed himself up ahead, ringin the doorbell.

I looked aroun at the size of the place. The convent was huge, an I looked back at the avenue. It was dark wit trees leanin over it, an it went fer miles, an there was a long black iron fence on the other side wit cows an horses munchin on grass, an a donkey. It spotted us an started roarin its head off an came flyin from miles down the end of the field up te see wha's goin on. I watched him gettin closer, wit his mouth wide open an his lip curlin up under his nose showin his big white teeth lookin like he was laughin. An screamin, 'He haw, he haw.' Like his chest was tryin te get breath an he had the whoopin cough, only without the cough. Jaysus! I wish I was him. I'd have nothin te worry me, but munch grass all day long an keep a look out fer someone te come along an maybe give me a pat on the head.

I looked over at the big statue of the Sacred Heart, wit his arms outstretched, an his heart bleedin in the middle of his chest,

implorin everyone te see it was bleedin fer the love of us. Tha
statue's like the one in Hairy's convent. This place even looks a
bit like tha convent. I shivered, listenin te the silence all aroun
me. There's nothin but miles an miles a fields, wit sheep on the
other side, very far away inta the distance. Even the donkey was
quiet now, he just rambled off back down the fields, gettin fed
up waitin fer someone te talk te him.

The door opened an I whipped me head aroun, lookin up inta
the face of a long skinny nun starin from me te the detective.

'Eh, ahem, Mother! This is the child, Martha Long,' he said,
lookin at the front of a bunch of papers he had in his hand,
then slowly handin them te the nun. 'She's been sent from the
Children's Court, Dublin Castle,' he said, seein the nun lookin
confused.

'Really! Is that right now?' she said, lookin at him very annoyed,
then starin down at me, lookin like she was tryin te make me
out.

'Yes. You have all the papers there,' he said, turnin aroun an
pushin me in the door, an tryin te make his escape down the
steps.

'One moment, please, Detective . . .'

'Shoe,' he said, smilin, hopin she'd get a move on an let him
get out of here.

'I would like a word with you, please, if I may.'

I stood just inside the door, wonderin wha's happenin. He came
flyin back up the steps an pushed me further inta the hall.

'Would you please wait inside here,' she said te me, puttin one
long bony finger on me shoulder an steerin me inta a big room,
then closin the door behind me.

I stood next te a big white marble fireplace wit a big black-
an-white holy picture of men holdin Jesus lyin dead in their
arms an lookin shocked, an some of them were cryin. Then
me eyes whipped aroun the room, takin in the long mahogany
table lined wit chairs, an a big silver tray wit a silver teapot an
other silver things fer milk an sugar sittin in the middle of the

table. I looked over at the big windas goin down te the floor, an I could see the cows an the donkey far away in the fields, munchin away te their hearts' content in peace an quiet. An I felt me heart droppin down inta me belly, an I wanted te cry. It feels like I'm suffocatin, locked up here! Jesus! Jesus! Will I ever be free? Please make the time go fast so tha I can get outa here, an wander where I like, an never be in trouble again, an have no one te bother me. I heard their voices gettin louder, an I moved a little over te the door te hear wha's goin on.

'No! That is not good enough,' the nun's voice said, still in a whisper, but I could hear she was annoyed. I heard him mutterin somethin back, an she said, 'Well! We shall have to see about that.' Then the front door opened an slammed shut again. I rushed back te the fireplace.

'So!' she said, comin in the door an shuttin it behind her. 'You have been sent to us!'

I looked up at her, me eyes flippin past her face with the big brown hairy mole, down te the toes of her shoes. Tha's all ye could see under the long black habit. I lifted me head, landin back on her face again, an we stared at each other. Her big grey goitre eyes glittered back at me through huge milk-bottle eyeglasses, lookin like she wanted te kill me. I stared at them, wonderin why she was annoyed. I'm the one tha should be annoyed! Wha has she got te complain about?

She lifted her chin, wrigglin her neck tryin te ease the tight linen collar wrapped aroun it, an jerked her head, flickin her veil aroun her shoulder like she thought she had long hair, an stretched herself up, makin herself look even taller, then crossed her arms, hidin them under her cloak, an looked down at me, sayin, 'We were not asked to take you, you know! Do you know that?' she barked at me, lookin shocked.

I still said nothin, tryin te make out wha she was talkin about.

'We do not take your sort here, do you know that? This is not the place for you!' She stared at me, lookin like she hoped I would come up wit an answer. But I just stared back, not knowin wha she was talkin about. Then she let her breath out through her nose an leaned her head towards me. 'Do you have your monthlies?' she suddenly whispered, waitin fer me answer.

'Eh! Wha monthlies is tha, Sister?'

'Your periods!'

'Wha periods would tha be, Sister?' I felt really stupid, not knowin a word of wha she was talkin about.

'Mother! You call me Reverend Mother,' she roared in a whisper, gettin very annoyed wit me. 'I am in charge here. I am Mother Mary Immaculate! Do you understand that?' She leaned her head down te me, lookin like she was tryin te figure me out. 'Are you slow?' she asked me, lookin even more confused.

I stared back, gettin more confused meself be the minute.

'Really! This is outrageous!' she said, straightenin herself up again, her head swingin aroun talkin te the walls. 'Are you retarded?' she shouted, lookin at me again, gettin all red in her long skinny face.

I knew wha tha word meant, an I felt meself gettin hot in me belly. The bleedin cheek a her!

'No, Sister, there's nothin wrong wit me head. I'm not backwards, is tha wha ye mean?' I asked her, tightenin me mouth an darin her.

She clamped her lips together an gave her veil another flip wit the back of her hand an said, 'Mother! Have you forgotten already what I just told you? Really! This is preposterous! I am not accepting this!' Then she took another big sigh, sayin, 'I am not sure where to send you. Whether you are menstruating or not, I think perhaps you might be better with the big girls. I won't put you in with the middle group; you might prove to be a bad influence on them. Stay here, I shall be back in a moment,' an she flew out the door, leavin me thinkin about the word monthlies, an periods, an other big words.

I wonder wha she's talkin about? Does she mean the monthly *Sacred Heart Messenger*? Is she wonderin if I'm holy? I read tha sometimes in the church. People tellin about gettin their special intentions answered when they prayed hard te the Sacred Heart! An others askin ye te pray fer them te get over a sickness, or someone short of money an they are maybe goin te lose their home. Yeah! I like churches. When I'm passin one, an if I have the time, I like te go in an sit down in the peace an quiet, an look aroun at all the statues an candles an talk te God up on the altar in the tabernacle. It always reminds me of when I was little, an it was just me an the ma, an she'd take me in te say a few prayers an light a penny candle if she had the money.

I stared at the floor, seein the picture of me an the ma together, rememberin the peace, an me mind flew back down all them days. Down, down I toppled, then lit on me ma's happy laughin face. Me chest started jumpin an me belly wobbled, an I felt me heart break an suddenly a hot gush a tears erupted down me face. Ma! Mammy, where are ye? I want them times te come back; I want ye when you were me old mammy, an it was just you an me, an then Charlie. All we had te worry about was gettin a place te stay an somethin te eat, but I wasn't afraid then, an ye used te laugh, an talk te me, an take me te the pictures when we got the money. 'I'm lost, Ma! I don't feel big any more,' I whispered, lookin aroun the big strange room, not seein it cos me eyes are all fogged up. I feel like a babby, an I'm lost, cos I'm on me own an I don't have her an Charlie any more. I felt the tears streamin down me face an I wiped them away wit the back of me hand. I'm not lettin tha nun see me cry. She's gettin nothin outa me. Anyway, there's no use in cryin. Them times is gone for ever, an they went a long time ago. Then I started te feel very old. Yeah! I have only meself te look out fer now, an her an tha Jackser fella is gone for ever, too, so tha's somethin te be grateful for, an I won't feel the time passin in this place; soon I'll be sixteen, an I'll walk out them gates an never look back. I'll bury everythin an everyone tha ever had anythin te do wit me, an start me own life. Yeah! Tha's wha I'll do.

I lifted me head, shakin me shoulders, lookin around the room, an took in a big sigh, lettin me breath outa me chest, feelin a bit easier in meself. Yeah! Things are never really tha bad, it just depends on how I'm lookin at them. Me mind wandered back te the skinny aul nun. Yeah, maybe tha's wha she's talkin about, the holy little books in the chapel. Nuns are always tellin ye te pray an read them things. But wha has tha got te do wit me comin here? 'Ah, fuck her,' I whispered, gettin back te meself. I'm not botherin me head about wha she thinks; let her do wha she likes.

I stared down at the silver things sittin on the table an wandered down te get a better look. Gawd! Them nuns sure know how te look after themself wit their eatin off silver. I lifted the lid off the teapot just as the door whipped open, an dropped it back down wit the almighty fright I got, an the skinny nun flew in wit a little red-faced nun trailin in behind her.

'How dare you touch those things!' she roared, snortin at me an whippin me outa the way te grab the tray offa the table. Then she lifted it up te examine it an make sure I hadn't done any damage or robbed somethin. She marched over te a sideboard an rested it down very gently an wiped away an imaginary bit a dust, treatin it like a newborn babby. 'Take her down to the institution, Sister Eleanor,' she said, wavin her arm at me then whippin aroun her veil, throwin her head from side te side like it was long hair an she was really beautiful altogether.

Jaysus, tha one really fancies herself no end, I thought, lookin aroun at the little nun.

'Yes, Mother,' the little nun said, goin even redder in the face an bendin down te me an takin me arm very gently an flyin me out the door.

CHAPTER 2

We flew inta the hall an through another door, the nun in an awful hurry. I looked up at wide stairs as the nun hurried me past, sayin through her breath, 'Come and see our lovely chapel, wouldn't you like that?' I wasn't bothered an said nothin as we turned left inta a big wide passage wit shiny brown tiles. Ye could see yer face in them.

'Now, pet! Come into our chapel and we will say a quick prayer,' she said, dippin her hand inta a holy water font an blessin herself an splashin it at me te bless me, too.

I was lookin up at the big long rope comin down from the ceilin. 'That is rung to call the nuns to prayers and announce the angelus,' she said, seein me lookin at it.

I'd love te have a go at ringin tha, I thought, lookin at it swingin in the air. She swung the door open inta the chapel an steered me in, collapsin herself onta her knees an bowin her head. I looked aroun at the chapel an it was very plain. I wondered wha she was makin all the fuss about; I've seen better. Then she stood up an breathed out again. 'Really, it is very beautiful, don't you think?' she said, bendin down te look at me.

I stared at the benches runnin the length of it, an the kneelers at the back wit priests' chairs behind them. The wooden floorboards were polished within an inch of their life, an the altar wit the marble floor was a bit smaller than normal churches. 'Yeah, it's lovely, Sister,' I croaked in a whisper.

She was delighted an gave me a big smile, noddin her head an squintin her eyes aroun like it was her very own palace an she built it all be herself. Gawd! It doesn't take much te make her happy, I thought, as she whipped me out the door an headed me down another passage.

'This is the convent passage,' she whispered. 'We have to be very quiet,' she said, puttin her finger to her lip. 'The children are not allowed up here,' she whispered very quietly, bendin down te me. 'We are passing the side of the chapel. So we must not make any noise,' she said, soundin like our life depended on it an waggin her finger at me.

We turned right onta another long passage. 'This is the sick bay,' she said, openin a door, an I followed her inta a room wit beds lined along the walls. 'The children come here when they are sick and need to see our doctor, Doctor Blightman.'

'Right!' I breathed, tryin te get me breath an take everythin in. I had a chance te count six beds before I was whipped out the door, an we were off, on the move again.

She pushed a door open an we were standin on a landin wit a long winda an a wide windasill. It was too high up te see out, an anyway, ye wouldn't be able te see out through it, cos the glass wasn't fer lookin through. I looked up the stairs wit another passage, an the stairs went fer miles up te more floors.

A door opened suddenly an I could hear a tilet flushin an a young one wit long white hair streamin down her back came rushin out. 'Sister Eleanor! Sister Eleanor, I have to talk to you,' she roared, rushin over te the nun.

'Not now, Jane Mary, I'm in a hurry,' an she rushed me down the stairs wit the young one screamin behind us.

'Sister Eleanor! I have to tell you something. I told that big gom Jean Clarke I was going to tell on her because she gave me a box in the ear for nothing!' she moaned, her mouth droppin down te her chest.

The Sister kept rushin, draggin me behind her. I was tryin te get a look back at the young one, an she gave me a dirty look as if it was all my fault the nun had no time fer her.

'It's real red and it's paining me,' she screamed, tearin down the stairs an pushin past me, gettin herself next te the nun.

'What? What is it?' the nun stopped, lookin distracted, an squinted inta the young one's ear.

'I think me eardrum is broke. I can hear a roaring in me ear!' she gasped in a whisper, outa breath, thinkin she's near te death's door. 'Can you see the red?' she asked, lookin hopeful, her eyes bulgin outa her head an her mouth hangin open, waitin fer the nun te tell her she has te be rushed te see the Doctor Blightman, an it's a real emergency.

I held me breath.

'No! You'll be all right,' the nun said an flew off again.

We tore off down another passage then she stopped an opened a door. I could hear shoutin an laughin an music, an I followed her through a room wit mahogany boxes wit lids on them, lined all along the walls, wit a big winda in the middle like the one on the landin, only this one had big black thick bars across it, an an old-fashioned sewin machine tha ye put yer foot on te make it go sat in the middle of the wall, wit a big old pine press like ye find in school sat behind the door. Young ones were sittin on a sofa an one was holdin a banjo. They all stopped talkin an gaped at me.

'Girls, this is Martha. Will you take care of her?' she said, smilin at them then puttin me sittin in an armchair. 'I will see you later,' she said te me an made te fly out the door.

'Wait, Sister Eleanor! What about me sore ear?' the blonde young one roared, flyin out the door after her.

I stared at the young ones an they stared back at me.

'Where are yeh from?' a young one wit fat freckly cheeks an roarin red hair asked me.

'Dublin,' I said, eyein the banjo.

She muttered somethin te the tall skinny one wit a red culchie face an the two of them laughed, eyein me. I eyed them back, not thinkin much a them. Laughin at me an I only in the bleedin door two minutes. Yeah, they better watch out, or I'll put the grin on the other side of their faces if they're not careful! I snorted te meself, feelin sick in me stomach at the thought of havin te stay here wit the like a them.

The fat one started te play the banjo an they all started singin, 'Oh, Polly wally doodle all day!' It sounded grand, an I watched te see how she played it. I could play tha easy! I thought te meself, an I jumped up te grab the banjo. 'Give us a go!' I said, whippin it offa her an sittin meself back down in the armchair an pullin the strings. It made an awful noise, an the others started roarin laughin. I didn't blame them, it wasn't easy after all, an I stood up an gave it back.

Yer woman still had her mouth hangin open an looked aroun at the others, sayin, 'She just grabbed it out of my hands! Huh! She's a street kid!'

They all started roarin an laughin again, an I looked aroun at them, gettin the picture of the four-eyed skinny nun insultin me be askin if I was retarded. They're all tryin te make an eejit outa me in this place. I suddenly felt meself gettin a red-hot fire in me belly an me chest tightened. Without warnin, I grabbed the banjo back an gave yer woman a smack on the head wit it, roarin, 'Who are you callin a street kid, ye culchie cow?'

The fat one leapt te her feet, still rubbin her head, an made a lunge fer me hair. I jumped back, holdin out the banjo, roarin, 'Come on, an I'll give ye another taste a this!'

Yer woman stood grindin her teeth an watchin the banjo an then landin her eyes on mine, an we locked on each other's faces, an I felt meself stiffenin, watchin fer the slightest move.

'I've a good mind to rip your hair off,' she said, thinkin better of it an lettin her shoulders drop.

I looked aroun at the others an they were lettin their breaths go an drawin up their jaws hangin down te their bellies. 'No one calls me names or threatens me, cos ye'll soon see wha I'm made of,' I said te the room, walkin out an headin fer the door.

I could hear them all shoutin at the same time, givin out about me. Te hell wit them! I thought, slammin the door shut after me, an walked down a passage tha looked dark at the end, wantin te put distance between me an them. I passed a door wit glass at the top an hesimitated. I could hear voices shoutin an little childre screamin. Jaysus, no! I'm not goin in there. I moved on an it was very quiet – good! No one aroun. I stopped at the end of the passage an looked at a door te me right, an one at the end in a corner, then I turned right then left again an went through an open door. I could smell disinfectant an came inta a row of doors wit tilets fer the childre. They look like the ones ye get at school. I went in an put the lid down on the seat an sat meself down te get a bit a peace an quiet.

God! Are ye listenin te me? I don't like this place. The people are not very nice an them young ones are very ignorant. They don't have the easy way of talkin te ye like the Dublin people do. No, they're very sour. Anyway! They're different from me. I think they're all a load a culchies in this place. An they don't like the Dublin people cos Dublin belongs te us, an we don't like them fer robbin all the jobs! Tha's wha all the big people do be sayin. Tha long skinny nun doesn't like me, an now I'm afraid of me life gettin locked up wit the whole lot a them. I know I shouldn't a grabbed the banjo, tha was a definite mistake. I made a right eejit outa meself. Then when I couldn't play it they all started laughin, then I knew I made a right gobshite outa meself. Then tha young one got annoyed an called me a street kid. Well! God, tha put the tin hat on it an I went fer her. Now I've made an enemy of meself when the last thing I wanted te do was get meself inta trouble. I was hopin te keep meself nice an quiet, an get on wit the people here. But now . . . I'm feelin all on me own wit no escape. God, will ye stay wit me an help me te keep outa trouble, an let me know I'm not on me own, cos I'm feelin lost again, as if I was a babby. Thanks, God, an I promise te be very good. An anyway, tha little nun wit the red face, I like her, she's very gentle. Maybe I'll take a wander an see where she is. Yeah! Good idea.

I stood up an let out a big breath an dropped me shoulders,

feelin better in meself. An headed out the door. Just as I got te it I heard laughin then runnin feet. I tried te open the door an it was locked. I pulled an pushed but it wouldn't open. The bastards! They've locked me in! I'm locked in. I felt meself gettin hot an bothered, I'm not goin te be able te get out!

'Open this door, ye bleedin ratbags!' I slammed me fists an kicked the door, screamin me lungs out, an the bastards were laughin their heads off outside the door.

'Let me out, I'm goin te fuckin tear ye's limb from limb when I get me hands on the lot a ye's!'

The door suddenly flew in, an a little woman wit long thin grey hair an wearin a blue overall smock stood blinkin an starin at me. I pushed past her an made fer the young ones.

'Where are they? Let me at them, the mean cows!'

'Glory be! Stop!' An she grabbed a hold a me. 'What happened to you at all?' she said, lookin inta me face.

'They locked me in!'

'Who?'

'The young ones.'

I was sweatin wit the fright, thinkin I'd never get outa there, an ragin at them makin a fool a me. I tried te pull meself free of the aul one an she held on tight te me coat. Me coat! She's pullin me new navy-blue gabardine coat I robbed fer meself, an I was wearin me new red an white check wool frock, this is me first time te wear it, an I robbed tha on Saturday te look respectable fer the court. She'll tear me coat!

I sobbed in a big breath an tried te ease meself, wantin her to let go. I wasn't goin te run after them young ones now. 'I'm all right,' I sobbed, takin in another big breath.

'Ah, that was very mean of them. Are you the new girl?'

I nodded me head up an down, happy someone was bein nice.

'Come along and I'll take you to Sister. She should be down now from the convent. It's time for the rosary. I'll take you to your group.'

We walked back along the passage an the little nun was rushin an pushin a load a kids ahead of her inta a room.

'There she is! Sister! Sister Eleanor!'

The nun shot her head aroun, lookin very distracted.

'I found the new girl, Sister Eleanor. She was locked in the toilets!' The tiny little woman laughed, blinkin an shakin her head, like she had more te say but couldn't get it all out at the same time. 'Some bold brats were playing a joke on her,' she laughed an coughed. She probably got tha from the smokin, I could smell it offa her.

The nun took me arm, sayin, 'Oh, thank you so much, Miss,' then let me arm go te move closer te the woman. They whispered te each other, watchin me, then the nun moved away, makin a hold fer me arm again, sayin, 'Oh! They are very bold children altogether. When I find out who was involved, I will certainly punish them. Tsk, tsk, it is shocking behaviour,' an she stared at the tiny woman, squintin wit her eyes half closed an clampin her lips together.

I felt better wit the fuss they were makin about me, an them agreein wit me thoughts tha them young ones were definitely mean cows! An I'm happy now havin the nun back, I feel more safe now she's here. I think she's very nice an gentle, an I really think I'm goin te like the Sister Eleanor.

The door opened an a pile a young ones came roarin out. 'Sister Eleanor! Tell that big gom to give me back my ruler. I need it to make a straight line for me English composition.'

'No, Sister! That's mine! She gave it to me for helping her with her sums.'

'I did not, you!'

'Yeh liar. You dirty filthy terrible liar!' the fat one wit the freckles roared inta the face of a young one wit long curly black hair streamin down her back.

'Sister Eleanor! Ivy Holmes robbed me rubber! I want it back this minute, or she's going te get it off me! She'll be sorry,' roared a young one wit lovely jet-black bouncy hair cut just past her ears, wit a thick fringe an lovely eyelashes tha look like sweepin brushes. Then she thumped a fat young one wit long gingery curly hair, it was lovely.

'Give me back that rubber!' screamed Bouncy-hair, wrestlin wit Curly-ginger. Bouncy got an unmerciful slap on the kisser, then was sent flyin when Curly put out her two hands givin yer woman an almighty push an ran back inta the room.

Sister Eleanor let out a scream. 'Stop this fighting at once!'

'But, Sister . . . me ruler! She has it!'

'I want to hear no more out of you, Dilly Nugent!' the Sister erupted, losin her rag an draggin hold of Dilly Nugent, pushin her inta the room. 'Or the rest of you,' she roared, swingin herself aroun te grab out at people.

'Sister Eleanor! I want me rubber back! Punish her for hitting me!' screamed Bouncy inta me ear.

'Get in! Get in!' an she dragged an slapped anyone she could get her hands on, an she started pushin an pokin them in the back te get them movin, an looked aroun at me, decidin not te slap me, an said, lookin very weary, 'Come in, darling,' then shut the door behind me.

'Gawd! I hate everyone!' moaned Dilly Nugent, lookin sideways at the nun like a dog tha's circlin ye just before it attacks ye.

'My God and my all!' moaned the nun, bendin herself in two an lookin at the ceilin. Then she picked herself up an rushed down the room, an started roarin, 'Put away all your school books; study time is over.'

'Sister! My knickers and vest got lost in the laundry,' whined a young one wit short cropped hair an a grey face lookin like a dirty ashtray.

'Duck Egg . . . I mean Sister Mary Innocent said she never left them down to the laundry,' roared a young one wit long black thin hair an the face like a back of a bus. She had thin lips an small beady eyes. Then she flicked her hair back an twisted her mouth an flashed her eyes, smirkin at the pasty one.

'You mind your own business,' roared the pasty one.

'Girls!' screamed the nun. 'Pick up everything from the work table and tidy your bags away at once,' an she made a run at the table, grabbin up things, an people roared, 'That's mine!'

'Clean up the workroom,' roared the nun, clappin her hands an tryin te get a bit of order.

I stayed close te the door, not likin this place at all. Some of them are very rough, an I'm goin te have te watch meself.

We got goin on the rosary, an I knelt meself down next te the nun. She held her rosary beads up fer everyone te see an tried te close her eyes an concentrate but had te flick them open when she heard the titterin. They were restin themselves against chairs an tables, an the Dilly Nugent one an her gang were holdin their hands up te their mouths an laughin an pointin at me. More people were joinin in, an I couldn't figure out wha I was doin tha was makin them laugh. I looked up at the nun, an she was sayin the prayers an squintin at them an shakin her head. I moved in closer, nearly sittin on her lap, wantin te be right beside her, an the others got very annoyed an started pointin. I couldn't understand wha was wrong wit tha, but they didn't seem te like it.

'In the name of the Father and of the Son and of the Holy Spirit, Amen,' the nun breathed, blessin herself wit the cross of the rosary beads an kissin it. Then everyone stood up an made fer the door.

'Come along now, pet, and we'll go down to the refectory,' she said, makin te take me arm.

Some of them were sittin an chattin an arguin, an the nun looked aroun an clapped her hands an shouted, 'Would you please all do as you are told! It's tea time for the love of God.'

'Sister! I swept the refectory for you at lunchtime today. That big mope Terry Brown was supposed to do it, but she went off an left me to do all the washing up an everything by myself!'

'Thank you, pet, you are very good,' whispered the nun, lookin very distracted an pattin yer woman on the arm an lookin back at the stragglers wit her face twisted as if she was in pain. 'Oh, give me patience,' she muttered te the ceilin, screwin up her eyes an takin me arm an holdin onta the other one's arm.

We made it down the passage wit the lovely shiny brown tiles an past rooms wit big glass windas lookin inta tables an chairs wit younger kids all shoutin an slappin, an the nun in charge was takin no notice an givin all her attention te a big young one cryin. The nun looked back as my nun passed, an waved an smiled an said, 'Sister Eleanor! I'll talk to you later about that other matter.' She had a lovely white face an sky-blue eyes an fair eyebrows, an lovely white teeth. Gawd! She'd be lovely if she was an ordinary woman, I thought te meself as I flew on te catch up wit the nun. Then passed another room wit the same glass winda, an lookin the very same as the other room.

I threw me eye in, an little kids all lookin about four te six years old looked out at us, sittin themselves very quiet, cos a tall dark-lookin nun wit lovely brown eyes was watchin them like a hawk. She glared out at us cos of all the racket goin on an went on about her business of seein te the tea. I wouldn't like te be in wit her, I thought te meself, rushin past wantin te catch up wit the Sister, who was gallopin ahead te break up a fight. Jaysus! They kill each other in this place. I don't really like fightin; I prefer te have the peace an quiet.

We went inta a room like all the others. An a big young one was pourin out the tea from a huge big kettle. 'You sit here, darling,' the nun said, sittin me down beside a young one wit glasses an lovely wavy roarin red hair.

'Gawd! Boiled eggs again!' moaned the redhead. 'Why can't we get something different? It's not even soft! I hate this group, I do! And I hate that Sister Eleanor,' she moaned, lookin sideways at the nun an takin me in an decidin she hated me, too.

'Olivia Ryan! If Sister in the kitchen hears you speak like that again, you know what will happen!' an the nun looked away, hidin the annoyance an the laugh on her face at the same time.

Everyone at the table started roarin laughin. 'Yeah! She'll bring back in the slop bucket for the pigs and land it in front of you again on the table for calling her cooking pigs' slop!'

'Yeah, well, that Sister Eleanor one is not fair. I was the only one to get punished at breakfast, and she said nothing to that thick mopey gom Aine Keeps, even though she ran out of the laundry, too, without helping Duck Egg!'

'Yeah! I know. She has her pets that one!' a young one moaned in agreement, droppin the corners of her mouth down te her belly an givin a dirty look over te the nun. Then she went back te starin at her long skinny face an a narrow pointy nose in a broken bit a mirror leanin against the plastic cup. She leaned in fer a better look, squeezin an scratchin at pimples on her face. Then the nun shouted fer everyone te stand up an say the angelus. The bells started ringin fer everyone te pray.

'The Angel of the Lord declared unto Mary,' moaned the nun in a long breath, soundin like she was very tired. I was exhausted meself an was dyin te get a bit te eat an find where me bed was. I watched as the nun disappeared out the door, leavin the room bare without her, an me stuck here all on me own wit these wild young ones.

A big shiny metal tray arrived carryin a load a thick-sliced buttered bread an landed on the middle table where all the older ones sat. Then the tray went aroun the room te the other tables. I counted five long tables wit about six or seven people sittin at them. One table was fer holdin the dishes fer the food, the cups an saucers an plates.

The bread arrived at our table an everyone grabbed two, an there was a few left an people at our table tried te grab it, but the tray was whipped away an brought over te the big young ones' table. I watched it go, hopin I might get another few slices, but no such luck. The big ones took it all, an Redhead roared over at them, 'It's just not fair! You big girls always grab the best of everything!'

'Yes! And you're just jealous!' cackled the one wit the back-of-a-bus face an long stringy hair tha she thought was beautiful.

Then the nun arrived back an said more prayers, an rushed

over te me an whispered, 'Come along with me, Martha, and we'll get you sorted out with your clothes.' Then she galloped outa the refectory, an I rushed after her, an a load a kids chased us up the passage all shoutin an roarin fer the nun.

'You'll need a nightdress,' she said, fittin up a long cotton white frilly-necked gown te me neck.

I looked down: it went te me feet.

'It will keep you nice and warm,' she laughed, seein me wonderin how I'd get aroun in this without breakin me neck.

'Now! Here are two pairs of knickers and two vests. You wear one set and leave the other down to Sister Mary Innocent in the laundry on a Saturday. This is your school uniform,' she said, fittin up a navy-blue gymslip an red jumper an white shirt an a red sash te go aroun the gymslip. I was delighted wit meself, thinkin I'll look lovely in tha. I always wanted te wear a school uniform; all the respectable people wear them. The only thing is I won't be able te wear them out an show them off . . . Only the gobshites livin here see them, an tha doesn't count. Cos they're all wearin them themselves.

'Now! Come along with me and I'll take you up to the dormitory.'

We climbed stairs, passin landins wit corridors an rooms an younger childre runnin aroun, an went up te nearly the top. We passed a statue of Our Lady holdin the baby Jesus an went inta a room wit ten beds then carried on inta a big long room wit loads a beds like a hospital. Only they were lengthways under the big windas tha ye couldn't see out cos they were too high up, an more beds down the middle, runnin the length a the room.

'Now, darling, this is your bed,' she said, puttin me stuff on the bed an openin a locker sittin next te it. I was down in the corner outside a door leadin inta another room, an there's only one bed beside me, sittin in the other corner. I looked at the black hairy blankets when she pulled down the red bedspread wit white roses in the middle, an I was delighted wit the lovely white sheets an white pilla.

'Now, darling, why don't you have a wash and climb into your bed before the others come up, you must be exhausted, you poor thing,' she said, bendin down an lookin inta me face.

'Yes, Sister, I'll do tha,' I said, feelin happy at the thought of gettin inta me new bed an gettin a bit a sleep, cos me head was painin me an I could hardly keep me eyes open. Too much had happened all in the one day.

'Look, darling,' she whispered, headin me over te a little room wit sinks fer the childre te wash themselves. 'This is the dressing-room, and the toilet is out on the landing. Now, darling, off you go and get yourself ready for bed,' an I rushed outa the room, headin fer me locker te get me wash things she gave me. 'Good girl, have a good night's rest for yourself,' she said, flyin out the door.

CHAPTER 3

I heard noise an felt someone shakin me. I opened me eyes an the nun was lookin down at me.

'Good girl! Wake up now and get yourself dressed, we have to be down in the chapel in five minutes,' she puffed, rushin off an clappin her hands. 'Now, girls! Please stop delaying; the priest will be up on the altar,' she complained, lookin very worried an rushin off talkin te herself.

I lifted me head an looked aroun me. Loads a girls were dressin themselves under their nightdresses. An some were pullin nylons up their legs. A big girl wit long wavy hair down te her waist caught me eye an smiled. 'Are you the new girl?' she mouthed over te me in a whisper.

'Yeah! Me name is Martha,' I whispered, happy tha she was nice.

'You were asleep when we came in last night. How are you feeling?'

'Not bad,' I whispered, lookin aroun me, just really takin in the place now; I was too tired last night.

'Don't worry, you'll find it strange for a while, but you'll get used to it. Now you better get dressed before Sister Eleanor gets back, she'll only start fussing.'

I jumped outa the bed an headed inta the dressin-room wit me wash things te get meself washed. I came rushin back out an bent down te me locker, takin out me new school uniform.

'No,' whispered the lovely girl. 'Just put on your after-school clothes, then when we get back you make your bed and get yourself ready for school, then go down for your breakfast.'

'OK,' I said, puttin the uniform back an gettin meself dressed in me own new woolly frock. 'Thanks fer tha, fer tellin me,' I said, smilin at her.

'No bother,' she said, puttin on her frock over her head.

Everyone made a stampede outa the dormitory, makin the floorboards hop up an down, the noise soundin like a gang of injuns comin te town, an tore down the stairs, makin a grab fer hats sittin in a cardboard box on the landin an stuck it on their heads still rushin, headin through a door, makin fer the convent passage wit the nun screamin in a whisper, tearin ahead a everybody. I looked at the hat, it was like the ones grannies wear when they're polishin churches, except they put fancy pins through them. Jaysus! This is very hickey, I thought, lookin at it, then slappin it on me head an rushin te catch up wit the others.

I got on the line an everyone moved in very quickly wit the nun standin guard at the door, her eyes flickin from us on the line pushin in, then flickin her eyes back te make sure everyone went down on their knees te the tabernacle before rushin inta the benches. I copied the others an pressed me knee on the shiny wooden floorboards an made fer a bench. Just as I got me foot over the kneeler an was creepin inta the bench, the fat freckly one, Dilly Nugent, twisted her elbows te her cronies an they all shuffled down, leavin me no room.

Right! I said te meself. I don't want te sit beside any a youse neither! An I crept down the chapel lookin fer a free space. I'm ragin. The bleedin cheek a tha one thinkin she can do tha te me an get away wit it! I'm goin te wrap tha smirk on the other side of her face before I'm finished in this place. I hope she stays a midget an all her hair falls out. Yeah! An she grows hair on her face instead, just like Hairy in the convent where I go fer the bread. I crept past all the other kids starin up at me an laughin behind their hands, feelin a right eejit.

Sister Eleanor caught me eye an was red in the face over the carryin-on of them young ones, an pushed the other childre up te make room fer me. I went te move in beside her, takin a quick look down the back, an all the nuns were kneelin wit their priests' chairs behind them, an some had their eyes closed, sittin straight up but lookin like they were still asleep. The long skinny nun lifted her head from her black holy Mass book an stared up at me, watchin me every move wit her goitre eyes hangin outa her head, an pinnin her lips together like she was still annoyed wit me cos they hadn't asked her if I could come here. Yeah! Hope ye're still worryin, Missus, cos I didn't ask either, te come an stay in this bleedin madhouse. I sat down beside the nun, glad te be sittin close te her, cos if I was on me own I'd go mental. This place would put years on ye!

I stood on the landin waitin me turn te get inta school. I wonder wha it's goin te be like! I looked down at me new gympslip an red jumper wit the white shirt inside an the red woollen sash wrapped aroun me waist, admirin meself. I look lovely. Pity the kids in Finglas can't see me now. They'd think I look very respectable altogether. Then I could play wit them an go te their houses! Yeah! Tha would be great. I've never been te any of their houses. Still, how could I do tha? Not wit the state a the ma an tha aul Jackser fella.

I took in a big sigh thinkin about it. Hm! Nothin ever works out the way ye want it to. Still! My day will come; this is the start of it. God is good, now I have no more worries. I don't have te rob the butter any more. No more worryin about Jackser wantin te kill me, or havin te look fer food for me ma an the childre an find the money fer tha bandy aul bastard's Woodbines, always thinkin an lookin fer ways te him keep easy, tryin te placate him so he won't go mad an kill everyone. I shivered in me skin thinkin about tha. Oh, thank you, God, fer lookin after me. I have a lovely warm clean bed an good food te eat. Yeah, it's a bit spare, they don't overfeed ye. But still an all, it's lovely grub. So fuck tha Dilly Nugent an her fuckin gang. I can knock the life outa them wit one hand tied behind me back. Tha's wha bandy aul Jackser says: 'Come on! I'll take ye's all on one be one wit one hand tied behind me back.' Cowardly fucker, he only says tha when he's drunk, otherwise he'd run fer his life! Anyway, them young ones are nothin but overfed windbag culchies! I was feelin happy in meself wit no more worries, an I rushed through the door inta the school.

I stood beside the other childre from the convent an looked aroun at the childre comin in from their own homes. They looked more normal than the convent childre, not as sulky, an I felt I could talk te them, not like some of the eejits from here, always backbitin an fightin an moanin an watchin each other.

The nun in charge of the school was sayin the prayers when she suddenly stopped, then started sayin the prayers slowly, an leaned herself te the side te get a better look at someone in the back row. Then she blessed herself, quickly finishin the prayers, an let out a roar. 'Dilly Nugent! Come up here this minute!'

We all looked aroun te see wha was goin on, an the nun shouted, 'Go to your classrooms, children,' an everyone started te leave except me.

'Come on! You're with us in our class,' Jane Mary wit the long white hair said, lookin at me wit a sour face an raisin her eyes te heaven like she was bein crucified at the thought a meetin someone so stupid. I followed her inta a room wit three rows a seats, an I made fer a spare place next te a young one I didn't think was from the convent. I sat meself down an took out all me books the nun Sister Eleanor gave te me an put them in me desk. I put me new pencil sittin in the holder on the desk an waited te see wha subject they were goin te do.

Jaysus! I don't know much about this school business; I hope she doesn't ask me anythin! I hardly ever set foot in these places an I know them convent kids are just waitin te have another good laugh at me. Ah, fuck them, let them laugh, I know more about some things than they do! They've had themselves wrapped in cotton wool most of their lives, an they'd probably get themselves lost in O'Connell Street.

I looked up at the teacher; she was an old woman, probably in her forties be now, wit a tight perm an her hair dyed black, I could see the grey roots comin through the top of her head. An her face was very purply lookin. Me ma says tha's a sign of a bad heart. I stared at her, an I could see she was probably nice.

'Yes, dear, hand back the test copies,' the teacher said te a young one wearin glasses wit stickin plaster holdin them together. She musta broke them, I thought, starin up at her gingery curly hair tha stood up like she got a fright. She doesn't look like a convent girl, I thought, starin over at her, takin her in. She looks more like someone tha would follow her ma aroun the kitchen, like she wants te be minded all the time. No! Definitely not convent. She's more normal.

'Now, open your English books, girls, and start on page . . . where did we finish on Friday? Yes! Page twenty-three. Now, who is going to read?' an she looked aroun the room an her eyes landed on me! 'You child, you are the new convent child,' she smiled over at me, leanin her head te hear wha I was goin te say. 'You are . . . let me see again,' an she made te look at her desk.

'Martha, Sister . . . I mean Miss,' an a roar of snorts of laughin came from the other side a the room, an the gobshite convent kids were laughin their heads off, callin me, 'Ye gom! Listen to her, she's really thick.'

I felt me belly tightenin an the heat runnin up te me chest. I sniffed air up through me nose, lettin it out slowly, an stared straight ahead, decidin te just ignore them. 'Gobshites,' I whispered te meself.

'Good girl, Martha. Now would you please read for me? I would like to see where you are in your reading.'

I took in another deep breath an read the story about the cowboy bein chased be the injun, tryin te catch up wit him te get his scalp.

'That was excellent!' she breathed down at me all smiles, an I sat down very happy wit meself an looked over at the gobshites, an they were ragin. Makin faces at me an mutterin, 'Noticebox, looking for attention.'

I didn't care. I had taught meself te read wit me comics, an now it paid off. The teacher, Mrs Basin, was delighted wit me, tha's wha matters te me.

'Now, can anyone tell me why the Indian couldn't catch the cowboy?'

Everyone jumped up wit the answer, includin me.

I couldn't believe no one was gettin the right answer. An I was delighted, cos maybe I'll get a chance te have a go. 'Me! Me! Mrs Basin, I know the answer,' everyone was shoutin, leppin up an down wit their hand in the air. She didn't look in my direction, an I was worried someone might get there before me. Then finally her eyes peeled on me.

'Cos the cowboy's steed was faster than the injun's . . . I mean Indian's!'

'Yes! Because the cowboy's horse was faster than the Indian's,' she said slowly te the class. 'You have wonderful powers of reasoning,' she said over te me. 'Now, children, if you read more books you would have known what steed meant.'

Me chest nearly blew outa me mouth it was hammerin so fast wit the enjoyment of listenin te the teacher heap loads a praise on me head. I looked over at the eejits on the other side an they were nearly chokin wit the sour faces they were makin at me. I was clampin me lips together, creasin me face in half wit the smilin over at them. Yeah! Tha shut youse up.

I spent the rest of the day in a doze, not knowin anythin about anythin else. I only know about readin an writin an spellin an doin sums in me head, I'm quick enough at tha all right; ye'd have te be wit me butter round, otherwise me customers woulda robbed me blind. No fear! I can work out numbers like greased lightnin. So I suppose there was somethin te be said about me havin te rob the butter after all. But tha's me lot.

I woke meself up when I heard her say, 'Put away your books, girls,' then she started the singin lessons. Tha was somethin I could learn. Everyone was singin away te their hearts' content, but I didn't know any of the words an I started scratchin me head an yawnin.

'You have nits!' a young one said te me, lookin aroun from the seat in front a me an laughin.

I stared at her long brown stringy hair an said, 'Well, at least mine keep lovely an warm. If they were crawlin aroun your head, they'd get pneumonia from the draught ye're so baldy! An mind you, I'm not sayin ye haven't got any.'

'My head is not baldy, ye tinker!'

'Yeah, I know, ye must be deaf as well as baldy if ye didn't hear the teacher say I'm a great tinker!'

She stared at me, wantin te say somethin back, but couldn't think of anythin, then she snorted air up her nose an said, 'Ah, shrrup, ye skinny little cow!'

'Loretta Winters! Stop that fighting at once and turn around in your seat! I will not tolerate you setting a bad example to that child. She's a beautifully behaved young girl.' Then she heaved in her chest an turned aroun te the convent kids an snorted, 'She is going to be a shining example to the rest of you,' then she smiled down at me.

The convent kids went mad an started roarin out big sighs under their breath. 'She's an awful noticebox.'

'Yeah! Suck up! I hate that new one, she thinks she's great.'

'Pet! She's licking up to the teacher,' they were all complainin like mad under their breath. I was screamin laughin inside meself, delighted te be the teacher's pet! Yeah, I really like Mrs Basin, she's very kind altogether.

The school bell went, tellin everyone it was time te go home; well, fer the kids goin home. I put me books in me bag an trailed out the door after the convent kids, not in much of a hurry te go back in there. Everyone was tryin te fly out the door at the same time onta the convent landin.

'Stop pushin!' A middle group young one turned te me. I just looked at her, not pushin anyone at all.

A big young one twice the size of everyone else lunged from the crowd an grabbed at her schoolbag, pullin it, an gave her a slap on the head wit her other hand. 'Ye can't catch me,' she laughed.

'Vanessa Andrewson! I'm tellin on you!' she screamed, lungin out an grabbin the big one be the jumper an tryin te catch a hold of her hair. The big one gave her an almighty push an the two of them were slammin inta me, tearin at each other, an I'm gettin flattened in the middle.

'Geroffa me!' I roared, pushin the two of them.

They stopped dead, still hangin onta each other, an looked at me. 'Who's she?' they asked, lookin an laughin at each other an lookin shocked at the same time.

'It must be the new one . . . Gawd! She's very rough!' the little one just a bit bigger than me said, wit her big buck teeth restin on her lip hangin down makin her chin look pointy.

'Watch it, you big mope!' the big one roared at me.

'Gobshite,' I muttered, not wastin me time, an movin me way through the crowd all flyin in different directions.

I wondered which way te go. Wha do I do now? Go upstairs te the dormitory or downstairs te wha? I wonder when they get somethin te eat. I'm starvin te death. Them fuckers sittin at me table put sugar on me dinner when I wasn't lookin. Yeah, tha was an awful disappointment. An the dinner was lovely an all. A bit a red meat, I don't know wha it was called, I think someone said corned beef, an they were moanin they didn't like it. Overfed pigs! It's a pity about them. Hm, tha woulda been lovely sittin next te the green cabbage an big potatoes not peeled, still sittin in their skins. I went te get meself a fork from the long table holdin all the stuff, an when I got back I knew somethin was wrong. They were lookin at me sideways, actin very shifty an smirkin at each other under their eyes. I couldn't figure it out an kept lookin at me dinner, but it was only when I tasted it. Aahhh, Jaysus! I nearly got sick. Bastards nearly poisoned me. They put a load a sugar in it. I tried te pretend there was nothin wrong wit it, not lettin them get the better a me. Me stomach was turnin, an they were laughin, starin inta me face waitin fer me te spit it out.

'Does it taste OK?' the one wit the white hair asked me, her mouth hangin open an her eyes dancin in her head, ready te split herself in two, wit the lot of them laughin their heads off.

'Yeah, it's lovely,' I muttered, swallowin it, tellin meself it's supposed te taste like tha so I could keep it down.

'Do you not taste the sugar we poured into it?' they roared.

'No! I think it's lovely,' I said, puttin down me fork, leavin most of it sittin on the plate. 'Well, whatever was in it I really enjoyed tha dinner,' I said, holdin me belly, pretendin I was full up te the top.

The smirks slid off their faces an they looked very disappointed altogether, not gettin the rise outa me. 'Gawd! She's real peculiar,' the white-haired one whined, tryin te figure me out.

I nearly cried, lookin at the lovely food sittin on the plate, an me dyin te get it down me belly. It's a cryin shame te waste good food like tha, but it was no use, I had te leave it. Yeah! But we'll see who has the last laugh. I'm not lettin them get away wit tha!

Right! Where will I head? Me eyes peeled down the stairs an the rest a me was just about te follow when Sister Eleanor came flyin outa nowhere, herdin a load a young ones ahead a her. 'Get up those stairs and change your uniforms!' she shouted, gettin all red in the face an lookin like she wanted te escape outa here wit her eyes lookin miles away.

'Sister Eleanor!' roared Dilly Nugent, escapin the hold the nun had on her an flyin past me, shovin me outa the way. 'Gerrouta me way, you!' she muttered, snarlin under her breath.

'Watch it, ye cross-eyed fuckin goofy cow,' I muttered.

'Come back here at once,' Sister Eleanor screamed, rushin after her, gettin herself even redder in the face, an grabbin a hold a her.

'I left me homework copy at school and I need to rush in and get it!' yer woman screamed.

'No! Get up to that dormitory and do as you are told,' Sister Eleanor whispered, narrowin her eyes an squintin at her, waggin her finger in her face. 'You are trying my patience, and I am going to count to three . . .'

'Gawd! That's not fair! You hate me, you do! You're always giving out to me, so you are!'

Sister Eleanor made a lunge an wit her two hands grabbed the young one an wrestled her up the stairs.

'Sister Eleanor!' I was delighted te see her an rushed after her. 'Do we have te change outa our school clothes now?' I asked her, tryin te pull her arm te get her te look at me, an rushin after her.

She kept goin, not hearin me.

'Do we have te change outa our school clothes now?' I asked her, pullin harder on her arm an tryin te get ahead of her te look inta her face.

'Yes! Yes!' she roared at the landin, not really seein me.

Then a big young one came flyin outa the convent passage swingin a bongin thing, bangin hell outa it. I stopped te look. 'Sister Eleanor! Sister Eleanor!'

'What is it?' she asked in a pained face, not lookin down te the young one but askin the air, an hangin on te some a the crowd she was tryin te keep movin up the stairs.

'Sister Eleanor!' I roared, delighted te have somethin te say te get her te talk te me. 'Tha big young one wit the bongin thing in her hand is shoutin fer ye!'

'Oh, for the love of God! I know that! What does she want?' she roared, moanin at me.

Ah, fuck! Now I've annoyed her.

'Sister Eleanor! I've been shouting around the house for the last hour looking for you! You're wanted on the phone. I have me work to do you know!' Then she gave the bong another bang an put her nose inta the air an swung her long ponytail, flappin it in the air, an wriggled her arse an slid back out the door te head off fer the convent.

Gawd! I'd love te be doin tha! Flyin aroun wit tha thing, bangin the hell outa it an talkin te the nuns like tha, an have me work te do an a lovely long ponytail like her. She looks about fifteen. No, probably sixteen. Jaysus! I can't wait te be big like tha.

'Excuse me!' Sister Eleanor flew past me down the stairs, holdin up her habit te stop her trippin, an shouted back at me starin after her, 'Will you please go and change out of that uniform, child,' then she gave one last look back, seein me still not movin, an shook her head in annoyance.

I watched as her face disappeared out the door, takin the rest of herself wit her an vanishin! I stood lookin at the spot where she'd been an felt me heart drop. Ah, she's gone! I was lookin forward te tellin her me news about the school an wha the teacher said te me, an now it felt a bit empty without her. I looked aroun the landin where the middle kids have their playroom, an they had their nun in there wit them, an she was sewin away an listenin te them. Everyone had disappeared inta the dormitories, an I could hear the shoutin an laughin comin all the way down the stairs. I'm the last one standin here, an I thought I'd sort meself out sooner than this an maybe go fer a ramble an see wha this place is really like, an I might meet someone I could play wit. I suppose tha's wha everyone else is doin now, havin a play time. Right! I'll run upstairs an get meself changed.

'You can't bring that bag in here!' Freckle-face roared at me, standin wit her hands on her hips, her eyes bulgin outa her head lookin from me te the bag.

'Wha do I do wit it?'

'Shove it up your jumper,' she laughed, lookin at Pointy-nose wit the ashtray face an the Jane Mary one roarin their heads laughin.

'Fuck off,' I said, makin fer me bed.

'Sister Eleanor will punish you!'

'Yeah,' they all laughed, 'and tonight it won't be a sugary dinner, because you'll get nothing if you're punished.'

'So where do I put it?' I roared, losin me patience.

'That's for us to know and you to find out,' they cackled, all sayin it at the same time an laughin their heads off.

'Right! Fuck the lot of ye's,' I said te meself, not carin any more.

I started te take me uniform off an was tryin te get me own frock over me head when they all started roarin.

'Gawd, she has legs like matchsticks!'

'Noo! More like a chicken!' Grey-face screamed. 'And she's showing off her knickers. You're supposed to get dressed under your nightdress! Not show us everything!'

'Yeah! And scare the life out of us,' Jane Mary laughed.

They all roared laughin again, thinkin themselves really funny.

'Gawd! She's terrible looking,' the Dilly one said, starin up at me like I had two heads.

I'm goin te be dug outa tha one in a minute if I lose me patience. I could feel me heart hammerin away in me chest, an shoved on me shoes an folded me uniform, takin good care te make sure I still had the nice pleats in the middle an wantin te get outa here as fast as me legs would carry me.

I heard footsteps an the little grey-haired woman came rushin in, blinkin an thinkin wha she wanted te say, her mouth movin before she could get the words out. 'Dilly Nugent! Jane Mary Wilson! And the rest of you! Get out of this dormitory immediately. Come on!' an she waved her arm out the door.

They started te move, moanin, 'Gawd! You can't do anything in this house without people giving out to you!'

'Out! Before I tell Sister Eleanor. You know it's forbidden to come up here. You should be changed long before now and down to study. Hurry! Come along now, child,' she roared up at me.

I closed me locker an checked everythin looked nice an tidy wit me uniform sittin on me chair an galloped off, takin me schoolbag wit me.

'You don't bring that up here; leave it in your locker in the playroom until you need it,' she said te me as I flew past her, wantin te make distance between me an the torments.

'OK, Miss, sorry, I didn't know wha te do wit it,' I said, makin me way down the stairs an headin fer the study.

I followed the rest a me group inta a room wit a long table an two long benches sittin beside it, an everyone made a rush te get themselves a place. I looked te see where I could sit; I didn't want te be beside tha Dilly one an her gang.

'Come along now, dear, and sit yourself down,' a woman wit short grey permed hair an wearin a blue smock said te me, pointin me te the end a the bench next te a young one wit brown short hair an a very red face. 'Move up there, Ellen, an let this child sit herself down like a good girrell.' An she gave her a push, cos yer woman was pretendin te be deaf.

'Now! I want ye girrels to get yer heads down to the books and don't be giving me any trouble today, because I'm not too long outa me sick bed at all, at all!' she said, feelin very sorry fer herself an hopin they'd have pity on her. 'Are ye all listening to me?' she asked them one be one, lookin the length a the table an bendin herself in two, restin her hands on her hips.

'Yes, Miss Farmers,' they muttered, laughin inta their chests.

'Good girrells,' she said, hikin herself up, tryin te stand. Then she wobbled, grabbin hold of a chair, an took herself off walkin on hairy bandy legs wit the muscles stickin out, lookin like she was tryin te balance herself on a very dangerous icy floor, wearin a pair of black laced-up shoes wit thick high heels.

'Oooh! I'm getting too old,' she moaned, tryin te lower herself inta a chair an sittin herself down beside a desk. 'Now! I want ye to be nice and quiet, children, and I might have something later on for the quietest girrell.'

'What will you give us, Miss Farmers?' they all roared up.

'Oh, now! Ye'll have to wait and see!' she said, pullin out a cloth te do her sewin on fancy little flowers.

'Ah, Miss! Go on! Show us! And we'll be very good for you, won't we girrells?' roared Dilly Nugent.

They all sniggered, shoutin. 'Yeah, Miss! We'll be very good girrells for you,' they screamed, laughin their heads off.

'Well, all right then,' she said, takin a hankie outa her pocket. 'I only have the one, mind!' she said, holdin up the hankie as we all watched. Then she opened it, showin us a lemon sweet stuck te the hankie.

'Uuhh! Yuk! That's disgusting! We definitely don't want that, Miss,' they screamed.

'Ooh! I'm going to be sick,' moaned Dilly Nugent, holdin her stomach.

'Well! You are not going to get it anyway,' huffed Miss Farmers. 'I think you are all very spoilt. When I was a child, I certainly would not think of refusing a sweet!'

I sucked on me pencil, lookin from me sum book back te me copy again. I can't make head nor tail outa them sums. Jaysus! How do ye do them? I looked down the table wonderin if I could ask someone fer help. No, better not look fer trouble; they'll only start tormentin me again. The young ones here are very sour altogether; ye'd think they had the world on their shoulders the way they jump at ye an the carry-on a them. Ah, fuck! An I can't make out tha geography either. I felt me heart sinkin. Ah, I was hopin te be able te learn meself an do sums an all the other things ye do at school. But it's too hard cos I don't know wha I'm doin. I'm only wastin me time! Te hell wit it, I'm not botherin me arse. I put me books in me bag an turned aroun.

'What are ye doing, child? Surely ye can't be finished already?'

'No, Miss! She's skiving!' the Dilly one an her gang all shouted, lookin shocked an annoyed at the thought of me gettin away an they still stuck here.

'Yeah, I'm finished, Miss,' I said, not lookin at her an makin me way te the door while I could still escape.

'Come back!'

I hesimitated, listenin te them all shoutin an screamin tha I was tellin big lies and it's not fair. 'Why should we have to stay?' they roared.

I put me head back in the door, sayin, 'I'm rushin te the tilet, Miss,' an I banged the door shut, hearin them say, '"I'm rushin te the tilet, Miss!" She's a real street kid, that one!'

An ye're all ragin I'm gettin out! I thought te meself, flyin down te the tilets then pullin meself te a stop, rememberin tha's where they locked me in. No! I'm not goin in there, they might come after me an do it again. I turned back, headin down the other passage, lookin in at the refectories. Nobody in, they must be all doin their study in their own places. The kids don't seem te mix; they keep the groups te their own parts.

CHAPTER 4

It's very quiet, not a sinner aroun or a sound te be heard. I stopped at a door on me right an turned the handle, walkin in. I could hear machines an smell washin. I walked down the little passage an turned the handle on another door, openin it very quietly in case someone let a roar at me.

The noise hit me straight away. I looked in, seein big machines groanin an moanin wit loads a washin slappin away. An a big machine wit rollers an a long runnin board fer puttin yer feet on te make it go sat in the middle of the room. 'I wonder wha tha's for?' I said, starin at it, then havin a good look aroun the room.

I looked over inta a corner, seein a skinny little woman wit grey hair slammin down an iron wit the flex hangin from the ceilin, an steam came outa the white linen cloth she was ironin. I walked over quietly, sayin, 'Hello, Miss, are you in charge a the laundry?'

'Oh my God,' she said, nearly droppin the iron wit the fright I gave her.

'Sorry, I didn't mean te worry ye!'

'Where did you come out of?' she said, still holdin her chest. Then a little tiny nun wearin a long rubber apron trailin the ground, an rubber Russian boots under her habit – she had tha tied up aroun her waist te stop it gettin inta the water runnin aroun her feet – appeared outa another room wit the sound a machines clampin behind her.

I stared. 'Gawd! She's tiny!' I whispered te the woman, not takin me eyes offa the nun. 'She's just like tha nun in tha Fellini fillum I sneaked inta.'

'Is that right now?' said the woman, carryin on wit her ironin an smilin an throwin her eye te me.

'Yeah!' I whispered. 'The Italian relations had te call out the midget nun from the madhouse te get the mad uncle outa the tree. He kept pissin his trousers, an climbed up te the top a the tree an wouldn't come down, an kept screamin an cryin. He kept roarin, "I wanta womm man! I wanta womm man!" An his mammy was standin lookin up at him, wringin her hands an cryin an shoutin at the daddy an everyone else, all the other relations, "Do some ting! Oooh! My poorre bam bino! Ped dro! You av to do some ting!" An he kept screamin and cryin, "Get me a womm man,"' I said, holdin me hand over me chest, an lookin up at the imaginary tree. 'Gawd! Tha was a gas fillum!' I shook me head rememberin, while the woman laughed her head off, an I had te blink, forgettin where I was, hearin the winchy tiny little nun screamin her heart out laughin at me.

Then the nun was sayin, takin her hankie outa her pocket an dryin her eyes an red nose, 'Are you looking for me? Are you the new girl in Sister Eleanor's group?'

'Yeah, Sister, I am.'

'Oh, you are very welcome. Goodness! You really are a hard case. I have not laughed like that since goodness knows how long. Now,' she said, lookin at me, 'are you settling in well?'

'Yeah, I'm grand, Sister.'

'Oh good! Now you better run along, and I think you are supposed to be in your group doing your study, isn't that true?'

'Yeah, I am. But I had te go out lookin fer the tilet. Now I'm lost!'

'Well, if you go back the way you came, you won't be lost. Isn't that right?' she said, smilin at me, knowin I was coddin her.

'Yeah, right, Sister,' I said, moochin away from her an turnin aroun te shut the door.

'Oh! What is your name?'

'Martha, Sister, me name is Martha.'

'That is a lovely name. You are called after Saint Martha, the worker. I hope you are a good worker?'

I nodded me head at her starin at me waitin fer me answer.

'Good! Because we will have plenty of work for you on Mondays after school. That is the big wash day, and we need all the hands down here. Oh, and don't forget to bring down your vest and knickers. You change them after your bath on Saturdays.'

'Yes, Sister,' I said, tryin te make me escape.

'Bye now,' she said, wavin me out the door.

'Bye, Sister,' I said, shuttin it fast behind me. I'm not very pushed about the idea a goin back in there. It looks like very hard work te me!

I carried on wit me ramble, passin me own refectory, an stopped on a long concrete passage. A big door seemed te go te the outside onta the grounds. I tried the handle. Locked! Pity . . . I'd a lovin te get outside. I turned aroun, headin down the passage. Loads a doors here, I thought te meself, but I'll keep goin, cos I could hear noise comin from a door near the end, an made fer tha.

'Did yeh nat finish washin me pots yet?' a huge culchie aul nun built like a bus, an a squashed face lookin like it was made outa hardened putty, was roarin inta the face of a young one wit cross eyes an short wiry-lookin roarin red hair tha stood up lookin like it had a mind of its own, wearin a long brown rubber apron an brown suede boots tha grannies wore on their day's outin when they were wearin their good stuff.

'I'm goinh as fast as I can, Sister Mercy! I habe a terrible cold in be head, an I'm not bery well at all,' whined the young one, snots streamin down her nose, an restin her elbows on the sink an lookin up at the nun, who gave her a dig, roarin, 'Look at all me pots, they're starting to grow mould from the want of a wash. Get a move on with yerself outa dat, yeh lazy good for nothing!'

She turned aroun just as I put me head back out the door. 'Come back here, you!'

I hesimitated, wonderin if I should run.

'Come in here and give me a hand. I'm expected to do everything by myself. Now! Watch them eggs biling in that pot. I won't be a minute, I'm just running over to the convent, I won't be long.'

I stood starin at the eggs hoppin aroun in the boilin water, wonderin wha I was supposed te do wit them. Then she came flyin back in, headin over te the eggs.

'Ahh! You stupid amadan!' she roared, givin me a smack on the back a me head. 'The eggs are like bullets!' she screamed, grabbin the pot wit a cloth an landin them in the sink. 'You were supposed to take them out!'

I stared at them, not knowin tha, then she gave me another clout an shoved the pot inta me hand. 'Here! Take dat into dat one an tell her to get a hurry on, I haven't got till next Christmas to wait on the likes of her!'

I rushed inta the scullery, droppin the pot inta the sink, hearin yer woman moan, an rushed back out again, headin fer the door.

'Here! Get back here, you, and give me a hand here.' She bent down te the oven, takin out a load a little cakes. I stared as she humped the big heavy metal tray onta the long kitchen table, the steam makin its way over te me nose, an the smell turned me belly te water. Oooh I'd a lovin te taste one a them.

'Here! Put that bowl in the press over dere,' an she aimed her head at a long press comin from the ceilin te the floor just behind the door. I grabbed the bowl in a hurry te get out, an opened the press. Me eyes landed on trays a cakes: rock buns, fairy cakes, scones an little jam tarts, all sittin on the middle shelf. I stared, then felt them! They're still hot! Oh, an the smell!

I threw one eye, givin a look back at the nun. She's bendin down te the oven again; now is me chance. I grabbed two in each hand an shot out the door makin fer the tilets at the other end a the convent.

I flew, me heart poundin, carryin the two cakes in each hand. I can't hide them; I've nowhere te put them. I shot past the study, hearin them arguin an bangin aroun, me eyes glued on the end a the passage. Nearly there, I puffed, outa breath. Then roundin the corner an went flyin in the door, slammin it shut behind me an sittin down on the tilet seat te enjoy me cakes.

I took a bite. Oh my God, this is gorgeous! I never tasted anythin as lovely as this in me life. Hmm! I took another bite, shovin the rest of it in me mouth, lookin at the three I still had left. I started on the rock bun, tastin the softness in the inside an all crunchy on the outside. This is marvellous. I'm havin the time of me life. An I'm all be meself not havin te share them, an no one te bother me. Wha more could a body want? I bet them eejits would be ragin altogether if they could see me now.

Then I heard noises. I stopped chewin, an held me breath, me mouth stuffed, an me heart started te pound, strainin me ears te listen.

'Have you seen her?'

'No! Where do you think she might have got to?'

'Smartha Long! Khum out! I know you're hiding somewhere!'

Jaysus! Ah, help! Mammy, I'm caught. I looked down at me last cake an swallowed down wha was in me mouth, an took huge bites, wantin te finish it before they took it offa me.

The door whipped in. 'Smartha Long?' An I saw someone bend down an I leapt up on the seat so they couldn't see me feet. 'Khum out! Cheese in here, Miss!' I heard the kitchen young one roarin through her nose te the grey-haired Miss.

I held me breath, not movin. Then a head appeared over the top of the tilet. I looked up at her grippin the top of the wall. Ah, Mammy! I was shiverin wit the fright.

'Khum out of nhere, you! Open knat door now!' screamed the young one from the kitchen. Then she tumbled down off the wall. 'Oh, me knee. I'll kill knat new one when I get me hands on her. Khum out of nhere quick! Sister said I'm to bring you straight back down to the kitchen,' she screamed.

Me heart was leppin wit the fright.

'Khum out here this sminute!'

'Martha Long! Please open this door,' shouted the aul one. I opened the door an flew past just as the aul one tried te grab me, blinkin an twitchin her mouth tryin te talk.

I flew meself down the passage headin fer the stairs, takin them two at a time, leppin onta the landin an flyin inta the tilet an lockin the door, tryin te steady me breathin so they wouldn't hear me. I heard shoutin an feet rushin down the passage, headin off in the wrong direction. Oh, God! Let me get outa this trouble an I promise I'll never do anythin like this again. I promise! Me heart was pumpin away like I'm goin te drop dead from the bangin. Jaysus! I can't keep meself outa trouble in this place. Them cakes wasn't worth all the bother. I didn't even get te enjoy them.

I kept listenin, an it was very quiet. Maybe they'll forget about me. Oh holy God, are ye listenin te me? Make them forget all about me robbin the cakes an I promise I'll never get meself inta trouble again!

I sat fer a long time, then I heard doors openin an runnin feet an the noise of the childre finishin the study. I crept out, lookin all aroun me. Right! I'll head back downstairs an pretend te be busy puttin away me schoolbag, an wait te see which way the wind blows. But I can't understand how I'm always managin te get meself inta trouble when I'm always tryin te be good!

I was sittin down waitin fer me tea when I heard me name gettin roared. The kitchen nun came flyin in all red-faced, an even her eyes was red.

'How dare you help yerself to my cakes?' she screamed, slappin me on the head an anywhere else she could get me wit a dishcloth. I kept me head down, an she turned te Sister Eleanor, who was rushin herself over te see wha all the bother was about.

'What is it, Sister?' breathed Sister Eleanor, tryin te get her breath wit the shock, an lookin at me wit her mouth open, not makin sense of anythin.

'Dis one!' screamed Sister Mercy, givin me another slap a the cloth. 'Rifled me kitchen press and made off with half of me fresh batch of cakes I made for the convent tea!'

'Oh, merciful!' moaned Sister Eleanor, bendin down te get a look at me, not believin her ears. 'Tsk, tsk, that's a very bold thing to do. She's a very bold child, Sister Mary Mercy. I'll see she gets punished.'

'Hm! Well, see you do, Sister.' Then she ran at me again. 'If I ever catch you within an ass's roar of my kitchen ever again, I'll skin you alive! Did you hear dat?' she roared, thumpin me an slappin me wit the dishcloth te get the message.

'Right, Sister, I'll never set foot near yer kitchen again,' I muttered. 'I'm sorry about yer cakes.'

'Half the press, Sister Eleanor! Half the press!' She shook her head, not believin it. 'Now there's not enough left for the poor nuns' tea!'

'Yes, Sister, I'm very, very sorry about this,' my nun said, tryin te placate her.

Then Sister Mercy wandered out the door, mutterin te herself the place was goin te rack an ruin. 'Law an order is breaking down completely. Where will it all lead to?' she muttered, shakin her head an still standin in the door.

'All right, Sister! I will see to this lassie,' Sister Eleanor shouted te her, tryin te get rid of her. Then she ran at me. 'I want a word with you, miss! Don't go disappearing after the tea.'

'No, Sister,' I mumbled.

Then the eggs arrived, an one was put in front of me. A lovely brown one. I was just about te give it a bang a the spoon when it was whipped from under me nose an disappeared.

'You're not having this!' Sister Eleanor puffed, vanishin over te the big girls' table an givin it te one of the big ones.

I watched a big young one grab it, sayin, 'Oh, thanks, Sister,' an cross her eyes, makin a face over at me, an lift it inta the air, wavin it back at me.

'Hungry fucker! I hope ye choke on it,' I muttered, turnin me head back te see wha was left te eat.

'You are being punished!' Sister Eleanor said, appearin up behind me again an wavin her finger at me.

I looked back at me plate, in case she'd robbed me bread. I still had me two slices a bread an grabbed one, takin a big bite, lettin it slide down me neck, tryin te get rid a them in case she took them, too.

CHAPTER 5

I flew outa the dressin-room hangin onta me wash things after gettin inta a big fight wit tha Dilly Nugent one. They wouldn't let me near the sink, an I had te push an roar me way te get a wash an get meself ready fer school.

'Martha!'

I looked up te see Sister Eleanor wavin an rushin herself down te get me. Ah, fuck! Wha did I do now?

'Listen, pet,' she said, breathin all over me an smilin an grabbin me hand. 'Come and get dressed quickly and put these on you. Miss is waiting to take you out, and we have a taxi coming in ten minutes to collect the both of you.'

Me mind flew an me heart started leppin wit excitement. 'Where? Where am I goin te, Sister? Am I goin back te me ma?' Me heart started te sink wit the fear now tha thought just hit me.

'Oh no! I declare to God! Where would you be getting that idea from?' she laughed.

Oh, thank God fer tha. I let out a big breath, feelin meself goin easier. 'But where then?'

'We don't have time for questions. Now hurry! Be a good girl and get yourself ready quickly. Come on!' an she rushed over te me bed, droppin the new stuff fer me te wear.

'Put these on you,' she said, eyein me own frock tha was gettin dirty. Then she whipped it over me head, leavin me standin in me knickers an vest. I hope tha Dilly lot are not goin te start laughin at me again.

I whipped the frock over me head an looked down at meself as Sister Eleanor buttoned up the back an tied the belt. 'Now put these socks on.' I put on the new long white socks an dived inta me shoes. 'Are they polished?' she asked, lookin down te see me brown leather shoes I robbed fer meself along wit me coat an frock. 'Tsk, they'll have to do,' she said, not likin the look a them. I think they're gorgeous. They have two straps across me foot, an now I really look lovely, I thought, admirin meself, lookin down at the long brown wool frock wit the big white collar.

'Now brush your hair,' she said, grabbin me comb then rushin me inta me coat, after puttin a pair a gloves on me an a lovely red an white knitted hat on me head. It has a long string comin outa the top wit a woolly ball at the end, makin it fly in all directions.

'Now come along and we better be quick. The taxi will be waiting.'

I swung me head flyin along wit the Sister holdin me hand an made the string fly from side te side, lettin me think I had a ponytail.

'Here we are, Miss!' Sister said, handin me over te Miss, the little grey-haired woman waitin at the convent passage an blinkin like mad when she saw us.

'Now, Sister, we will go directly there, and will the taxi wait for us?'

'No, Miss, the office will call for the taxi when you are ready to leave,' she said, leanin over te Miss an breathin at her in a whisper.

'Oh, good, that's all settled, so,' she laughed, an coughed an blinked. 'So I will wait for her and come directly back.'

'Yes, Miss! Oh, thank you! I better run and get those children into school. Goodbye, Martha,' she whispered te me, an waved, turnin te run back up the stairs.

We drove down Talbot Street an I looked at all the people goin inta the shops, an me stomach felt sick at the thoughts of havin te go in an rob all the butter. Jaysus! Thank you, God, fer makin tha stop. Now I can forget all about tha. I let me shoulders drop an let out me breath, happy at them times bein gone fer ever.

The taxi pulled up outside the Department of Education. I remember this place, I thought, lookin up at the steps. Tha's where I robbed the chairs fer the ma tha time Jackser was locked up! 'Are we goin in there, Miss?'

'Yes,' she said, leanin over te the taxi man, sayin thank you an openin the door, flingin her cigarette butt inta the middle a the road an leavin the inside of the car lookin like it was on fire!

I leapt out, thinkin me new hat wit the woolly ball will be stinkin wit the smell a smoke.

'Come along,' she said, grabbin me arm an marchin me up the steps.

We went inta the hall an a man said, 'Up to room four.'

'Here we are!' she said, wheezin like a bagpipes an collapsin onta the door, knockin on it wit her knuckles.

'Come in!' a culchie voice barked, whippin open the door.

'This is the child from the convent, Martha Long,' gushed Miss, blinkin an coughin an smilin, waitin fer him te say somethin.

He stared down at me, then lifted his big roundy bald head wit a few strips a hair across the front, wrappin themselves aroun his ear, an said, 'Fine! Good, would you take a seat downstairs, this won't take long. Come in, sit,' he barked at me, flyin aroun te a big swingin armchair wit the horse's hair burstin up through the seat an planked himself down, pushin papers outa his way an foldin his arms across the desk an stared at me, thinkin before he said anythin.

I sat up an watched him.

'So! You've been giving the nuns trouble!'

I looked at him, wonderin wha nuns he was talkin about. I was good fer the last week, not a bit a trouble, except them gobshites, the young ones. But not the nuns!

'We are going to send you to a reformatory!' he roared, sniffin an sittin back again, foldin his arms, lettin the word fly aroun the room, bouncin against the walls, then waitin fer the ringin te stop an see wha I thought about tha.

Not much! So I stayed quiet an watched him, feelin meself go cold. Fuck you, pig face, if tha's wha this is all about . . . then youse can all go an fuck off!

I sat starin without blinkin, an he did the same. Then he jumped at me again, shoutin. 'Reformatory!' he barked, suddenly snufflin an rubbin his nose, tryin te get rid of a long bunch a grey hair stickin down, then sat back again, watchin me like a hawk te see how I was takin this. 'You should never have been sent to that convent in the first place! The Reverend Mother is right. So what do you think about that?' he asked, waitin te hear wha I had te say.

I said nothin. I don't give a curse! They can send me where they like, so long as it's not back te tha bandy bastard Jackser! Nothin they do will ever be as bad as tha.

'So! What do you have to say for yourself?'

I sat starin, keepin me face still, sayin nothin.

'Do you know what a reformatory is like?' he asked, tryin te put the fear a God inta me.

'Yeah, they beat the hell outa ye! An make ye work.'

'Exactly! So that's where you are going. Where you should have been sent in the first place. I never heard the like of it, sending the likes of people like you to a convent like that!' He was gettin himself all worked up, hopin I'd start floodin inta tears an askin fer mercy, hopin I'd get a second chance.

But I'm not goin te do tha. If they don't want me in tha convent, so te hell wit them. I'll still do the same amount a time in the reformatory, an hard work never kilt anyone. An I'm used te Jackser beatin the shite outa me. So I'll manage till me time is up.

'Have you any questions? Do you want to say something to me?' he asked, wakin me from me thoughts.

'Right! Will I be goin down be train?' I asked him, thinkin about the time I went on one te the Sunshine Home. Me heart dropped fer a minute, thinkin tha was a really lovely time I had then.

He scratched the back of his baldy head an lifted his lips like he wanted te touch the hair growin outa his nose an snorted, lookin aroun the room. 'Listen! You are hanging on by a string there in that convent! One more complaint about you, and we will get that court order struck out. Yes! Our hands are tied at the moment; there is not much we can really do about getting you moved. We haven't got sufficient grounds. Unfortunately, the judge made the order specifying you be sent there, and not for punishment. But! And mark this,' he said, wavin his finger slowly at me. 'You give us the grounds by not behaving yourself and you will be moved to a reformatory where you belong before you can say Flash Gordon! Now get out of my sight, and I don't want to see your face in here again, or you will definitely be heading your way to a reformatory tailor-made for just the likes of you: in the heart of the country, out in the midde of nowhere, miles from the nearest town. Go on, scat!' An he waved his papers at me, jumpin up te open the door an goin out te tell the Miss I was ready.

She came rushin herself up the stairs all smiles fer the man, an he said te tell the Reverend Mother he would be in touch in the near future.

CHAPTER 6

I woke up an the sun was shinin in the dormitory winda. Lovely! I stretched meself, feelin the warm comfortable sheets, an I still don't have te move. Nobody called us. I looked aroun at the empty beds. Only a few of us left. School is finished fer the summer holidays an all the torments are gone off on their holidays te stay wit their godparents. Pity I never got te get godparents, I could go off on me holidays, too.

Ah, it's goin te be great just havin the few of us aroun. I wonder wha's goin te happen now I'm fourteen? Yeah! I made sure te remember tha, I had me birthday last week, an I went aroun tellin everyone it was me birthday; they were fed up listenin te me. But they didn't understand it meant the world te me te remember fer the first time in me life the day I was born. Yeah! I waited fourteen years, an it was great. I felt really special. Everyone said happy birthday te me an sang happy birthday in the refectory at teatime. Sister Eleanor gave me a holy picture as a remembrance, an a slice a cake. Hm! Me first birthday!

I wonder will I get sent te the technical school? I've no chance of goin te the secondary school; ye have te be very brainy fer tha. An I only got te stay for a little while at the primary school, sittin in the fifth class learnin nothin. Cos I didn't know anythin te begin wit. Pity tha, I woulda loved te be able te sit an learn. But ye have te spend years learnin yer way through all the classes, an I only got te go te tha fifth class, an not knowin wha was goin on aroun me, ye can't just know how te do long division without someone showin ye, an I was supposed te know tha be the time I got te tha class! Yeah! I really do regret tha. Oh well! Could be worse I suppose; lucky I taught meself how te read. Some of them here can't even do tha. I managed te get ahead of them in the English, an I'm good at figures, so tha's all tha matters. I can do a lot fer meself be teachin meself how te speak properly for a start. Yeah! I must get goin on tha. Even if the others laugh at me. Lately I've been practisin when I answer the prayers at rosary time. Fuck them! I'm goin te get meself ahead in this life. Yeah!

I leapt outa bed an threw on me clothes, headin off te the refectory te get somethin te eat. I bounced down the stairs takin them two at a time, feelin light as air inside meself. Me hand was slidin along down the lovely shiny mahogany banisters, an I leaned over te slide down the rest a the way, when I got a fright. Not on yer nelly! Last year I nearly lost me life doin tha. I tumbled over backwards, sailin through thin air, straightenin up as I fell, an grabbed out instinctively, me hands landin on solid wood, grabbin hold a the banisters, seein meself swingin over an almighty drop. Jaysus! It must be a hundred feet drop down te the bottom onta the tiled passage.

I was shakin like jelly when I kicked out at the banisters an got me foot under, an hauled meself back up te the land a the livin, te survive an tell the tale. Ahhh! I learned me lesson good an proper. I shivered me shoulders thinkin back on tha time an floated on, landin on the landin. I stopped te listen te the silence an watch the early-mornin sun comin in an floodin the whole passage. The only sound I could hear is the birds havin their early-mornin get togethers te meet an eat an fight an have great gas, screamin an chatterin, all tryin te get their own point across!

'No! Quick! Over here! Lookit! The best spot, lots a crumbs down here, it's safer, there's a cat up tha end!'

'No! Listen the lot a ye's. Head for the kitchens: that's where ye get everythin!'

'No! There's a big black fuckin cat over there. An a dog! Yeah! An a dog!'

Then the sparrow lost his crust. I could hear the almighty screams.

'Ehhhh! Gimme back tha! Get yer claws offa me grub!'

'Catch me! Ha, ha!'

'Bleedin robber!'

It sounds like the pack a young ones in this place.

I took in a sharp breath, holdin it an lettin it go. Oh, it's lovely, nothin te worry about, an nearly the whole place te meself, wit only a few of us left. The heat from the sun was great, warmin me from head te toe. Jaysus! This place would freeze the arse off ye in the winter. We all trail aroun like hunched-up aul biddies lookin fer a bit a heat. The big metal storage heater in the playroom is no good. When you do get a chance te hoist yerself up an sit on it, ye either get the arse roasted offa ye, makin ye leap down, or it's lukewarm, an the bigger ones sit nestin on it, an let a roar at ye te get lost. Tha's when I get inta the hair-pullin fights. No one tells me te get lost! But it's usually me an half the convent all jumpin in, an I'm stuck under a pile a bodies, all tryin te kill me. I manage te come up fer air be holdin onta the leader, takin no notice a wha they're doin te me. I ignore the pain an wrap me fingers an anythin else I can wrap, puttin all me strength inta it, an makin her call off her hounds! It usually works. But no one calls me names, or starts a fight, or throws anythin at me when they're on their own. Oh no! They would be afraid a their life, cowardly fuckers. Or not even if there's two a them. No! I'll never be one a them. I didn't grow up in this place. Even the nuns keep their distance. Yeah, well, I'm not dependent on them. I can take care of meself, thank you very much!

I took off flyin down the rest of the stairs, jumpin onta the passage, feelin the hunger rise in me. I wonder wha's fer breakfast? Now I'll have all the bread te meself; I can eat as much as I want. I flew past the empty refectories, catchin sight a two young ones eatin their breakfast. Oh! There's only two a them left in the middle group, an the youngest ones, the little four te six year olds, must be all gone, I thought, slidin me eyes past the glass winda seein it empty. I flew inta our refectory an two a the older girls who go out te work in preparation fer when they leave at sixteen were finished their breakfast.

'How're ya, girls?'

'Oh! How're you?' Camille Lambert said, smilin at me as she dried her dishes.

'Are ye off te work, Camille?'

'Yeah! Better hurry, or they'll dock me wage packet at the end of the week.'

'Can ye not sneak in?' I asked.

'No! You have to clock in.'

'Do ye ever get te eat any a them biscuits ye make in Jacob's Factory, Camille?'

'I don't make them, I pack them, Martha, but they don't let you take any home; some of them do, on the quiet, but I don't want to lose me job.'

'Yeah, yeah! Better bein safe than sorry. When will you be leavin this place, Camille?'

'Oh, it won't be long now, they're tracing my mother, and when they find her . . .' She dropped her head slowly, dryin the plate, thinkin about it. 'She's somewhere in England, that's the last address they have for her,' she said wit a slow sigh, liftin her head, lookin off inta the distance, a worried look in her eyes.

Poor Camille, she'd love te meet her mammy, I thought, starin at her lovely greeny-blue eyes. She's real nice, very gentle. I like her.

'Anyway, I'm hoping when they do, I can go and stay with her for a while.'

'How long is it since ye last saw her, Camille?' I asked her, lookin at the worried look in her eyes, seein them change, watchin a pain comin inta them, sensin the lonely feelin comin through her.

'Gawd! It was a long time ago, Martha,' she said wit a faraway look in her eyes. 'I remember her dressing me, I couldn't have been more than three, probably less, and she'd put me good coat on me with the matching hat, the pixie one . . .'

'I remember havin one like tha!' I shouted, gettin all excited.

Memories started te crowd back at me, too. Bein on the boat, headin fer Liverpool, or probably comin back, about the same age Camille is talkin about. Me ma wakin me up from the two chairs she'd put together, an showin me the new blue coat wit the fur collar an the matchin blue pixie hat. Me heart started te fall te pieces seein an feelin the time an the place an me mammy smilin, all excited, her eyes shinin down at me, holdin up the hat an coat te show me, an me grizzlin, wantin te go back te sleep, but starin at me ma's face, likin her smilin, an lookin up at wha she was smilin about. Peelin me eyes on the hat an the coat. Oh, Mammy! Mammeee! Bring back them times! An I suddenly wanted te cry, feelin a terrible loss inside me, an a hunger leavin me empty. Then a pain hittin me, cos I could hear a loud bang, not in me head but down in me heart, of a big steel door slammin shut. Closin tha time an happy place fer ever. I can never get back te tha time. I wanted te open me mouth an cry me heart out until the pain an the loss eased in me, but it's no good. Cos tha's how it is. I dropped me head an squeezed me eyes shut, lettin tha thought push away the memory, then lifted meself an went on listenin te Camille.

'I was put into a big black car and me mammy stood on the footpath, waving like mad, while some woman held me up, lifting my hand to wave back at her, and I was shocked, not even able to cry at that minute, watching me mammy waving and smiling and the car was taking me away from her . . .'

'I still see her standing there . . . waving at me,' Camille said in a whisper, starin at the floor, her eyes starin back through time, seein her mother fer the last time.

I saw the movement shift her eyes, takin her back te here an the tears burstin out, then slowly roll down her cheeks.

She sniffed an gave a little laugh, wipin her nose quickly wit her hand, sayin, 'Gawd! It must be after eight o'clock, I'm going to be late.'

She threw the tea towel on the sink, grabbin her handbag, an rushed out the door.

'Come on, Camille! We'll miss the bus,' shouted Sammy Tyler, tearin out the back door.

'I'm coming! Wait!' shouted Camille, tearin after her.

I watched her go, thinkin it was very hard fer poor Camille an the rest a them. No wonder they are always goin mad te get Sister Eleanor's attention, an goin mad when they don't get it, an callin ye names if ye're nice te the nun, jealous cos they know tha's the way te get attention. But if ye do get yerself inta trouble, then tha's it, she has nothin te do wit ye! Everyone gets inta trouble sometime, an tha's when ye get left out in the cold. I'm always in trouble, so she hasn't much te say te me, an I ramble aroun most of the time, waitin fer her te come down from the convent, hopin she'll notice me an maybe be pleased wit me. But I'm not one of her pets an I'd give me right arm te be, yeah!

I have te be honest wit meself. It's awfully lonely, an the pain of not bein liked be Sister Eleanor cripples me somethin terrible. All I want is a mammy, an she's the one I want. Even if I'm too old fer all tha caper now! I still want te be made a fuss of, an have her call me pet an darling. Whether I'm too old or not! An waitin fer Sister Eleanor te appear back down from the convent takes all me time. An the hopin an the wishin an the lookin an the waitin, walkin the length an the breadth a the place. Just waitin te clap eyes on her keeps me goin. Rushin when I see her, an tryin te get meself squeezed in an be next te her, an distract her from all the other young ones hangin outa her, moanin about their complaints an lookin at me wit the rage in their eyes cos their chances of gettin a look in are lessenin wit another one joinin the pack te trail after her an shout about their wants.

Usually it comes te nothin cos she loses the rag an flies off talkin te herself about all the things she has te do an the things not done, an lets a roar at us. Then flies back te the convent an we stand on the convent passage watchin the door close wit a whoosh an know we can't follow her through there. She's taken the light wit her, an the hope an the expectation, leavin the place suddenly turnin dark an empty an cold. We stare at the door fer a few seconds, then everyone starts.

'I hate that one!' somebody suddenly turns aroun an shouts, starin at nothin, wit their mouth hangin open, feelin the rage in them at bein robbed.

'Yeah,' we mutter, me wishin I didn't need her. Then just wander off, some wit their heads hangin down, trailin the floor, an others wit disgust, a sour look on their face, an find somethin else te do, an wait fer the next time she comes back.

I found a way te get her attention. 'Do ye want me te do somethin fer ye, Sister Eleanor?' I shout, flyin like mad up te her when I see her comin. Tha always gets her attention. Even when ten other people are all shoutin at her at the same time.

'Oh, yes! Would you ever go . . .' an sometimes she might even hold me arm while she thinks! An I feel lovely an warm wit her hand on me while I wait te hear wha she wants me te do. 'Would you ever like a good girl,' she says, lookin inta me face, seein me, 'go into the refectory and wash up those plates those bold girls left behind, and would you sweep the floor for me and tidy up? Will you do that for me like a good girl?'

'Yes, Sister Eleanor!' I smile happily. Then she lets go of me arm an flies off, talkin te herself an lookin worried again. I fly off, racin down te the refectory, washin an cleanin an thinkin how happy she's goin te be wit me fer doin such a good job, leavin the place spotless so it will bring a smile te her face an she will look at me tellin me I am very good. Then I know she likes me. When she is happy wit me, then me whole world is lit up! Tha's wha keeps me goin! Until I do somethin wrong, then I'm out in the cold.

I turned aroun feelin the emptiness of the place fer a minute, noticin the tears on me face an wipin them away; I didn't know I was cryin.

Ah, stop! Ye were happy only a few minutes ago, sure wha have ye got te be belly-achin about? Life is great, an if ye want something, then ye know wha te do: go after it. Right! No more carryin-on, an Camille will be grand; sure, isn't she goin te be goin her own way in a few months? She can make her own life. The important thing about life is tha as long as we have the breath in us, we always have a chance. When I'm gone, I'm gone! An I only have one chance at life, so no matter wha happens, I'm grateful te be alive. Wha more could I want?

Yeah! I felt the happiness risin in me again. Food! Now wha's fer breakfast? I spotted the big metal pie dish wit the cornflakes sittin in it, an the big metal jug a milk. Lovely! An I have it all te meself; it's nearly full.

I slurped me way through three bowls a cornflakes, enjoyin the cold creamy milk an the lovely smell a the cornflakes goin up me nostrils, when I spotted Loretta Winters makin her way past the glass windas headin in here.

'Oh, I should have known you'd be here stuffing your face,' she laughed, turnin her face te the wall te complain.

'Ah, shrrup you! You're just ragin I got here fer first pick.'

'Hm! Yeah! What's for breakfast?' she asked, stickin her head in the cornflakes dish, askin fer the want te hear the sound of her own voice.

'How many of us are left in the group, Loretta?'

'What? Oh, Ellie is lookin for you!'

'Me?'

'Yeah. She's giving out the new jobs, for the ones leaving school.'

'Wha do ye mean?'

'Well, there's five of us being kept back to work aroun the house. An you're one of them.'

I am? Me heart sank. I'm not goin back te school. So tha's me lot! Sure, I barely got a foot in the bleedin school door. Now I'm out again.

They said I was thirteen when I got here, a year older than me ma said, the silly cow! Surely it's not tha difficult te keep track a thirteen years. She doesn't know her arse from her elbow tha one. I had te wait until I got here te have me fourteenth birthday, an I've just had tha. The first one in me whole life. I never knew when it came aroun. Ah, tha means I'll never be able te get past fifth class.

I was only ever in the fifth class, no fourth or third, or any fuckin class . . . just the one, sittin there like a gobshite, not knowin wha it was all about. But I mighta learned! So tha's it fer me whole life! Just one class! An the fuckin ma not tellin me I was thirteen. If I had known tha, I woulda taken off long ago! Flyin like the hammers a hell on the next banana boat outa this country, an well away from them. She's a cute aul fucker! She probably knew tha full well but was gettin worried seein it comin aroun the corner. Knowin I'd take off as fast as me skinny legs would take me, leavin her stranded. If I had a known tha, I woulda kept me mouth shut. Not go mutterin tha I was gettin the hell well away from tha mad bastard as soon as I hit fourteen. Hm! So now it's too late. I've landed meself in this place! An tha's put a stop te me gallop fer a while. But on the other hand. Well, I won't have te spend so long in this place, only another two years. Yeah! Me heart lifted; I can't wait fer tha day.

'I don't care!' Loretta laughed. 'I hated school anyway.'

'Yeah, I know, ye weren't bothered doin anythin. Jaysus, Loretta, you can hardly read!'

'Shrrup you! You did nothing either. You spent all the time playing oxo with me.'

Yeah, I thought, thinkin of the square boxes. Ye have te get three Xs or Os in a line te win. Still, I would have been happy te understand how te do the lessons, but it doesn't work like tha; ye have te know yerself. Ah well, I suppose there was no point in me goin te the technical school if I would be only wastin me time.

'So tha's it then. I'm always in Sister Eleanor's bad books, so I bet I'll end up pot wallopin in the kitchen wit Mercy havin a fit an bangin me over the head wit the bleedin pots,' I laughed.

'No! I got that job, I get on really well with Sister Mercy, and I can eat what I like.'

I looked at her, seein her lovely blue eyes sparklin at the thought a bein left school an gettin first go at the best grub.

'So, what am I on? Wha job am I gettin?'

'Dunno,' she said, shovellin half the bowl a cornflakes inta her mouth. 'Allanah got nursery, and so did lanky Mary Lemington, and the pet, Harriet Miller, got odd jobs around our group, working with Ellie, Sister Eleanor.'

'So wha does tha leave?' I said, tryin te think.

'Dunno! Go and find out.'

Right! I leapt up rushin me dishes te the sink an rinsin them out, an dried them quickly, puttin them on the long table. 'Bye, see ya!'

'See ya! You'll probably end up with the farmer, helping him clean out the cows' shit,' she laughed.

'Fuck off, Loretta Winters. Sister Eleanor has two hopes if she thinks she's gettin me out there: Bob Hope an no fuckin hope!'

CHAPTER 7

I tore up through the passages dyin te know wha job I got. Jaysus!
I hope I get somethin good; I don't want te end up wit Mercy in
the kitchen. Two of them were sent te the nursery wit the babbies.
Tha job woulda been lovely, pity I didn't get tha one, I love the
babbies. So maybe they will want two in the kitchen, tha means.
One te help Mercy wit the cookin, an one fer the pot wallopin – tha
will surely mean me. She would love tha. Get the chance te get her
own back be bangin me over the head wit the pots. Anyway, I don't
know how te cook, not even how te boil an egg! Ha, ha! Tha's wha
started the whole trouble in the first place. I can still see her face
after me eatin her cakes. Yeah! Everyone got a good laugh outa tha
one!

I looked aroun – not a sinner te be seen. Where is she? Damn!
Probably up in the convent gettin her prayers, prayin her life away.
I'll probably have te cool me heels, as she says, an wait, holdin me
patience. Maybe she's in the playroom gettin a bit a sewin done
while she has the peace an quiet. 'Sister Eleanor?' I put me head in
the room lookin aroun. Nope! Not here. I dashed up the stairs an
headed up te the dormitory. I'll knock on her door; maybe she's in
her room. It's right next te me bed, an she has another door in her
room tha leads right out inta the convent. Just as I hit the landin
an was about te fly through the dormitory, she came rushin out.

'Martha! Ah, Martha. Listen, I have something to tell you,' she
said, smilin an takin me arm.

'Yes! Is it about the jobs?' I puffed, anxious te know wha I was gettin.

'Yes, darling, it is.'

DARLING! An she's smilin at me. Hm! She's only sayin tha cos she wants something. She's a bit like the ma in tha. Soft soapin when they want somethin outa ye. Still, it's better than a kick up the arse.

'Yeah! Wha did I get, Sister?'

'Well!' she smiled. 'Mother Pius has asked especially for you to work on the hall door! That is a great privilege, Martha,' she said, narrowin her eyes an shakin her face, thinkin I truly am blessed. 'Mother Pius obviously thinks very highly of you to ask for you, so run into the convent quickly and gong for her. You will see the nuns' listing for how many gongs you give, and she will come to see you. Now, Martha! Only use the gong once and wait, don't upset her, because she is very important!' Sister Eleanor said, starin inta me eyes, lookin worried I might let her down.

'No, Sister, I'll behave. I'll be very good – on me best behaviour!'

She stared at me, not lookin too sure.

'Promise!' I said, dyin te get movin.

'Now remember, she is very important, and treat her with the same respect as you would the Reverend Mother.'

'Oh, right!' I said, thinkin I'm definitely goin te be in trouble in no time at all. Tha Reverend Mother has no time fer me. No wonder Sister Eleanor is lookin so worried. She gets all red at the mention a the Mother's name; she treats her like God!

'OK, run along and remember what I said.'

'Right! Thanks, Sister Eleanor. Don't worry, they won't even know I'm there!'

I headed meself up te the convent, passin the chapel, an arrived at the gong standin in front of the nuns' little passage leadin right inta the heart of the convent. I stared at the size of it. It looks like the one yer man on the fillums in the Rank advertisement bangs te announce the start of the fillum. Now I get te have a go. Right!

I lifted up the board covered in the plastic sheet an looked fer the number of bangs ye give te get the different nuns. One fer the Reverend Mother – no fear! Don't want her. Two fer Mother Pius. Right! Two! Here goes.

I picked up the long wooden mallet wit the ball at the end covered in calf's leather an swung it at the big round metal drum thing hangin from a leather rope. I gave it two unmerciful whacks, makin it fly like mad an listenin te noise soundin like every plate in the house was bein smashed. Me arm was still goin, wantin te give it another good belt, but I stopped meself an put the mallet back carefully, rememberin wha Sister Eleanor said. Jaysus! I don't want te lose me job before I even got a chance te get started!

'Yes?' A red-faced nun wearin very fancy black leather shoes wit soft-leather soles squeaked her way down te me, comin outa the office beside the telephone.

'Martha? Wonderful! You are going to be my new steward,' she roared, soundin English, but she's not, I heard she's German, I thought, watchin her sweepin herself down te grab a hold a me. 'Let me see you,' she said, grabbin me arms out in the air an spinnin me aroun. 'Yes! We shall have to get you a nice smock to wear while on duty. I shall go into Clerys store this afternoon and you shall have it ready for tomorrow morning. Now! Let me educate you on the rules. Incidentally, why are you not in the choir? I have been listening to you for some time now in chapel. You have a wonderful singing voice, very sweet, soprano, with a little contralto!'

I stared at her wit me mouth open. 'Eh . . .' I was thinkin tha's not a good idea.

'Do you think they will throw you out?' she whipped at me.

'Eh . . .' was all I could get out.

'I am all too well aware of your little tête-à-têtes with the other children. Really! It is ridiculous! You would be one of their most gifted. I will recommend you join the choir right away. We can't have this nonsense. You are very gifted, and you have a duty to see you do not waste these God-given gifts,' she snorted, wavin her finger at me.

'Yeah,' I said, shakin me head slowly, lettin her think I agree. But mutterin under me breath, 'Not on your nelly. Ye're not gettin me inta tha choir.' Havin te learn the Latin, then stand there singin our lungs out, soundin like a pack of crows on our last gasp! An she thinks we sound lovely? Gawd! She gets enjoyment outa nothin. No, I wouldn't be able fer all tha shoutin an messin an fightin wit all them gobshites! I'd sooner or later lose the rag an end up throwin one a them over the gallery te end up splattered on top a the Reverend Mother, dozin in her prie-dieu, supposed te be prayin.

'Yes,' she rambled on, 'I did so ask for you especially. I believe you are the best of the bunch. I'm surprised you are not continuing with your education, you are far too bright not to be allowed to do so,' she said lookin at me, her eyes starin inta mine, lookin very annoyed. 'Hm! I think I shall speak to Mother about this; some of the girls are being sent off to boarding school. I think you would benefit greatly if you continue with your education. Yes!' an she stood thinkin about this, forgettin about me waitin te start me new job. Then she woke up. 'OK! Come along quickly, don't dally, I have a lot of work to get through . . .'

'Now! This is the telephone. When it rings, you pick it up,' an she picked it up, 'say good morning or afternoon, whatever the time of day, and give the name of the convent.' Then she pointed te the gong. 'Familiarise yourself with the signals for each nun, and please . . . only call once. If the nun does not respond, take the small silver one and hunt them out in the grounds, where you will probably find them along the Cloistered Walk praying. Have you got that?'

'Yes, Mother Pius!'

'Good! Now the door. At all times you must be the essence of politeness! Remember you hold the reputation of the convent in your hands; this burden is placed on you when you present yourself at the front door. You will be the first person they will meet. So at all times you must be very polite and courteous. Also, the poor man who turns up looking for a cup of tea is also to be treated

with the same respect you yourself would like to enjoy. Do you
understand that?'

'Yes, Mother Pius!'

'Good! Now come along with me and I shall show you your
duties . . .

'You will arrive here at nine a.m. sharp, not a minute late. I do
not tolerate lateness, idleness or bad workmanship. If you must do
a job, do it well, or not at all! Do I make myself perfectly clear?'
she said, swishin her habit te look aroun at me as I followed her
down the little passage again an inta a big sittin room.

'This is the nuns' sitting room; you sweep and dust this room
every morning, and on Fridays you wax the furniture and floor.
Come along.'

I looked at the size of it, wit the long table an the chairs – I
counted six – an the big bookcase from ceilin te floor stuffed wit
holy books. An the sideboard, an four leather red armchairs each
side of the huge white marble fireplace, an big oil paintins of God
an the Apostles an all sorts of saints.

I followed her through a long passage wit brown tiles. 'This
must also be waxed and polished and dusted and swept every
morning.'

'Do I wax it every morning, Mother Pius?' I said, shocked.

'No, sweep and dust every day, and everywhere waxed on
Fridays.'

'Right! I said, followin her up the stairs.

'This will be scrubbed once a week also.'

Then we stepped off a little landin wit a winda, an up more
stairs an onta the longest passage I ever saw.

'These are the nuns' cells, where they sleep,' she said, bouncin
along the corridor, wavin her arms at a long line a doors. 'Swept
and dusted, waxed on Fridays,' she said, wavin at the long corridor
floor.

Me eyes looked the length a the passage. It must be the length
of O'Connell Street! Jaysus, how will I find me way aroun this
place, never mind clean an scrub it?

We got te the end a the passage an went down more stairs. 'These must also be scrubbed on Fridays and swept and dusted every day.'

We arrived back at the gong an flew down more stairs an inta a tilet. 'Clean this every morning, and of course if the floor needs mopping . . . in fact, you had better wash the toilet and basin every morning, using Vim. And those stairs,' she said, pointin te the ones we came down, 'must also be scrubbed, and they do tend to take a lot of traffic. Give them a mop out in the mornings after you have swept, and dust along the edges of the staircase there. I shall run my finger along to be sure you have dusted, so no shortcuts, please!' she said, pointin her finger at me.

We traipsed on down more stairs an finally ended up on the last passage. It was dark down here, no winda te throw in the light. 'These old Victorian tiles must be scrubbed and waxed; they need constant care or they tend to become shabby . . . dull and dirty-looking. Now! You will finish by twelve-thirty in the afternoon, then you go for lunch, and please be back by one-thirty to resume your duties. You will receive five shillings every Friday; this is not wages, it is your pocket money. In the afternoons at one-thirty, you will go to the convent kitchen where you will wash up the dishes and sweep and clean the floors, then you may be called to help the Sacristan Sister Benedict to wax and polish the chapel; after the nuns' office, prayers. Then you may go in to sweep and dust . . .

'Now! Our retreat will be starting shortly, and our nuns from the convents around the country will be arriving here to take their retreat. It will go on for eight days, and this is taken in complete silence. The nuns do not converse with anyone; they will spend the time in prayer and listening to lectures from the visiting Benedictine monk taking the retreat. So, when you see a nun coming towards you, please make yourself scarce and above all do not speak or make eye contact, and you must do your duties in absolute silence. Is that clear?'

'Yes, Mother Pius!' I said, lowerin me head, already feelin the holy an solemn occasion of it all.

'Now! One more thing. You really must improve your diction. Do open your mouth when you speak and stop dropping your endings of a word! Start practising now – AND, ING, TH – it will come to you quite easily. This should not pose problems for you, you are quick and bright, and I see great promise for you . . .

'Now we must start right away. Our Matron Millington, she takes care of the nuns. She will be wanting you to give her a hand to set up the cells for the visiting nuns in preparation for the coming retreat. Some of them will arrive early, perhaps two days before. So you must start to scrub and wax the convent from top to bottom straight away; the nuns will be arriving in six days. So you must be finished at the latest the day before. Now come along, I shall take you upstairs to meet Matron Millington.'

We climbed the stairs again, walkin along the corridor with the nuns' bedrooms, or cells as Mother Pius called them. I could hear bangin comin from the far end.

'In here, dear.'

I could see a very old woman humpin iron beds aroun the room. There's loads a them stacked against the wall.

'Mona! This is Martha; she is the new child taking over the convent duties.'

'Ah! You're very welcome, Martha. Come over here till I get a good look at you. My! Aren't you a lovely girl? You have lovely hair, God bless you!' An she made a dive te feel me shoulder-length hair wit me fringe hangin over me eyes. 'Oh, we'll have to cut that fringe,' she said, moppin it offa me forehead.

Not on yer nelly, I'm thinkin te meself, lookin her up an down the length a the floor. She has te be ninety if she's a day, I thought te meself, lookin at her wisps a grey hair stickin outa a white frilly linen bonnet tha they wear te bed in the cowboy fillums when they're well off an livin in the town. Her face was like melted dough tha was beginnin te harden. Soft an wrinkly an hangin down te her chest nearly. She was wearin a white smock an black laced-up boots wit very thick nylons tha fell down in rolls an wrapped themselves aroun her ankles.

'Well!' she said, standin back an examinin me. 'You and me are going to get along like a house on fire. I can see the mischief in them blue eyes. Sparkling with the devilment and mischief they are. Ahh! We should have some great laughs.'

'Yes, Matron, I shall get a move on,' the nun said, movin herself te the door, not likin the sound a the idea of me an the matron havin a laugh. 'Yes, she will be a great help to you, Matron.' Then she vanished in a whish of floatin black an disappeared down the passage.

Matron Mona gave me a dig wit her elbow, laughin, an whispered, 'What did she say to you?'

'Eh . . . she told me wha me work was.'

'Don't be mindin any a them! They would put years on yeh with their fussing and carrying on,' she said, laughin an winkin.

I like her, I thought, grabbin a hold a the spring an puttin it sittin on the black bars already waitin.

'Come on, we have to get these into the rooms ready for the big contingent arriving any day. Oh, the curse on them, why they bloody have to come here I'll never know! It's just more work for us. Here! You go first and I'll steer,' she said, grabbin hold a the bed an heavin me out the door. I was headin fer the door opposite, she was movin so fast! 'Turn left, Martha! Before yeh put a hole in the wall and end up sitting on top of one a the aul nuns in the cell,' she laughed.

I kept goin, me head swingin in all directions, wonderin which was me left. I hardly had time te think, she was movin so fast.

'Now!' Matron Mona breathed, liftin her head an tryin te straighten herself, rubbin her back. 'Just run the duster along the irons and we will make up this bed. Oh, that's the last a them beds, thanks be to bloody hell! I'm too old for this malarkin about! Then you can sweep the floor and run the duster over the room and finish off with giving the floorboards a quick run over with the drying-upper to bring back the shine. I wonder what time it is. Hurry! I think the bell may go any minute for the dinner, and

I want to be out of here by then. I'm not bloody humping meself
back up here to mess around.'

I shot aroun the iron bed wit the duster, an we banged the
mattress on top an put the sheets on, then the black hairy blankets,
an Matron said, 'Now, Martha, I'm going to show yeh how to make
up a bed properly. Here! Grab a hold of the sheet an blankets from
the bottom, and lift the top. Now hold it up an put the end ones
underneath, and now fold that under, and tuck it in all along the
sides. Now stand back and take a look, it's called an envelope!
Taking the corners and tucking them in like that. That is how we
were trained to make hospital beds.'

'Did ye work in a hospital, Matron?'

'Oh, indeed I did, child! I worked in Belgium during the Great
World War. Yes! I went out in November 1915,' she said, lowerin
her voice an droppin her head, her eyes not seein this place any
more, gettin lost in herself in a time long ago.

'But, Matron,' I shouted, wantin te know, havin so many
questions all in a flash. But I just couldn't get any words outa
meself. I just stood, lookin at her wit me mouth wide open. Then
she came back te me, liftin her face, an she laughed wit her eyes,
standin back wit her chest thrown back an her hands on her hips
studyin me studyin her. 'But the bombs must a been flyin in all
directions,' was all I could get out, me head flyin at the idea she
was a . . . hero!

'Yes, I worked side by side with surgeons fighting to save a man's
life and cutting off limbs.'

'No? Gawd!' I breathed.

'Yes! And more died than we could save . . . Oh, enough of
that,' she said, shakin her head te get rid a the memories. 'You're
too young to be hearin what I saw and did, you'll have your own
troubles soon enough! Now come on! Let's get this bloody room
finished before I drop from me standing.'

We trailed down the passage just as the bell went fer dinner.
'Bloody hell! Come on, Martha! Hurry! Let's go down the back
way; I don't want to meet all them bloody nuns, I see enough of

them day and night.' An she giggled an took off tryin te run on her black boots, draggin me behind her be me frock.

I roared laughin at her, 'Gawd! Ye're gas, Matron Mona. I'm havin a better time wit you than I do wit the girls in me group! Ye'd think you were very young, because ye're game fer anythin.'

'Yeh can say that again,' she laughed, grabbin me arm an gettin me up beside her.

'How long are ye here, Matron?' I whispered, hearin the nuns come outa their room an head off in the other direction as we headed down te the nuns' sittin room. We clattered along, her hammerin the floorboards an makin them shake in her big boots. Then out te the passage an down the back stairs, an onta the old Victorian grey tiles.

Matron opened the back door from the convent tha leads straight inta the concrete passage where our kitchen an refectory are. An loads of other rooms: the staffroom; an the little Holy Family room; an the pantry room; an the bread room, where all the bread is kept locked behind a cage. Otherwise we'd get our hands on it an eat the lot. An there's the dairy, where the farmer brings in the buckets a milk wit thick yella cream sittin on top, covered wit muslin be Sister Mercy.

'Well,' Matron Mona puffed. 'I came here many a few years ago now, after the war, looking for peace, for a rest,' she huffed, outa breath. 'I was only intending to stay a little while, but here I am . . . still here. Now, love, go and get your dinner, you're a great little worker, and I'm delighted to have yeh up in the convent. We'll have some great times together. Now go on,' an she gave me a push. 'Go and eat up everything they give yeh, you're going to need it,' she cackled.

'Oh, go on, Matron! It's not as bad as tha,' I laughed.

'No! You're right! It's worse,' she laughed, bangin the door shut an disappearin.

I turned aroun an headed up the passage, not wantin te be late fer me dinner. They might leave me nothin, the greedy fuckers!

CHAPTER 8

I dragged the metal basin wit the soapy water, landin it on the second-last stair, an slopped in the scrubbin brush, swirlin it aroun. Then rubbed the big bar a Sunlight soap through the brushes, sendin a shower a soapy water flyin at me face an hair. I wiped me stingin eyes wit the back a me hand, an rubbed the wet hair outa me face. It was all stuck, dried hard from the washin soap, an I was hot an tired an me bones ached like mad. Then I slapped the scrubbin brush down on the white heavy rubber coverin the stairs an started te scrub, tryin te get the black marks off from the nuns' rubber-soled shoes. They're filthy; I'm never goin te be able te keep these stairs clean!

I scrubbed like mad, runnin me hand up an down, an the soap was makin me hands even more raw from all the dippin in an out a the carbolic soap an washin the place from top te bottom. I finished an dropped the brush back inta the cold dirty water an squeezed out the cloth, runnin it over the stair an dried it. Then standin meself up slowly, I stretched, tryin te get me back te straighten. I leaned meself back against the banisters, stoppin fer a minute te take a rest an look down the rest a the way. 'Nearly there,' I breathed te meself. Just tha last Victorian passage te scrub an tha's it. Jaysus! At last I'll be finished. I've been goin mornin, noon, night an day te get this convent finished fer them retreat nuns, an draggin meself outa here banjacksed. Gawd, I can't wait te get stuck inta me tea, I'm starvin wit the hunger. Christ! It must be nearly tha time now! I better get a move on.

I reached up an dragged the basin onta the tiled floor an dropped te me knees an started te scrub the last step. Right! Tha's it, better get the bucket an clean water an get them grey tiles done, then tha will be it fer another week. I'll only have me ordinary work te do from then on.

'Hurry! The nuns are arriving! We need to have this chapel finished by lunchtime, and the retreat will be starting tonight at ten o'clock.'

'I'm goin as fast as I can, Sister Benedict! Why won't ye ask Sister Eleanor te send up someone to help me te polish, while I polish an dry it in wit the dryer-upper?'

'She has nobody,' she said. 'Now stop arguing and get a move on, Martha Long! You are wasting valuable time.'

I looked the length a the chapel, an me heart dropped, an me eyes settled on the benches all piled together, stacked one against the other. 'Then ye better get someone in here te help push them benches back, Sister. I won't be able to do it on me own.'

'Oh, stop wittering and get a move on, or I'll go and get the Reverend Mother in here immediately.'

'OK! I'll get movin,' I said, feelin very tired after all me scrubbin an polishin until all hours at night.

I reached down, liftin the wooden spoon an dug it inta the bucket a wax an flung it at the floor, grabbin the big heavy dryer-upper an pounded it over the polish, spreadin it up an down an workin me way from one side te the other. Then got the polishin one, diggin me feet inta the floor an heavin it over the wax dryin inta the floor. I pulled an pushed until it began te shine an the wax dried in, makin the floor come up in a shine lookin like glass. I dug in, flyin the heavy block up an down, faster an faster, bringin up such a massive shine I could nearly see me face in it. Halfway there!

I grabbed the first bench an swung it aroun an went te the

other side an did the same, gettin it down te the end where me floor was now lovely an shiny, ye really can see yer face in it!

'Are you still not finished?' aul Sister Benedict roared in a whisper, comin in an huffin up the chapel, swingin herself from side te side in her black Hush Puppy slippers.

'Nearly!' I puffed, pushin the last bench inta place an standin back te admire me lovely work.

The chapel sparkled, an me floor glowed wit a red hue. 'Now, Sister Benedict, did I do a good job?' I said happily, feelin I'd never be able te stand straight again. But I was happy wit all me hard work.

Sister Benedict said nothin fer a minute. I watched her walkin along the side a the benches an flyin her watery grey old tired eyes aroun, lookin te see if I missed anything or there was somethin outa place.

'No! That's grand,' she said happily, lookin more at ease now an throwin herself back te lean her hands on her hips, an let her head swing aroun wit more ease an take in the place. 'Yes! You did a good job, Martha Long. Thank you very much. Now! Did you get your dinner?'

'No, Sister. I wanted te get this finished. I hope they kept me somethin.'

'Run along, child, you must be starving! You should never miss your meals. That is very bad for you at your age; you are still growing. If you want to live as long as me, then you should eat well, pray, get to bed early and be up with the lark, ready to do a hard day's work.'

'What age are ye, Sister Benedict?'

'I am not telling you that! It is very impertinent to ask an older person what age they are.'

I laughed, 'Are ye nearly ninety, Sister?'

'No! I have a few more years to go! Now be gone with you. I have work to do.'

'Right, Sister, I'm off fer me dinner.'

I took the convent stairs two at a time, admirin me lovely clean white rubber I scrubbed last night, an landed on the lovely grey tiles sparklin wit the polish. An the lovely clean smell went up me nose, makin me feel at peace wit meself. Feelin I had everythin in its place, an there was nothin botherin me.

I whipped open the back convent door an rushed onta the grey concrete passage, headin inta the kitchen fer me dinner. I stopped suddenly at the sight a Sister Mercy stoppin te glare at me. 'Eh, I've come fer me dinner, Sister Mercy.'

'Did yeh get dat tea for the poor man yet?'

'Wha poor man?'

'The one sitting out in the hut for the last half hour!'

'No! I didn't know anythin abou tha.'

'Well, go and make it now! You'll find the tea canister and the mugs on the poor man's tray dere!'

'Where?' I asked, spinnin me head aroun the kitchen, not seein it.

She stamped over in her hobnailed big black boots an rattled the tray wit the dishcloth in her hand, roarin, 'Open your eyes! We haven't the time to be dancing attendance on you!'

'Right!' I said, makin a dive fer the tray. 'But, eh, wha about me dinner, Sister? Did ye . . .'

'Get a move on and make the tea! He's not going to wait on your pleasure! The poor man's out dere with his tongue dragging along the ground for the want of a drop.'

'Right,' I said, grabbin the big heavy kettle wit the steam pourin outa it an pourin it inta the teapot.

'Put the tea in first, yeh amadan!'

'OK,' I said, lettin go a the kettle an splashin it down, burnin me hand.

'Get outa me way,' she roared, takin the little egg cup filled wit tea an sendin it flyin everywhere in her hurry te get it inta the little teapot. 'Now take dis, and don't come in here fustering around my kitchen again!'

'Right, Sister Mercy.'

I headed off up the long passage an out the top door, carryin the tray out te the grounds. The light blinded me, an I felt like a vampire seein the day fer the first time in years.

'God bless ye, little one,' an aul man wrapped in loads a jackets an coats wit a bit a twine wrapped aroun his waist te keep them together, an a pair a boots wit more twine tied aroun the soles te keep the top of them tha was tryin te stand up cos they were split at the toes, an ye could see his black feet wit the long black toenails stickin out, an the socks aroun them was in ribbons.

'Eh, I wonder, little one, would ye err have a bit a bread te go wit the tea?' He looked down at me, leanin his face inta me, an his teeth was black, an I stared at the long black hairs growin outa the top a his nose. The dirt was grained inta his forehead, an his face was covered in huge blackheads. The smell a him nearly knocked me out. But I couldn't move meself back, because I knew it would only hurt him. The whites of his eyes was all bloodshot, an his faded grey eyes looked out at me wit terrible kindness in them, an he looked at me like I was the most important person in the world, an I was a lovely person altogether.

'I . . . the nun in the kitchen is a bit mean,' I said, thinkin. Knowin I wouldn't be able te get him anythin.

'I wouldn't be askin ye, only I missed out on the bit a dinner up in Cabra. I had longer te walk today, ye see. I was far from me rounds over be Adam an Eve's church down on the quays . . .'

'I know it!' I said, thinkin tha's nearly beside where me an Charlie an the ma were born.

'Well, ye'll know then wha an awful aul long walk it is. Especially when ye're in a hurry. So I carried on down here . . .'

'Hang on,' I said. 'I'll see if I can get ye somethin.'

'Ah, God bless ye, I'm very grateful,' he smiled happily.

I raced down past the convent door, lookin at the retreat nuns all stoppin an laughin an talkin te each other, delighted te be meetin each other again. An flew aroun the back door an headed inta the nuns' convent kitchen. I opened the door quietly an put me head in. No sound – good! I think Sister Thomas is gone. I raced through the scullery an inta the kitchen, an made straight fer the fridge. Two cooked chops sat in tinfoil – wonder who she's keepin them fer? Me! I picked up a lump a cheddar cheese, then went te the bread press an took down a brown soda bread, it smelled lovely an fresh. Then grabbed another one. Two's better than one when ye're hungry! Then I saw somethin sittin on the side a the counter. Two fish done in breadcrumbs. Right! I'll take them, an went back te the fridge an grabbed a block a butter sittin in greaseproof paper an looked through the press fer tinfoil.

Fuck! Hurry, I hear someone. I grabbed the tinfoil, tearin a long bit, an threw everythin in together an flew like greased lightnin out the door, headin back te the hut.

'Here! Don't let them see ye wit tha,' I puffed outa breath.

'Oh, ye're a God-sent angel! May God an his Mother make sure ye never go for the want of anythin for as long as ye live! God bless ye, child, an I hope ye have great luck.'

'Thanks, Mister! I better run!' An I took off thinkin, ye should have tha, not them bleedin fats nuns, they have more than enough, an I know better than anyone wha it's like te go hungry. God help tha poor man, he looks like he's on his last days.

I tore back inta the kitchen; the sight an smell a the grub I just robbed made me really hungry fer me dinner. The hunger is makin a hole in me belly; I wonder if the aul fucker kept me somethin te eat.

'Your dinner is in the oven,' she roared as I put me head back in the door.

I grabbed the dishcloth from the steel bar over the Aga an took out the hot plate, whippin off the metal dish cover. Lovely! Roast meat an two sausages, an carrots an mashed potatoes in gravy. The smell went up me nose an the steam covered me face. I headed outa the kitchen holdin onta me hot plate wit the dishcloth, an was just on the passage when I heard a roar.

'Come back here, Martha Long!'

I turned, headin back inta the kitchen.

'Yeh better scrub dat passage after tea this evening. It has not been done in weeks!' she roared, starin at me.

'Wha passage, Sister Mercy?'

'The long kitchen passage,' she roared, pointin te where I stood.

'But!'

'No buts! Dat's part of your work. Now I want it scrubbed from top to bottom dis very evening, and yeh have to do it at the same time every Friday.'

'OK,' I said, lookin miserably at the length a the passage.

I finished me dinner an started te rinse the plate under the hot tap when Sister Eleanor came flyin in. 'Oh, really and truly, this refectory is disgusting! Look at those plates still sitting in the sink,' she said, making a grab te take them out an pile them on the draining board. 'Oh, listen, darling, will you ever take charge of this refectory after the dinner? Wash the dishes and wipe down the tables and sweep the floor, there's no one to do it. Will you do that for me, pet?' she said, lookin inta me eyes an pleadin wit me, lookin lost.

'OK, Sister,' I whispered, wonderin if I have the time after me dinner. I have te run over te the convent kitchen an work over there.

'Oh, thank you, darling! That will be a great help to me,' then she vanished out the door.

'I better get a move on,' I muttered, lookin aroun the room.

CHAPTER 9

The nuns helpin te clear the convent refectory table came ramblin inta the kitchen one be one an left their plates on the drainin board fer me te wash.

'Oh, you're a wonderful worker!' gushed the nun in charge of doin the rounds helpin the poor in their own homes.

'What's that, Sister, you're saying?'

'I was just saying what a great girl Martha is! She's always on the go!'

'Oh, yes! Indeed we would be lost without her,' roared the aul head nun from the school, Sister Ursula.

I looked at her examinin her plate te see if she had cleaned it enough. It looked like she had licked it clean, but she found somethin te stick on her tongue, an moved her teeth an tongue wit her mouth flyin up an down tryin te find it, then she gave the plate one last look before landin it down beside me, not really takin a blind bit a notice of wha the nun was sayin te her.

'Oh, yes indeed she is,' she said, tryin te bring herself outa her trance, her eyes crossin, an looked up, stretchin her face te see better at the nun talkin. 'Eh! Oh, yes,' an her head flew aroun landin on me, sayin, 'Oh, yes, our Martha is a Trojan worker. She was the same with me at school, is that not right, my dear?' she said, restin her hand on me back as if she thought I was the greatest thing since sliced pan.

I said nothin an just carried on wit me washin up. Tha aul

one has a short memory! She made it her business every mornin te roar her head at me, sayin, 'I hope you have your homework done, Long!'

Course I hadn't! I didn't know wha I was supposed te be doin. Anyway, I'm glad te be away from her; she hated the sight a me. Any trouble goin an of course it was my bleedin fault! Ah, she never bothered me, because I don't even like the woman.

I put the sweepin brush an dustpan an handbrush back in the press an looked aroun the convent kitchen. Finished. Better get up te the hall door. Ma Pius will be waitin fer me te take over the door an the phone. I could hear her voice ringin in me ear if I was one minute late.

I sat in me own little waitin room leanin me face in me hands, restin me elbows on the wide windasill, an stared out at the orchard. I dropped me shoulders, lettin out a big sigh, feelin the contentment in me, lettin the peace an the lovely sweet soft sound of the nuns singin in the chapel lull me inta a lovely doze. They sounded so sweet an melodious. It ran through me, takin me te a world where there's no pain, no sufferin, no hurry an no worry. Just feelin a stillness. Calm an peaceful an dreamy, makin me wonder wha all the fuss an the bother is about.

I didn't notice the phone ringin away fer a minute, I was so lost in meself gettin carried away wit the picture of meself wrapped up in a black habit covered from head te toe, the white bonnet hidin under the veil givin me a bit a colour.

I saw meself gazin up at the altar, singin the Gregorian Chant, just like they're doin now. I would float outa the chapel wit me hands wrapped under me wide sleeves, or under me cloak. Lost in a fog of holiness, seein an hearin nothin. Then glide up te me little cell on the last bell, tellin me me work is done fer the day.

I sighed, liftin me head seein the garden again an thinkin, yeah, I might like te be a nun. Then the janglin rattled me nerves. The phone! I jumped up an crept fast up the chapel passage, makin sure not te make a sound. Then made fer the little phone box an picked up the phone. I held me breath, then shoutin out in me best voice, hopin te sound like Ma Pius, 'Hul..lo! Gud..after..nune! Dis..is dee Ho..le..Re..De..mer Cun..vent speekink!' Then listened.

'Cud I spake te the nun . . . gabble . . . charge . . . gabble . . . butter . . . R . . . der.'

'Wha? I can't hear ye! Wha did ye say?'

'Tsk' . . . big breath . . . 'tsk . . . I want te spake te . . . babble . . . butter ORDER!'

'Eh, just a minute, please. I shall go now an..dt ge..dt someone fer yew!'

I dropped the phone an rushed te get the gong, wonderin wha the hell they were sayin. I picked up the mallet an then remembered just in time. Ma Pius said I wasn't te gong when the retreat nuns were in the chapel! I looked aroun. Wha'll I do?

Sister Benedict came swingin herself outa the chapel headin fer me. 'Martha Long! Who is that telephone call for?'

I looked at her, thinkin. 'Eh, it's for Sister Butter Order.'

'Who?' she gasped.

'Sister Butter Order! A woman on the phone said she wants te speak te her.'

'Oh, can you not take a simple message?' she huffed, swingin herself past me an draggin herself up te the phone. I disappeared back te me little waitin room. Tha aul one on the phone was speakin very fast, an I couldn't understand her culchie accent!

I went back te lookin out the winda; it was beginnin te look like rain. The sky was gettin dark, an the room was feelin a bit chilly. I watched the apple trees beginnin te wave wit the wind blowin up. Gawd! We're always dyin te get our teeth inta them apples, but the only look we get at them is watchin them from our playroom growin on the trees. Last year I got meself inta terrible trouble when the older young ones put the big idea inta me head te climb out the winda an grab a few.

'Go on! Go on! You're skinny and small enough to fit through the bars,' they roared, eggin me on.

I looked at the bars, sayin, 'Then youse better mind the door an watch fer Sister Eleanor!'

'Yeah, yeah! Course we will, hurry! We'll keep watch!'

I climbed out, stuffin meself through the thick black iron bars, an flew inta the orchard, gallopin fer the first tree. I grabbed a hold of the lowest branches an shook the hell outa them. Apples flew down in all directions, landin on me head, an I grabbed a handful.

'Throw them in!' the big ones roared.

Me head was flyin, lookin an listenen te them an wonderin how I'd carry the rest still sittin on the ground.

'OK!' I shot te the winda, sendin them flyin in, then suddenly I heard a load of shoutin.

'Look, Sister! She's robbing the orchard!'

Jaysus! The big ones were munchin on me apples an laughin their heads off, an the others were stampedin in wit the nun! Oh, help! Mammy! The nun is comin. Me heart is goin so fast it's tryin te fly out through me mouth. Ahh! I looked aroun me at all the apples still sittin on the grass. All this is fer nothin! Fuck! I'm gettin somethin for me trouble. I bent down, flyin aroun the grass, pickin up apples an shovin them down me knickers, an flew at the winda just as Sister Eleanor came flyin through the door, all black veil an the wings of her sleeves an habit flyin out behind her, screamin, 'Where is she? Martha Long! GET OUT OF THAT ORCHARD AT ONCE!'

I got stuck in the bars tryin te get meself back in a hurry.

'Get in!' she roared, draggin me through the bars an landin me hangin offa the windasill face down, lettin the apples roll outa me big navy-blue knickers. She grabbed them up, slappin me arse wit the other hand an tryin te hold onta the apples, while the young ones tried te grab them offa her. 'You are very bold! That is strictly forbidden. Get in! How dare you? Dilly Nugent, give me back those apples at once!'

I whirled meself aroun an leapt te the floor, runnin before me feet even hit the floorboards, an made fer the door, while the nun wrestled Dilly Nugent an her gang fer the apples. The big ones were screamin their heads laughin, an Sister Eleanor was screamin, hysterical an all red-faced, an Dilly Nugent an her gang was screamin at losin the apples.

I grabbed the door handle te make me getaway, an the big young ones blocked me way. 'Stay here, Long! You're going nowhere!' they laughed, hangin onta me fer the nun. She grabbed hold a me an marched me next door an locked me in, takin the handle a the door wit her so I couldn't get out.

'Stay here until I get back and decide what to do with you,' she roared through the door, an I could hear her marchin off, flyin up the stairs.

Oh, gawd! She's probably goin te the convent te get the Reverend Mother fer me! Ahh! Help, I'm really for it now. I'm not stayin here. I looked in her sewin machine an took out her big shears she calls it, a big scissors, an put it through the lock, an it opened.

'Get back in there!' the big ones roared, waitin outside the door fer me.

I lifted me head lookin aroun me little waitin room. Yeah, I got meself inta an awful lot a trouble tha time. Sister Eleanor didn't speak te me fer weeks over tha. She said I was a very bad influence on the other childre! But I'm bidin me time. Them young ones have had it their own way fer long enough, an one of these days I'm goin te find a way te turn the tables on them. Yeah, see if I don't, ye ratbags!

I heard the rustle of a habit an the shakin a rosary beads an the squeakin a soft leather shoes – Mother Pius! I sat up straight in me chair wit me heart givin a jump. Wonder wha she wants? Hope I'm not in trouble.

'Ah, Martha. Here you are. Well, really, you gave us nuns quite a laugh. Ha, ha! You are so funny,' she said wipin her red nose wit a big white hankie. 'Sister Butter Order! Well, I have been called many things, I am sure. But Sister Butter Order? Oh, we did laugh! You are a hoot! Listen, my dear, they were asking for me. I am in charge of the butter order. My job as Mother Pius is to take charge of the money. So refer all those calls to me, hm?' she said, lookin down at me an pattin me head.

'Yeah, right, Mother Pius.'

'Yes! You must say yes! Now start improving your diction; open your mouth, dear. Now I should get you on to some reading. Meanwhile, I have a lovely present for you.'

Me eyes lit up as she landed down a Clerys bag on the little table, openin it an pullin out a plastic sheet wit holes in it, an another bag wit balls a different colour wool. Me mouth dropped as I watched her take a crochet needle she called it, an pull the wool through an inta the hole an pull it back out again. 'Now! You see?' she said smiling. 'It is very simple. You can make me a lovely rug to put beside my bed. Wouldn't that be lovely?' she said, all smiles, showin me her big horses' teeth, shakin her shoulders wit the excitement.

'Eh, yeah . . . yes.' I wasn't feelin very excited meself as I looked at it, takin it from her te examine wha she did.

'Go on, do have a try, it really is easy, you know.'

I put the needle inta the hole, wrappin the wool through, an felt meself wantin te go te sleep already.

'Good girl! Now you will have something exciting to look forward to when your cleaning duties are finished. You can be doing something really useful and enjoying yourself at the same time. We must have fun: all work and no play makes Jack a dull boy. Ha, ha! Now I must be off!' An she twirled herself, makin her habit swing aroun the edges, an took herself off out the door, leavin me lookin at balls a wool an a bit a plastic.

Ah, fuck ye, Ma Pius, you an yer rug! I hate makin things! I stared at it then made a start, an after a few minutes stopped te get a look an see how much I'd done. Five holes! Ah, I'm not botherin me arse wit tha. An threw it down on the table, lookin out the winda again, seein nothin had changed.

I wandered up aroun the phone, starin at it fer a minute, hopin it would ring, but still nothin happened. Then I wandered out te look at the front door, an nobody called. I can't open the door te get a look outside, the nuns would skin me alive. Then the big parlour door opened an a monk in long brown robes stared down at me. He was nearly the height a the top a the door. He had jet-black wavy hair an laughin blue eyes tha danced in his head.

'Hello there, little lady!'

'Hello, Father,' I said, hopin the nuns wouldn't come along an ask me wha I'm doin here disturbin the monk.

'What is your name?' he said, smilin at me.

'Martha, Father.'

'Ah, Martha. Saint Martha!' he said te himself. 'I hope you are not a saint!' he said suddenly, lookin down at me very seriously.

'Eh, no, Father! Definitely not tha. The nuns would let ye know tha fast enough,' I said, laughin.

'Good! We have enough of them around here,' he roared laughin, throwin his head back. 'I see you around here beavering away. Quite a busy little bee, aren't you?'

'Yeah, Father. I have me work te do, an I have te get it done quickly, or I miss me dinner!'

'Oh, take as many shortcuts as you can. Dinner comes first,' he said, tryin te look serious. 'I think it's time for a little reward. Would you agree with me?'

'Yeah! Oh, yeah! Definitely, Father!' I said, shakin me head up an down, wonderin wha he was goin te give me. It couldn't be any worse than the knittin Ma Pius gave me. Anythin is better than tha.

'Would you like some sweets?'

'Eh, yeah I would,' I said happily.

He pushed open the door, wavin over te the table wit bowls a sweets an fruit an everythin fer yer heart's desire. Me eyes flew along the table, takin in the big slab a yella cake Sister Thomas must a baked fer him. An yella butter from the dairy, an crusty-lookin soda bread, an jugs a cream an bowls a strawberries, an Jaysus! I couldn't take in half the things, there's so many!

'Come on in and help yourself,' he said, seein me hesimitate an look aroun te see if a nun was comin. 'Come along, quickly! Get the sweets anyway! You don't want to get caught before you even sampled some of the stuff. Here!' An he lunged at the table, grabbin a handful of sweets an stuffin them in me smock pocket, then reached over fer another handful, stuffin me other pockets, an laughed, sayin, 'Come in and have some cake while you are thinking about it.'

I made up me mind an shot inta the room, waitin fer him te cut me a big slice a cake wit a wide silver knife an put it on a red flowery plate wit gold aroun the rims. 'Eat that,' he said handin me the plate. I lifted it up an took a big bite while he sprawled himself in an armchair, sayin, 'They give me far too much; it's much more fun watching you get enjoyment from it. I'm not a particularly good sweet eater. What are you doing at the moment?'

'Eh, I'm waitin fer the door an phone te ring, Father,' I said, sendin a shower a cake crumbs flyin outa me mouth, watchin it fly in all directions. I felt meself lookin very foolish, an I grabbed me mouth te hide them, an nearly choked, cos the cake was too dry an went down me windpipe! I was eatin too quickly.

'Here, take a drink,' he said, laughin an standin up an pourin me a glass a orange from a big sparklin bowl wit slices a fruit floatin in it. It slid down me neck, makin me face shiver. I drank the lot in one go, an he filled it up again, sayin, 'Have as much as you want.' Then he leaned back in his armchair, sayin, 'What age are you?'

'Fourteen, Father.'

'Have you left school?'

'Yes, I just started workin here on the hall door.'

'What was your favourite subject at school?' he asked, leanin over in his chair, waitin fer me answer.

'Eh, English, Father. Readin an writin an spellin, an sums ye do in your head. Mental arithmetic they call it. But I didn't get far in school, Father. I came in an they put me inta the fifth class, an I hadn't been te school before tha, only in an out fer a little while. But I never learned anythin, cos I wasn't there long enough.' Then I took another big bite of me cake an a sup a me drink. Enjoyin meself no end. Eatin an havin the monk talkin te me was better than sittin wit aul Ma Pius's knittin.

'Do you read?' he asked me, soundin really interested in wha I had te tell him.

'Yeah! The *Bunty* an *Judy* . . . they're comics. But I don't get them any more.' I didn't say tha's cos I don't go te the shops any more an rob me own!

'Hm, and what were your favourite stories?'

'Wee Slavey! She was a little young one back in them Victorian times, an she worked in the big house down in the kitchen. An they made her do everythin. She was blind bothered an bewildered tryin te keep up wit all the roars outa the cook an everyone tellin her te do this an do tha. Yeah, tha was good,' I said, thinkin back on it. Then I let out me breath, gettin more at ease wit him.

'Hm, very apt,' he mumbled, lookin down at the floor. 'Would you like me to give you something to read?'

'Ye mean ye have comics, Father?'

'No!' he laughed. 'But I tend to re-read over and over again some of the old classics. Did you ever hear of Charles Dickens?'

'No, Father! Who's he?'

'Well, he wrote that stuff you are talking about. Wee Slavey, for example, would be his time. Here! Take a look at this,' an he jumped up, goin over te his leather bag an took out a book, showin it te me. 'This is called *Oliver Twist*. Read it, see what you think. It's about an orphan boy left in the workhouse, and some bad people getting their hands on him.'

Tha sounded really interestin, an I took it happily, thinkin now I have somethin te occupy me.

'I put that in my bag as an afterthought. I suppose it had something to do with me coming here, to an orphanage,' he said, scratchin his head wit a faraway look in his eye fer a minute. Then he looked at me an patted me head, sayin, 'You must run along now, back to your post. I hope you enjoy reading that. It will take a little perseverance, you may have difficulty with the way they speak, but keep at it, you will grow to enjoy it.

Reading books will open up your mind, stretch it, and a whole new world will emerge. Never waste your time on rubbish, stick to the classics, and educate that fine mind you have,' he said, lookin very serious.

'Thank you, Father!' I was delighted wit all me stuff an thought he was a very kind man altogether.

'Bye,' he said, shuttin the door gently behind me until I turned an ran fer me little room.

Just as I was about te open me book, the telephone rang. Ah! Just as I was about te enjoy meself. I galloped off, divin inta the box, an picked up the phone. 'Hu..lloooo! Gud after..nuneee! Holy Re..d..mer Convent speak..ink!'

'Yes! Get me Sister Eleanor, I'm in a hurry,' a grumpy aul one barked.

'Jest a minute, please!'

I flew outa the box straight inta the Reverend Mother. 'Come here a minute, please,' she said, takin me arm an steerin me away from the phone. 'Will you please stop talking nonsense!' she said, starin at me fer a minute. 'You do not say "Convent speaking". The convent is not speaking, is it now?'

'No, Mother,' I said, thinkin about this.

'Yes! And stop with that ridiculous voice! Speak properly!'

'But I'm tryin te improve me diction, Mother! Like Ma . . . Mother Pius is always tellin me te do!' I said, gettin very annoyed at the cheek at her, sayin I'm soundin foolish.

'Yes, well, that voice does nothing to improve your diction!' she said, straightenin herself up an slippin her hands under her cloak, an floatin off te the chapel.

Hmph! An fuck you, too! I thought, starin after her.

Later on, I was scrubbin away fer all I was worth on the long kitchen concrete passage when Ma Pius came whippin out through the convent door an stopped te stare at me. 'My goodness, child. It's eight oclock on a Friday night! Are you still working?'

'Yes, Mother Pius. I'm nearly finished,' I said, standin up an tryin te straighten me back, an flingin the wet hair outa me face an tryin te blow back the hard bits tha stuck te me face.

'Well, I never!' she said, flyin inta the childre's kitchen te talk te Sister Mercy.

This mornin I couldn't straighten me back, I don't know wha's wrong. I stooped down te sweep the back convent stairs, glad it was Saturday, an I'm nearly finished me work, I can have the rest of the weekend off, when Ma Pius came flyin down the stairs, an I couldn't stand up te let her pass. I half stood, still holdin the dustpan in one hand an the brush in the other, the top half of me bent, trailin me head on the floor. I tried to lift me head te look at her, feelin very stupid lookin, an she said, 'Excuse me, please!' But I couldn't move over. I felt really foolish, an she roared, 'What's wrong with you?'

'Eh, me back is sore, Mother Pius.'

'I can see that! I also saw you last night scrubbing that kitchen passage. You have more than enough to do with your work in the convent. Now look at the state of you! How dare they? Your convent duties come first. Come with me this minute. I intend to put a stop to this instantly.'

'But, Mother Pius! It's not cos of tha!'

'Follow me!' she roared, marchin down the stairs. I dropped the dustpan an handbrush an crawled after her, trailin me head along the ground, feelin like an aul one wit a hump.

'SISTER MARY MERCY! HOW DARE YOU TAKE ADVANTAGE OF MY CONVENT GIRL?'

'What are you talking about?' Mercy asked, lookin very confused.

'HER!' Ma Pius roared, pointin at me crawlin in the door. 'The passage is your responsibility. That is part of the kitchen duties! And you all know that!' she roared, pointin her finger at the young one, Loretta, standin wit a pot in her hand gapin from Ma Pius te me an back te Ma Pius again, rubbin the pot up an down wit a tea towel, dryin the hell outa it. 'YOU KNEW WHAT YOU

WERE DOING WHEN YOU PRESSGANGED THAT CHILD INTO DOING YOUR WORK FOR YOU.'

I thought she was goin te have a heart attack be the way her face was turnin purple.

'And WHO is supposed to do the cooking, might I ask? If we have to scrub the passage,' screamed Sister Mary Mercy.

'You have enough lazy lumps hanging around the place! Get them to do some work. And furthermore! From now on she is not to set foot in this kitchen. The kitchen staff will from now on make the tea for the poor man!' Then she whirled aroun, grabbin me an pushin me ahead of her out the kitchen door, an told me te go back an finish me work, she was goin te have a word wit Sister Eleanor.

I couldn't believe wha I just heard. So I wasn't supposed te be doin tha passage after all. They were makin a fool a me all this time! No wonder tha kitchen young one was always laughin at me when she saw me scrubbin it!

I finished putting the brushes an cleanin stuff away in the press just when the back convent door came flyin in an Ma Pius charged through wit her arms swingin down be her side an her hands clamped in fists. She had a face on her like mustard an mortal sin.

'I have told them in the institution you are not to do any more work over there,' she roared, pointin her fist an slingin out her finger over te the childre's part.

'Right, Mother Pius,' I said, agreein wit her, thinkin they'll think twice before they mess me aroun again now I can threaten them wit Ma Pius!

'There is to be no more washing up in that refectory. Let the big lazy lumps she has lying around the place do some work for a change. Good gracious! You are practically the only child doing any work in that whole institution, and then the convent would suffer! I am expected to accept the wreck they left me!' An she looked me up an down, shakin her head like someone decidin, no, they won't buy after all. An flingin me back in me box!

PART II

*

Chapter 10

I held me breath, me eyes flying over the page. Mr Rochester is just about te propose te Jane! Then the door bell rang. I lifted me head, not wanting te leave me book. Bloody hell! It really is getting very exciting. I put me bookmark inta the page and closed the book gently. I love that book, *Jane Eyre*, by Charlotte Brontë. That priest was right! You can't beat the classics, I thought as I ran for the door, me ponytail swinging out behind me, making me feel I'm the bee's knees!

Yeah, once I persevered with *Oliver Twist*, as the priest advised, I really got inta the story, and ended up loving it and searching through the nuns' library looking for more. It has even helped me te improve me diction, as the Reverend Mother likes te say.

I opened the door and stood staring at two little travelling girls.

'Hello, Miss. Would ye have a sup a tea for us? The legs are fallin offa us for the want of a drop. We've been walkin all day.'

'Sure! Will you wait in that hut over there, and I'll get someone te bring it over te ye,' I said, smiling at them.

'Gawd bless ye, Miss,' said the big one, only about fourteen years old. 'Come on, Biddy!' And the little one, only about eight years old, trailed after her wearing a big pair of Wellington boots that would comfortably fit the farmer. I watched them go, not quite closing the door, and pulled it back when I heard the little one say 'Maggie! Wha about them cows there? They have tits hangin down. De ye think we could get a drop a milk outa them?' And she was trying te hurry after Maggie, tripping herself up and falling outa the boots.

'No! Wait till we see if they give us anythin yet! An they may be watchin us! Them windas all have eyes! Anyway, wha use is a drop a milk? Sure, we've nothin te carry it in.'

Take the whole cow, I thought, staring after them. I would! Then I started roaring me head laughing as I shut the door and headed down te the kitchen, thinking they remind me of meself not too long ago, and I felt me heart slipping. Poor things. It's hard work begging. And they probably have te bring something home te the other children. No wonder the little one is keeping her eyes peeled, hoping te get something, anything, they can bring back te put food on the table. The children here don't know how lucky they are. On the other hand, it is lonely, very lonely, when you have te fight for the attention of one poor aul nun. She's blind, bothered and bewildered trying te keep track of the lot of us.

I put me head in the kitchen door, shouting te the kitchen girl, Loretta, 'Tea for two in the poor man's hut!'

'You make it!' roared Loretta. 'Sitting up there on your arse like Lady Muck!'

'Really!' I said, raising me eyebrows, driving her mad with me airs and graces I got from watching and listening te Ma Pius! 'Then I will have to report this to Mother Pius. We'll see what she has to say about it!'

'Get back here, you!' roared Sister Mercy, lifting her head outa the oven, with her big arse stuck in the air, and trying te straighten herself by pushing her elbows back and sending her arse flying forward.

'Yes, Sister?' I asked, poking me head around the door again with me eyebrows raised, like Mother Pius does when she's waiting for you te answer for yourself!

'Stop giving me your cheeky looks! Yeh can take dat look off your face for a start, and don't be coming into me kitchen and threatening us!'

'Will that be all, Sister Mercy?' I asked in me best Ma Pius voice.

'Get out! Get out, ye cheeky cur!' she roared at me, throwing the dishcloth after me.

I leapt and bounced inta the air, feeling light as a feather, and grabbed the door handle, sailing back up te the convent, leaving the roars behind me. Ha! That'll teach you fuckers not te mess wit me. I'm moving up in the world, giving meself an edumacation, as that aul bandy bastard Jackser would say! Hm! He was right about that. Edumacation is the key te getting on in this world, and having the protection of aul Ma Pius is doing me no harm at all. Ha! If ye can't beat them, join them an beat them at their own game! Yeah! I can now speak the 'Queen's English' as Ma Pius calls it, when it suits me!

The angelus bell rang and I shut me book, standing up and stretching. Teatime! Another working day over! I walked past the chapel and stopped te watch Sister Clare John Mary swinging outa the bell. I walked over te get a closer look. 'Can I have a go, Sister?' I whispered.

'OK,' she said, handing me the rope.

I grabbed hold of it, giving it a yank – nothing happened.

'No! Tug it like this,' she said, grabbing hold again, 'then let go. See!'

I watched and listened, then had another go. I was swinging away like mad, having a great time, when the Reverend Mother came marching over from her office, sneaking up behind us.

'What on earth are you doing, Sister?'

I let go, getting an awful fright with the roar she gave. 'Sorry, Mother,' I said, lowering me eyes, looking very chastised. 'I was just having a practice, in case you ever want me te ring it.'

'Get out of here and go back down to the institution. You are now beginning to lose the run of yourself. You must think you are one of the nuns! The idea of it, indeed!' she snorted, and little

Sister Clare John Mary coughed, wanting te laugh. She was bright red at getting caught! I took off, racing down the back stairs, leaving the poor young nun getting herself eaten alive.

'The Angel of the Lord declared unto Mary!' moaned Sister Eleanor, flicking her eyes over me as I bombed inta the refectory, wanting te be on time in case the grub was gone. 'In the name of the Father and of the Son and of the Holy Spirit, Amen,' everyone drawled, blessing themselves quickly te get it over.

Sister Eleanor reached for the stainless-steel pie dish and started serving the sausages, going from table te table. 'Thank you, Sister,' I said, looking down at the size of the sausages, and looking te Olivia Ryan's plate te see if her sausages were bigger.

'"Thank you, Sister!"' Ryan mimicked, shaking her head at the table and giving me a sideways glance.

The rest of them roared laughing. 'Yeah! She's a right suck-up,' Ashtray-face laughed, staring down at me.

I took no notice. Ha! Let them laugh. Since I threw me lot in with the nuns and managed te keep me head down and stay outa trouble, they can't get at me. I've even found ways of getting them, I thought, landing me eyes on me bread, ready te put me sausage on it and make a sandwich.

'Have some salt!' Powers suddenly said, shaking half of the eggcup onta me plate. I stared at the mound of salt sitting on me sausages and felt me belly going red-hot. 'Ye scabby fuckin cow,' I snarled, grabbing hold of her plate and switching the sausages.

'Give that back, you tinker!' screamed Ryan, reaching for me new plate.

I held it up in the air outa her reach and stood up.

'Ha, ha! We knew she would revert to being a street kid! Did you hear her?'

'You bitch,' snorted Ryan, grabbing me ponytail and yanking me back.

I let go of the plate, letting it smack te the floor, walking in the sausages and slamming against the table, sending cups of tea flying, hearing it pour onta the floor and the roars of people getting tea in their laps, hearing them shout, 'We're going to tell Sister Eleanor! You are in big trouble now! Wait until Eleanor hears what you've just done,' they all screamed. '"My refectory, the floor! It was just cleaned and polished," she'll scream. "I'm reporting you te the Reverend Mother!"' they mimicked, laughing.

'Go on! Get her, Olivia!' they shouted, watching as Ryan swung me by me hair.

I whirled around, going with me ponytail, getting me closer te Ryan, and slammed me elbow inta her stomach, feeling the softness just under her ribs and the air flying up and outa her mouth with a whoosh, satisfying the madness pumping around me veins, feeling a white-hot rage.

Her hand let go as she bent, dropping in pain, collapsing on her knees, and I went straight for her hair, swinging her around. 'Bullying cowardly bastard,' I screamed as I let go, steadying meself on me feet. I was suddenly flying te the floor with hands grabbing hold of me hair, smashing me face down te me knees, and hearing her scream as she came at me again, fighting flying hands trying te tear at me as others tore me te the floor, and more from behind kicking and punching me. I heard shouts as Miss came tearing in from the staffroom, screaming, 'Stop!' trying te pull everyone apart. But even more joined in and were pulling me hair and kicking me. I rolled inta a ball, protecting me face with me arms and holding the roots of me hair with me hands, stiffening meself, waiting for the pummelling te stop.

'Stop! Stop this at once, or I'll send for the Reverend Mother this minute. Let go!' She was slapping hands away, trying te disentangle the fingers caught in me hair. I could feel the pain shooting through me head, with hands pulling me in different directions. And the kicks te me back and the laughter, and the heavy breathing of people trying te get a punch at me. Then we were apart.

I lifted me head, feeling me face sore and me head throbbing with the aching, as people moved away with hate and laughter in their eyes, and Miss was looking shocked from me te the rest of them. I headed out the door without thinking, hearing them laughing and shouting, 'Go on! Run, Long! You're nothing but a street kid, a skivvy for the nuns, and that's what you'll always be, while the rest of us go to good schools and we'll all get good jobs. Yeah! Run, skivvy!'

I could hear their voices still laughing after me but growing fainter now as I neared the back door and made for the convent. I tore up the back stairs and wandered inta the linen room. I won't go inta me little waiting room, because the nuns will see me there.

I shut the door quietly, knowing there was no one around; they will all be at their tea. I sat down on the floor in the corner, looking around at the clean white sheets and pillowcases belonging te the nuns. It's nice and warm in here, and most of all peaceful. The pain in me head and back was beginning te pound, and I could hear the throbbing in me ears. I felt an ache in me chest. Me heart felt like it was breaking from the pain, the loneliness. They just don't like me.

I looked down at me smock seeing the pockets torn. I'll have te sew it before Mother Pius sees it. Now Sister Eleanor won't speak te me for weeks. Because one way or the other, she feels closer te them than te me. She has had them since they were small, and I just blew inta the place. She'll think in her heart I'm te blame, I brought the trouble here, even though the cows are always fighting with each other, but they love te have a go at me, especially if there's a crowd of them, then one will jump on me, and the others will all dive in, and I end up under a pile a bodies!

Bastardin cowards! Me heart was flying with rage and pain; the bastards never leave me alone. I looked around at the little room. Jaysus! I can't stay here for ever, but me heart is fluttering like mad at the thought of going back and facing them. God! Are ye there? I wonder if I'll ever be happy? I thought when I got away from Jackser an havin te rob the butter everythin would be grand! But it's not, God! Now I'm very lonely. All I want these days is te have Sister Eleanor like me. Since I got here, all I want is a mammy. I want her te love me, because she's like a mammy. But she has too many hangin outa her, an I get mad jealous when she ignores me an makes a fuss of the other kids. It pains me in me heart all the time. I feel cold an lonely. That's one of the reasons I work so hard, just te get the nuns te smile at me an tell me I'm a grand girl. But I know they don't really mean it! It's only cos they see me work very hard an bein very polite an not speak te them until they speak first, an clean everythin an make it shine until ye can see yer face in it.

Every evenin when I'm finished me work, I'm hauntin an huntin up an down the place lookin for her. It's too cold an lonely down there without her. While the others sit wit their gangs in their own groups, they don't want me cos I'm an outsider, an I don't want them. So I mooch along the cold empty passages passin the time until we go te bed. I'm hangin round lookin for Sister Eleanor, then she gets me te do some work for her, an she might call me pet an tell me I'm very good, then she disappears an I'm left empty again. So ye see, God! I swapped one set a problems for another. I don't know which pain is worse: livin wit the Jackser fella an all tha went wit it, or this kind of pain, wantin te be loved by someone. Will I ever hear anyone say, 'Leave her alone. Stop tormenting my Martha, she belongs with us. You're not on your own, Martha! You have me,' an I won't have te do anythin te please them! Because they love me just for meself. Yeah! It's the pain of not bein wanted, tha's wha is killing me.

Tha never bothered me before, no! Tha only started when I came here! But I'm goin te tell ye one thing, God! When I do get outa here, I'm not goin te end up as a skivvy, as them bastards said I will. No, God! I will work hard! An I will get te the top! That I will do! I am goin te be somebody. An no one will ever look down on me again. Yeah! I'm improvin meself all the time! I know how te behave, I can speak properly. I use me Oxford Dictionary I robbed from the nuns' library, an when I'm readin an don't know a word, I look it up in me dictionary. Yeah! That reminds me! I must ask Sister Eleanor for some of me money she's saving for me. I let her keep me five shillings a week wages; that's another way of getting te the top. I never want te be short of a few bob, so I intend savin all I can. Anyway! I'll ask Ma Pius te buy me me own dictionary, an Oxford one, an put theirs back in the bookcase before they miss it!

Yeah! I have me plan already workin te get meself ahead in this life; them fuckers can go te their schools. I'll do it me own way! Without any help from anyone! I'm watchin, listenin an learnin all the time.

I stopped thinking for a minute, hearing meself going back te the way I always spoke. It's because I feel the same as I used te after Jackser beat the hell outa me: that nobody wants me, and I'm all on me own. That's what I'm feeling now. Oh well! My day will come; it won't always be like this. So don't worry, things will be better one day when I get outa here.

Right! I better get meself moving. Thanks, God, for taking care of me. I will try te be good! I lifted meself up, feeling aching all over, but I'm feeling a bit better in meself. No! I won't be here for ever. I'm nearly hitting fifteen now, then it's only another year te go, and that's it. I'll be on me own, making me own way in this life, and I'll never look back!

I was throwing the wax on the lino, looking around at the big square passage outside the chapel, wanting te see how much more I had te do, when Ma Pius came flying along all in a hurry, with her long outdoor black coat buttoned from the neck down te the floor. 'Martha!' she beamed, rushing over te me. 'I am going on my holidays back to our convent in London, so I shall be out for the afternoon. I must do a last-minute shop in preparation, so do take a message and leave it on the hall table.'

'Yes, Mother Pius,' I said, staring inta her face. She's wearing face powder, I'm sure of it. I stared, moving a bit closer te get a better look, pretending I needed te be closer te hear what she was saying, and stood gaping up at her with me mouth open.

Yeah, definitely! She's plastered in the stuff! Imagine that! She really fancies herself!

'Now!' she was saying. I shook me head te get meself outa the daze.

'Yes, Sister!' I said, blinking at her.

'I would like to bring you back a present from my holidays. What would you like?'

'A present! For me! You are going te bring me back a present?'

'Yes, yes!' she said, pleased I was delighted.

Gawd! I couldn't think! I wanted loads a things, but she said only pick one thing. Right! Me mind was made up. 'Eh, Sister, I would love a watch!'

'A WATCH!' Her mouth fell open. 'Good gracious, no! I was thinking something smaller! A watch would be frightfully expensive!'

'Oh! All right! Sorry, Sister. I wasn't really thinking! Bring me whatever you like to pick yourself.'

'Yes,' she said, letting out her breath, 'I shall do that,' shaking her head and deciding that would be safer!

You gobshite Martha! A watch would have cost pounds! Still, it was a nice try! I wonder what she'll bring me back? I thought te meself, as I humped the dryer-upper down on the polish and whacked it around the floor, rubbing the hell outa it. I was dying te get started on that new electric polisher the Reverend Mother bought me. It's supposed te shine the floor, but it keeps breaking down, and now it's arrived back from the factory. I could hear the Reverend Mother giving out hell te them on the phone the last time it broke down. 'Now! Either it will do the job it was intended for, or we shall be asking for our money back forthwith!' Then she slammed down the phone on them.

Matron Mona came te inspect it when it first arrived. And the Reverend Mother was demonstrating it te us, and she wouldn't let me have a go. She nearly polished the whole floor herself. 'You see!' she kept saying, 'There's no work involved at all!' her eyes spinning with the machine as she sailed around with it, smiling and keeping up a running commentary of the joys of modern machinery.

'Modern machinery, me eye!' muttered Matron Mona, waving her duster at the air and taking off on her high-heeled black boots, muttering, 'I've no time for new fangled things meself, ye can keep them.'

Finished! Now for me polisher. Here goes! I put in the plug carefully, not wanting te get blown up like the last time. Jaysus! I was nearly blown te kingdom come! As soon as I went near the socket, sparks flew, an there was an awful explosion. They picked me up off the floor, dazed, not knowing what happened or what day it was! Matron Millington said it was because I had wet hands, and I must have stuck me finger in the socket not looking at what I was doing! I shivered in meself thinking about it.

Right! Ready for take-off. I pressed the little red button and the machine purred inta life, and I pressed the lever, letting the handle fall down, and we're off. It slid around the room with the greatest of ease, and me just having te follow and see the shine appear as if by magic! This is great! Better still! I grabbed two dusters, putting them under me shoes, and stood back, sending the machine flying and me flying after it, holding on.

'Martha Long! What are you doing with the Reverend Mother's new machine?' I looked around, getting an awful fright with the voice coming outa nowhere! 'Oh, Sister Benedict, I didn't see you coming.'

'Evidently you didn't! Now stop your capering around this minute and get into my chapel and bring that new machine with you and polish my floors! Come on! Get a hurry on yourself!'

'Right, Sister, I'm coming up behind you!' I said, switching it off and grabbing up the wires.

CHAPTER 11

I sat reading *Great Expectations*, ignoring the noise around me and the eejits on the sofa trying te kill each other. I wish it was *The Virginian* night on the television, then they could all go down te the television room and watch it, and I could sit and read me book in peace and quiet. I don't watch that. I prefer te read a book than watch television.

I took in a deep breath, snorting out me annoyance through me nose, looking over at the three ratbags making mincemeat outa each other. I could see Karen Bingley lying on her back while two big gobshites sat on top of her, one holding her down and pinning her arms by her sides, while the other one held her nose and mouth, covering her face, blocking off her breathing. Bingley's face was turning blue, and she was desperately struggling, trying te kick her legs and bucking her back. The two fools were laughing too hard, getting carried away with each other and their enjoyment, te notice Bingley's terror.

I stared for about three seconds, seeing her face turn a darker shade of blue, then leapt up, dragging Ashtray-face and Nugent off her, sending them flying. Bingley tried te haul herself up, not able te get a breath.

'She's trying te breathe!' I screamed at them, watching as they drunkenly staggered back te have another go at Bingley. I dragged Bingley te her feet, and she landed out her foot sending Nugent flying, and the other one wiped the sickly smile off her face, sobering herself up.

'You bloody bitches,' Bingley roared, the colour now leaving her face.

She's turning very pale, I thought, staring at her te make sure she was all right. I looked from her te the other two watching her, thinking it was very funny, hiccupping and staggering around like they really were drunk. Jaysus! This place is doing me head in; those bitches are stark staring raving mad.

I was about te take off when I heard Sister Eleanor coming in the door, saying, 'Where is she? Have any of you seen Martha Long?'

Uh oh! Sounds like trouble!

'Yes, Sister, I'm coming. What is it?'

'Martha, darling,' she said, taking me arm and leading me out the door, whispering and smiling. 'Do you know who is up in the parlour? Waiting for you . . .' she hinted, as I stared at her, trying te figure out what she was talking about.

'Your mammy and, eh, Jackser!'

I stared, me heart in me mouth, not believing what I was hearing.

'Run up to the parlour quickly, they are in the small parlour.'

Me heart was beating like a sledgehammer. The ma! And fuck-face Jackser! What do they want? They haven't come here for the good of their health, that's for sure! Nor te enquire after mine! Right! I took in a deep breath, slowing down me breathing, and straightened me shoulders, heading up te the parlour, prepared for whatever they're up te. There's nothing much they can do te me now. I'm outa their control, come hell or high water, I can look after meself, me days of being pushed around are over! Right! No one can tell me what te do! No!

I felt meself beginning te shake. Jaysus! I don't want te see them. I have a bad feeling they're up te no good!

Yeah! OK! Ye know that. I better go up and face them. There's no getting outa this.

I pushed open the door, and the two of them were standing by the window.

'How're ye, Martha?' the ma said smiling. I stared at her, seeing the big belly and her thin grey face, her cheekbones sticking out from lack of nourishment. She looked smaller. And the buttons on her tweed coat wouldn't close. Only the two top buttons. Her ankles were swollen and she has varicose veins sticking out. Oh, Ma! I wanted te cry looking at her. She kept looking at me and smiling, and took a little cough and chewed the inside of her lip, and made a little mewling sound te Jackser, looking up at him, saying, 'She got big! Ha, ha. Doesn't she look lovely?'

'Yeah, ye got big enough all right!' Jackser muttered, flicking his eyes over me and turning his head away, feeling suddenly shy. 'We have a present for ye,' he said, whipping his head te the ma. 'Give it te the young one, Missus! Fer the love a Jaysus! Will ye wake yerself up outa tha!' he roared at me ma, getting annoyed with her because she couldn't read his thoughts.

'Yeah!' me ma said, smiling, taking out a brown little paper bag and looking inside, carefully taking out a watch. 'Here! He bought tha in the pawn office fer ye!'

I hesitated, looking in shock. A watch! They never bought me a present, not for as long as I've known that Jackser fella. Jaysus! That must have cost them at least two quid in the pawn office! They're so stupid with money. They could have spent it on the children, or even on the ma herself. That coat looks like it's seen better days: the pocket is ripped at the side, and the hem is hanging down in different lengths. Someone took it up and didn't do a good job, I thought, eyeing it. No wonder they dumped it; now the ma's wearing it.

'Come on! Here! Take it,' me ma said. 'Lookit! It's lovely.'

I took the watch, looking at the little face with the hands saying twenty-five past seven, and examined the silver bracelet. I put it on me arm, wanting te please her.

'It looks lovely on ye,' me ma said, admiring me arm held out for her.

I always wanted a watch, but not this way, from him! And at the expense of the children.

'Listen!' Jackser said, dropping his head and shutting his eyes tight and rubbing his hands together, like he was trying te get a bit a heat inta them. 'Now,' he said, straightening himself and getting down te business. 'Yer mammy here,' and he waved his arm at her, pointing his finger like he had a big announcement te make, 'is goin inta the hospital te have a new babby. An she needs ye at home te look after the childre an take care a the house!'

I felt meself going very cold, then heat rising in me chest and settling down in me belly like a red-hot fire! I stared at him, keeping me face still, not moving a muscle. He stared at me with his mouth in an o shape like he was turned te stone, his eyes staring outa his head, wondering why I wasn't jumping inta the air, shouting, 'Right, Jackser! I'll get workin on it right away an see about gettin meself outa this place!'

'Well! Did ye hear wha I just fuckin said te ye?' he roared, coming back te life, an astonished at me lack of interest.

'Of course I heard ye, Jackser,' I said quietly, not wanting te upset him, because he would only take it out on the ma and blame her, because I'm her bastard!

'She's already lost one, ye know! Right after she had the last one!'

Last one! I thought. Oh, I wasn't around for that, thank God! Oh hell! The poor ma can't look after herself. I stared at her, thinking she's me ma! My mother! But it doesn't feel like that; it never did! I was always her mother . . . looking out for her, minding her, telling her wha te do, making decisions for her. God, Ma! I feel very sorry for ye. God knows you are my mother, you had me . . . But no! Ye're on yer own! I'm not looking back; it's my turn now te make something of meself.

'Ma, I have te go.'

'Wait! Wha did ye think about wha he said?' she asked me, her eyes staring inta mine, her mouth in a half nervous smile, afraid te breathe.

'I don't think they will let me go, Ma. I'm in here until I'm sixteen,' I said, feeling me heart break looking inta her worn-out poor face. But I can't help her any more. I gave her enough!

She pulled her head back, looking over at him and chewing her lip, her face falling with disappointment, the hope going outa her eyes.

'Well! Tha's where ye're wrong!' Jackser announced, waving his arm at me like he had a card hidden up his sleeve and now he was pulling it out. 'Because I have already had a word wit tha Reverend Mother one. An she says she is goin te put it under consideration. So there ye are! Ye're comin outa here! You mark my words! I'd say ye should be out be the next week, if not sooner.'

I looked at me ma, shocked at even the mention the Reverend Mother would consider letting me back te them. The ma lifted her head, knowing I was looking in her direction, but dropped it again, searching the floor for an answer te her disappointment, knowing even if the Reverend Mother did let me out, I would take off. She knows I always wanted te get away from him; I was just biding me time, waiting, even as a young child. Yeah! From the first moment I clapped eyes on him I didn't like him. Yeah, Ma! You know me better, I thought, seeing the bond we had – even if it never did me any good. But I came from you, Ma, I can never take that away from you. You gave me life.

I moved me head, turning for the door, feeling the weight of the world on me shoulders. I never could refuse me ma anything! Now for the first time in me life I'm doing just that. When what I really wanted te do was te turn around and cry me heart out because she looks so lost and helpless, and wrap her in me arms and tell her it will be all right, I'll take care of her. Te do with her what I always wanted from Sister Eleanor: someone te mother me.

'I'm sorry, Ma. I'm going.'

I turned back, slipping the watch off me arm and slipped it inta her pocket, whispering, 'Take it te the pawn, Ma,' while Jackser looked out the window with a scheming look in his face, his eyes narrowing and his jaw working up and down, thinking. No! He's not getting the message yet. He's so fucking sure of himself, he thinks he's still dealing with a helpless child and he only has te look at me and I'll go running te do his bidding.

Fuck you, Jackser! Ye mangy little bandy midget. You would be afraid of me if ye didn't have me ma and the kids te use as blackmail. I'd have ye shitting in yer trousers, ye little coward. It really is all over.

I shook me head, barely moving it, pleading me sorrow silently inta the ma's eyes, telling her no! She has seen the last of me. Then moved quickly, whipping the door open, saying, 'I'll get inta trouble, Jackser! Wait until we see what the Reverend Mother says.' And I shut the door quickly and ran for the Reverend Mother. No! Wait until they are gone!

I went quickly down te me little waiting room, sitting meself down, feeling me heart in me belly. Jesus! What will happen now? Will the Reverend Mother force me te go back te them? She can! But I'll take meself off te England. I won't set foot in Jackser's house again. Thank God I have a bit of savings, five shillings a week is not much, but it must have amounted te a few pounds by now.

Right! I better make sure Sister Eleanor doesn't hand over me money te him. That should get me the boat ticket one way. I'll go te London, Euston Station, and look for work around there straight off the train. I can give a false address, find out an address when I get there! Otherwise I won't be taken on in a job homeless. Now, I haven't much stuff, anyway. I don't want te be dragging a heavy suitcase around the place. I would really stand out then. I wonder if there's a shopping bag hanging around the convent. That might be better than a bloody suitcase.

Right! First things first. Find out which way the wind is blowing. See what that nun has in her mind. Good! That's settled. I'm fifteen years old and definitely old enough te take care of meself. No fear in that!

I could hear voices, and the bandy bastard's voice was rising. I crept out onta the chapel passage te listen. 'Yes! Yes! I understand,' the nun's voice was saying.

'Well! I'll leave it te you, Sister! It's in your hands.'

'Yes! Goodbye now!'

Then I heard the front door slamming. I took in a deep breath and straightened my shoulders, taking off te catch the Reverend Mother.

'Oh, there you are,' she said smiling. 'I wondered where you got to!'

'Yes, Mother,' was all I said, and waited for her te say something.

'So! Did you have a good visit?' she asked, smiling, jerking her chin and throwing her veil back, her milk-bottle glasses reflecting the light; I was seeing double her eyes. 'Did they tell you they want you to go home?'

'Yes, Mother.'

'And? What do you think about that?'

'I am not going back te them, Mother.'

'But your mother needs you!'

I said nothing, and she stood there staring at me, trying te figure me out.

'I think we will send you home now. You can be a great help to your poor mother. She has a lot on her plate, you know,' she said, looking at me with a pained face.

'Yeah, but I'm supposed te be here until I'm sixteen. That was the judge's ruling,' I said, getting very annoyed and letting the gloves come off. This fucker didn't like me from the word go! And now I know I'm right. She can't force me out until I'm sixteen, then I can walk out the gate under me own steam and tell them all te go and fuck themselves! 'No, Mother, I'm not going back te them. I will stay here until I'm ready te leave at sixteen. Is tha OK with you?' I said with a stony face, making meself perfectly clear: she can't get rid of me that easily.

'Well . . . if you're sure, then,' she said, sounding very disappointed. 'I'll tell them when they phone me tomorrow.'

'Thank you, Mother,' and she headed inta the chapel and I headed off down the back convent stairs, wondering if it's worth me while waiting until I'm sixteen te get outa this place. I could be living in England this time next week . . . but no! That's only running away. I want te make sure I'm free as a bird when I do leave here. Fuck it! I'll just have te make the best of it here. Keep away from those young ones and keep me head down and stay outa trouble. That bleeding woman is waiting for an excuse te throw me out given the first opportunity. She doesn't like ye te cross her. So, fuck ye, Missus. We'll see who bests who! So far, I'm besting you! Ha! When ye can't beat them, join them! And beat them at their own game. That's what I've learned in this place. So far it's working!

I skipped down the stairs, happy at the thought, this time next year I'll be free as a bird. No Ma, Jackser, nuns or young ones tormenting me!

The sudden thought steamrolling inta me head made me heart lurch, and I wanted te run in different directions at the same time. The ma! Wait! Fuck! She'll be gone down the avenue and halfway te the bus stop by now. I leapt back up the stairs, taking them two at a time, me legs trying te stretch te three. I heaved meself up on the banisters, making fer the front door, and tore out through it, banging it shut behind me, and flew down the avenue, seeing no sight of them. I belted around the corner and saw them at the end of the road, just about te turn a corner.

'Ma! Ma!' I raced after her, screaming, 'Mammy! Wait!'

She turned, looking down te see where it was coming from, and spotted me flying after her.

'Wha? Wha is it?' she asked me, turning pale, her eyes blinking, and I could see the light appearing, thinking maybe I've changed me mind and I'm coming back after all.

'Ma!' I couldn't get me breath. 'Wait!'

'Wha is it?' she asked, her face shaking and her eyes getting anxious te hear what I wanted. I glanced up at the aul fella, and he stopped with his hands in his pockets, his head turned, screwed straight ahead, while his body was sideways, trying te look the hard man with the hard-as-stone-cement face on him. He knows I'm not coming back. He's fucking raging! Me ma has said it te him.

'Ma! Please come back fer a minute. I have somethin I want te give ye!'

'Wha is it?' she said, disappointment and curiosity showing all at the same time. 'I can't,' she said, looking up at him. 'The kids are waitin, an he won't wait fer me.'

'Come on outa tha!' he roared down at me ma, waving his fist and curling it back te himself, but ignoring me.

'Fuck him, Ma! I want te give ye somethin.'

'Wha . . . Wha is it?' she roared, getting annoyed.

'I might have a few bob. I don't know how much I have, it may not be a lot . . . but ye can have it.'

'Where is it?'

'The nun has it. She was savin it fer me.'

'Come on, then!' she said, moving towards me. 'Listen! Martha has a few bob she's givin me,' me ma shouted up te him, a half laugh coming outa her, not sure whether he would wait or what he would do.

'Fuck off then,' he waved his fist and shouted down te me ma. 'I'm havin nothin more te do wit tha whore's melt! You do wha ye fuckin like.'

Me ma's head swung from him te me and back te him again. 'Jaysus! He won't wait.'

'Ma, fuck him. Come on! I'll see what I can get ye!'

'Right so! But I better hurry. I don't want him startin any more trouble. He's fuckin ragin because ye're not comin back! Would ye not even come back fer a little while, Martha?' me ma said, looking at me with desperation.

Me heart was breaking at the thought of her and the children suffering. 'I can't, Ma.'

'But why? Surely ye don't want te stay locked up in this place?' she said, looking up at the huge old convent that stretched for building after building.

'No, Ma, of course not. But I'm staying here until I'm sixteen, then I'm off!'

'Where will ye go?'

'I don't know yet. But I'll make it somewhere, Ma!' I said, looking at her worn-out face, old before her time, with a mad man that needs her more than she fucking needs him.

'Wait here, Ma,' I said, running around te the back door and going in along the kitchen passage.

'Where will I wait, Martha?' me ma said, lowering her voice and looking around at all the doors of the refectories and staffrooms. Doors that stretched the length of O'Connell Street, disappearing inta the darkness at the end of the long concrete passage with no windows te throw in the light; it was like entering a tunnel.

'Ma! Don't let them see ye. Here! Come on with me quick.' I rushed her out te the green with the hedges all around, hidden from view where the nuns hang up their vests and big long navy-blue knickers. 'Sit down on tha bench, Ma, an wait for me; I won't be long,' I puffed getting outa breath with the hurry on me, and me heart flying, wanting te be quick as greased lightning, before I got caught!

'Don't be long, Martha!' me ma moaned, warning me, getting very anxious.

'No, Ma. Wait here, don't let them see ye! I'll be very fast.'

'Where are ye goin?' she called after me.

'Shush, Ma! I won't be long.'

I put me head in the staffroom, looking around – nobody here! And crept in, grabbing the Miss's bag hanging up behind the storage door, looking at it. It's a long canvas bag she uses for her bits and pieces of shopping. She can buy herself another one! She's nothing te spend her money on!

I whipped out, tearing down the kitchen passage, and stopped outside the kitchen, listening – nobody here. I flew inta the dairy, grabbing slabs a butter sitting on greaseproof paper, home-made! Lovely, I shoved that inta me bag and opened a parcel with strings a sausages and black and white pudding and a slab a rashers, with a big lump a bacon still waiting te be put in the fridge. Jaysus! Somebody left them sitting there! Probably the butcher. I grabbed them, putting them inta me bag and tore inta the kitchen, seeing lumps a chopped steak sitting in the fridge covered in a bowl. Tomorrow's dinner! I looked around for something te put it in, flying over te presses, yanking them open, and took out a roll of tinfoil and tore it off, wrapping the steak pieces of meat in it, shoving it inta me bag.

What else has she got? A huge lump a cheese sitting in a fancy dish. I tore off more foil, throwing the cheese in, and flew te the storage press. Tea, packets – I grabbed three – and jars a home-made jam with greaseproof lids on te keep it from going off. Two will do! Then I spotted the big bowl a tomatoes sitting on the kitchen table. I threw them inta the tinfoil. Fuck! Might as well be hung for a sheep as a lamb. I grabbed four loaves a soda bread cooling on the wire rack sitting on the windowsill and shoved them inta me bag. It's full! Nothing else? Me head swung around the kitchen, me eyes peeling over everything. No! Nothing left that I can carry; the sacks of potatoes out in the scullery are too heavy. That's enough.

I put me head out the door, looking up and down, and tore up the passage, knowing if I'm spotted now, the game's up! Me feet won't touch the ground I'll be outa here so fast. That Reverend Mother will have me out the door before I can take me next breath. Gawd! I'm sweating. Me face is pumping sweat, and I can feel it red as a berry.

Fuck! I stopped te creep past the long passage coming from me right, and listened. No footsteps; nobody coming. Now past the staffroom; they're not really nuns, though they think they are, the way they carry on. They're just the bleeding staff that help the nuns with the groups.

I flew out the door and over te the ma. 'Ma! Hide this!' I shoved the bag at her. 'I'll be back! No! Come on,' I said whipping back the bag and hurrying her off.

'Wait! Where are we goin?' she asked, laughing and looking

at the bag. 'Wha have ye got in tha, Martha?' she puffed, trying te keep up with me.

'Ma, let's get outa here. I'll talk te ye later!'

We shuffled fast past the convent hall door entrance then around the bend, praying no nun will happen te appear outa the side entrance.

'Wait here!' I said, leaving her standing at a tree. 'No! Better still, go te the end of the avenue an wait around the corner. I won't be long.'

'I can't wait, Martha! I have te go,' she said, shaking her head, getting all wound up.

'Wait! I need te get ye the few bob! Go on, wait down the road for me!'

I raced back, heading in the side entrance through the nuns' convent passage and up the back stairs and onta the landin with the convent entrance, and looked at the gong. No! Try the chapel.

I put me head in the door and saw her kneeling in her prie-dieu and crept over.

'Sister!' I whispered, creeping on me toes.

She looked up, getting a fright at being disturbed. 'What! What do you want, Martha?'

'I need te speak te ye straight away, Sister!'

'Can it not wait? I am getting my prayers,' she said, twisting her face and getting annoyed.

'No, I'm sorry, Sister! I have te talk te ye now!'

She shook her head in annoyance and blessed herself looking up at the altar and followed me out, stopping te genuflect and bless herself, then rushed out while I held the door open for her.

'What is it?' she asked. 'Why did you get me out from my prayers? Can I not even get time to say a few prayers without the lot of you hunting me down?'

'I am sorry, Sister. But me mother needs a bit a money, and I want te know how much ye have saved for me.'

'What? Now?'

'Yes, Sister.'

'But I don't know how much you have! I have to go up to my room and check,' she said, staring at me, looking very fed up.

'Sister! Will ye please get me all me money; I want te give it te me mammy!'

'But where is she? I thought they left ages ago?'

'No, she came back.'

'Oh!' she breathed. 'My God and my all!' rushing herself up te her room.

I took off, racing te the dormitory, trying te get ahead of her, even though I go miles around the house, while she just has te go up the stairs and along the corridor lined with all the cells, as Ma Pius calls them. I took the stairs, belting inta the dormitory, and knocked on her door just beside me bed in the little corner, and grabbed me brand-new long coat with the band a fur around the big wide hood attached te the coat and lifted it up, feeling the weight of it. I looked at the silver clips that fasten inta each other te button it; they use wooden ones for duffel coats, but these are like long hoops that clasp inta each other. It's navy blue and sort of heavy corduroy, and midi-length: they're all the fashion, ye wear them long now. This will keep the ma lovely and warm! I can save up for another one. God love her, she won't have that chance.

Oh! And me lovely earrings Ma Pius brought me back as a present. Little gold ones that dangle down! I only wear them for good occasions, because they clip on, and I'm always afraid of losing them, or they might get robbed! Some of the young ones here would take the eyes outa yer head. They're terrible fucking robbers! Me ma loves rings and earrings! She'll go mad when she sees these, I thought, feeling very happy at the thought of making her happy.

I could hear Sister Eleanor opening her drawers in the room. I knocked quietly. 'Sister Eleanor! It's me, Martha.'

'Wait one minute, please!'

I turned the coat inside out and laid it down gently on me bed, waiting for her te come out. There will be hell on earth when Sister Mercy finds all the stuff robbed. I'm saying nothing!

I might mention I saw some poor man hanging around . . . No! Better te say nothing. Let them rant and go mad! If I wasn't seen, then they can suspect all they like. But they can't prove it was me. There's no hope in hell I'm going te hang meself by admitting te anything. It's not like anyone in this place was going te starve. Me little brothers and sisters need the food, so te hell with them! I snorted te meself.

The door opened, and I jumped up off the bed. 'Here! You have five pounds and ten shillings!' she said, handing me over the money. 'Do what you like with that,' she said, annoyed I was taking me savings back.

'Thanks, Sister,' I said te her back as she went in closing her door. I grabbed up the coat and took off flying down the passages and out the back door. I hope it's not locked when I get back, I thought, rushing off and heading down the avenue.

'Here, Ma! Put tha on ye,' I said, taking off her old coat.

'Where did ye get tha, Martha?' me ma asked, laughing and blinking and chewing her lip, her face shaking.

'I bought it, Ma, last summer in a sale. I was keepin it fer the Christmas. Do ye like it?' I said, putting it on her and pulling up the zip in the middle, and buckling it from her neck te down past her legs, then pulling up the hood.

I stood back te admire her. 'Ye look lovely in tha, Ma,' I said, taking a big sigh of contentment inside meself at seeing me ma looking lovely and warm, and a bit more respectable.

'Gawd! It's lovely an warm, innit?' she said, looking down at herself.

'An here's the money. I managed te save five pounds an ten shillings. Tell him ye only got ten bob from me, will ye, Ma? An keep the five pounds for yerself.'

'OK!'

'Will ye promise me ye won't let him get his hands on the money, Ma?' I said, leaning inta her.

'Don't worry! He'll be off back te the pawn wit the watch he bought ye. Where is it?'

'Stop frettin, Ma! Here's yer stuff outa the pockets of the old coat. I'm takin this in case he gets the idea of pawnin that one on ye, Ma.'

'Wha? Will I not keep tha one, Martha?' she said, eyeing the old coat, thinking it might come in handy.

'No! If that's the only one ye have te wear, then ye won't be able te pawn it. Now come on! Ye have te hurry. Oh! An here's a pair of earrings for ye, Ma. They're nine-carat gold!'

'Where did ye get them?' me ma asked, her eyes lighting up.

'Someone gave them te me as a present,' I said, eyeing them and beginning te miss them already! 'I'll walk ye down the road; give me the bag. I'm not supposed te be out, Ma. I'll get inta terrible trouble if I'm caught, so we better hurry!' I said, looking at her admiring her new coat. 'Gawd, Ma! Ye look lovely an warm in tha.'

'Yeah, it's lovely,' she said, feeling the velvety softness.

'Right! I'm goin te leave ye here,' I said, looking down te the bus stop, wondering where the bandy aul bastard was. 'Oh! There he is, Ma! He's waitin for ye, hidin himself in the doorway beside the chip shop!'

'Right! I better go,' me ma said, smiling and looking and hesitating, wanting te say something else. 'Eh,' cough, 'when will I see ye again, Martha? Will ye come back te see me when they let ye out?'

'Ah, that's a long way off, Ma. We could be all dead an buried by then . . .'

'No! Next year! This time next year ye'll be well out,' me ma said.

'OK! Let's see what happens, Ma. Go on now! Get home outa the cold.'

'Bye now,' she waved after me, then turned her head towards the bus stop and that hell-on-earth aul fella.

I stopped te watch her go, trying te rush with the heavy bag and the baby in her belly, pulling herself along, moving the air around her but not really moving herself very much at all. It helped the heaviness weighing me down te see her wrapped up with the hood covering her up nicely, and she could button it up and know she had a bit of warmth inside her with the bit a grub for the kids and the money in her pocket and something for herself. The earrings would make her happy for a while!

I turned back towards the convent, feeling the weight of me ma and the children, and the rage inside me for the cowardly bandy bastard. He would flop on his belly and scream for mercy if given a good hammering by someone. I could do it! But the ma wouldn't thank me for it. When push comes te shove, it's him she wants. I learned that a long time ago, when she ran back te him after that time we escaped te England. Anyway, that's all behind me now!

I walked on, heading back te the convent, feeling the cold hitting me. I looked down at meself wearing me light working smock and stopped te throw me ma's old coat over me shoulders, and walked on with an empty feeling inside me of going back te nothing. I felt the heaviness of not having someone te go back te in the convent, someone who would smile and their eyes light up, happy te see me. Someone like Mrs Dunne from long ago, who took us in when Jackser tried te kill the lot of us, and me ma ended up in the hospital, and Jackser was taken away. Yeah! She was a real mammy. They might say, 'How are you? How did you get on?' I could tell them what happened, and they would listen and tell me I did the right thing, and say, 'Don't worry yourself about the ma. Sure, she knows what she's doing. Now! Forget about that. Do ye want something to eat? Here! Come over to the heat here, ye look frostbitten.' And put their arm around me, saying, 'I don't know what I'd do without you! You're the light of me life.'

Yeah! Someone who was interested in me for meself, not because I worked hard or was polite or behaved meself. I want someone who doesn't want something from me te make them happy, just happy because they like me, because I'm special te them. Te be in a place where I belong. Jesus! That's what I want!

It's only dawning on me now! I've never been in any place where I belonged. It makes me feel very lonely, God! Because I want te belong here, with Sister Eleanor, and have the other kids accept me. But I just have te wait for that. It's never going te happen here. God, I'm so lonely!

I stopped and pulled the coat off me shoulders and threw it inta the dustbin sitting outside the kitchen door. Then rambled off down the passage, looking up at the high windows, hearing the sound of a dripping tap in the ancient old bathroom at the end of the passage, waiting for Saturday, bath day. The crying of small children hit me as I passed the nursery; they're keening for the bit of comfort of a mammy's arms. Ye'll be crying a long time, little ones. The fucking ache for that never leaves ye.

Still and all, Martha! Ye could be a hell of a lot worse off! Think of the poor children waiting in fear for the ma and that bandy bastard te get back. At least no one is going te kill ye here! Not without me being able te put up a fight first. Yeah, and think of poor Charlie. I bet he would give his eye teeth te be here! But then he'd probably end up being lonely, too. Ah, fuck it, stop yer whingeing. Ye could be like the poor ma! Stuck with Jackser! I roared laughing te meself, not knowing why. But the thought made me laugh.

Chapter 12

The six o'clock bell rang for the angelus and I stood up wearily. Thank God it's Friday! Tomorrow, after the convent kitchen, I'll be off for the weekend.

I stretched and yawned, feeling banjacksed. Jaysus, I never want te see another scrubbing brush as long as I live. The amount of cleaning this last week! The nuns want the place shining for the Christmas. My gawd! Only two weeks away; the days are flying. I better get moving or I'll get no tea.

I walked up the chapel passage and stepped up te the brown-tiled passage just in time te see the Reverend Mother lift her head and bless herself after saying the angelus. She looked at me and mumbled, 'Goodnight.'

'Goodnight, Mother,' I mumbled back, not caring about her sulks because I wouldn't go home te the ma. That's the first time she's even looked at me, silly aul cow. Ye'd think she would have more sense at her age. She must be in her fifties by now. Jaysus! The nuns live in the land of Tir na nog, or whatever ye call it – 'the land of youth'. They never become aul ones even if they are; they still titter and act like girls, looking shocked when a man looks at them. Fucking eejits!

I dragged meself down the back stairs and headed up the long passage, passing the kitchen, hearing Mercy shout at Loretta. I stopped te listen, keeping well outa the way.

'Will yeh bring me in a clean pot! Are yeh making dem in

dat scullery? I only asked yeh to wash dem!'

'But it's tea time, Sister Mercy!' roared Loretta, sounding like she was either going te cry or lose the rag and throw the pots at Mercy. 'And I'm missing my tea!' she wailed.

'Aarh! I'm missing my own tea as well, you amadan! Haven't I a mouth on me, too? Here! Get out now and come straight back here as soon as yeh get something to eat. Yeh still have your passage to scrub! So don't forget dat!'

'No, Sister Mercy! Yes, Sister Mercy! Three bags full, Sister Mercy!'

'Get out, yeh cheeky brat,' Mercy roared, making a run at Loretta.

I leapt up the passage just as Loretta came flying up behind me, hearing me roaring me head laughing.

'Did you enjoy that, Long?' roared Loretta, trying te take her spite out on me.

'Yeah! I haven't had that much of a laugh since I saw ye scrubbing the kitchen passage!' I cackled.

As soon as I whipped me head in the door, Sister Eleanor pounced.

'Martha, pet,' she whispered, taking me arm. Pet! What's she after? 'As soon as you finish your tea, I'll be back from the convent, and I want you to come down to the nursery with me.'

Ah, Jaysus, no! I was afraid te ask her in case she told me. I'm not in the mood te sleep with the babies tonight. She knows I love them, but having te sleep with them . . . Nah! Not a good idea. I'm banjacksed after that week of scrubbing every single day.

I gave a big sigh, feeling fed up. I can't say no, or she'll go off in a sulk and won't speak te me. 'All right, Sister Eleanor,' I sighed.

'No! There's no need to look so worried,' she laughed. 'Just wait until I get back. Now go and have your tea like a good girl.'

I cheered meself up at that news. I wonder what she finds so interesting, then. Maybe she wants me te start painting something down there during me spare time over the weekend, in preparation for the Christmas.

Last year, during the summer, she had me painting every chair in the house. She had them all stacked up in the spare room leading inta the laundry. So now I know how te paint! Nuns are great for finding work for idle hands; it was during me weekends at that. 'The devil makes work for idle hands,' they bleat, showing ye how te do a job, as if they're going te help ye! Then they beetle off, leaving ye te get on with it! Crafty aul cows. I was hoping te get stuck inta me new book, *Pride and Prejudice*. Sorry, Jane, you shall just have to await my pleasure, to admire your wonderful ability to swoop me out of this place and take me to another era, as you would say!

I stopped te listen te meself. Merciful hour! T'is true. I am becoming a lady of letters! I must remember te say that again. It will impress Ma Pius no end! Gawd! I'm really coming on with me learning. And, of course, me diction.

Right! Where's the grub? Boiled egg – bulletproof, of course! I tapped it with the spoon and it hopped onta sour-face Blondie's lap sitting next te me. I grabbed it.

'Get your dirty filthy hands offa me, you lesbian!' roared Blondie.

'Whoo! Wah!' the big ones roared over from the table next te me.

I held up the egg, 'Sorry! Flying egg! Desperate dopey dolly here thinks she's being molested by a chicken's droppings!' I announced.

'Jaysus, Long! Did you swallow the dictionary?' Hatchet-face from the other table roared.

That one thinks she's gorgeous! I sniffed te meself, looking back at her with the long stringy hair and the sharp bony face with the ferret eyes. I turned back te me egg and ignored her.

After I finished, I dropped me dishes over te the sink, leaving them on the draining board.

'Here, Long, you stupid mope! Stack them properly! I'm not your slave!' roared Miller at me, staring at the mound of dishes piling up.

'You stack them, Miller. It will make a change for ye from scratching yer arse!'

'Say that again one more time and I'll throw this kettle at you,' she snarled, grinding her teeth and holding up the empty big heavy kettle.

I walked on a bit, heading for the door, keeping me distance te make it more difficult for her te aim the kettle, then stopped just inside the door. 'Miller! Ye may scare the shite outa Sister Eleanor! But one box from me would demolish half of that disgusting greasy fat ye're dragging around. Ye're supposed te be on odd jobs, but I've been doing yer work long enough; now it's your turn, ye fat, lazy slut!' Then I ducked, seeing the kettle flying through the air and landing on the pillars holding up the ceiling. I watched it collapse onta the floor, landing in a battered heap.

'Now look what you made me do,' she screamed, her eyes not believing she might be in real trouble for once.

I laughed, skipping outa the refectory and heading up the passage te wait on the landing for Sister Eleanor, before she gets the bad news about her kettle and forgets all about me.

'There you are!' Sister Eleanor puffed, her eyes spinning around the landing and up te the other floors, seeing if anything or anyone was outa place and needed her ordering. She stooped te pick up a coat dropped on the cloakroom passage. 'Tsk, tsk, those children are very untidy,' she muttered, getting all red in the face and pained-looking, working herself up inta a tizzy.

Gawd! Will ye ever stop fussing, Sister Eleanor, I muttered te meself. I wish ye would be easy in yerself. Jaysus! She's going te go mad over that kettle! I better make meself scarce when I find out what she wants. Miller is her pet and can do no wrong. Sister Eleanor will even do the work herself – well, sort of! – knowing she can get no good outa Miller. I can't see what her attraction is meself; she has a poison personality, drags her fat bulk around looking like she's had fifteen kids and they've taken it outa her, and she's not even sixteen yet! Hm!

'Sister!' I let a roar outa me.

'What! What is it?' she said, lifting her head from the floor, purple veins sticking outa her temple, trying te sort out the boots and shoes, putting them back on the shelf. 'What? . . . Give me a hand here with these shoes, for the love of God,' she whined. 'Those children are really filthy!'

I looked around. Any minute now someone is going te come screaming up that passage roaring I smashed the kettle. Poor Harriet was only standing beside the kettle, and it was me that made it fly through the air. Eleanor will go mad with me for upsetting her precious Harriet.

'Sister Eleanor! Are we going down te the nursery?'

'Yes! Yes,' she smiled, standing herself up, then fixed her veil on her head, taking off for the nursery at a bracing gallop.

Oh, I love the way that word came te me – bracing! I rushed up behind her, hearing the noise before we got there.

'Oh, God almighty! I can hear it from here,' muttered Sister Eleanor, belting in the door with me on her tail dying te know what all the mystery is about.

'Here we are!' she said, stooping down te a little tiny baby girl with a mop of curly gold hair and a tiny little white face with big blue velvety eyes looking like they were too big for her face. She was standing in the middle of the room on a little miniature pair of matchstick legs, roaring at a big young one.

'No! Youse buck off! I'm not sittin on tha! I want me ma!'

'OK! I give up,' sighed Vanessa Andrewson, giving me a dirty look, saying, 'Sister Eleanor! That child has not stopped screaming since she was brought through that door,' and marched off, taking the potty with her.

'Agnes! Look who's here to see you,' crooned Sister Eleanor, dropping on her knees te wrap her arms around the tiny little body.

Agnes stopped roaring te stare inta the nun's face, her mouth dropping open te take in what the nun had te say. 'Is it me ma?' she asked in a high-pitched squeak.

I can't believe she's well able te talk at that size, I thought, dropping down on me knees te touch her and grab her up in a tight hug. Ah, now I know what Sister was after. She wants me te placate this little one. She gets me te mind the new little ones who arrive here terrified and making strange. Eleanor is always telling me I have a wonderful way with the little ones. Yeah! It's because I'm used te looking after little children. I understand them.

'This is your big sister Martha!' Sister whispered, smiling and pointing at me.

I nearly fell over; the shock knocking the stuffing outa me. 'Me sister! How? When? . . .'

'Yes, this is Agnes, your little sister! Isn't she a little dote?' she said, squeezing Agnes. 'She's just over two years old.'

'Bar ta! Me big sista?' she asked the nun in a squeak, looking at her. Then she looked at me, staring at me, taking me in from head te foot, deciding the nun was telling the truth; she could see a bit of the ma in me!

I laughed, watching her staring and deciding if she trusts me or not.

'Bar ta!' she suddenly roared, throwing herself at me. 'Me ma said ye're te mind me!'

I scooped her up in me arms and she weighed a feather! I could feel her little ribs under the thin skin and I looked at her tiny white matchstick legs, feeling them. I squeezed her te me and I felt her taking the air inta her lungs, flying down through her, sinking inta the bottom of her belly, then letting go a big sigh, her little frame collapsing, losing the rigid tension and melting inta me, fitting herself snugly inta me arms and dropping her head onta me chest, totally at peace, feeling safe.

I stood rocking her, watching Sister Eleanor get te her feet, saying, 'We'll go up to the middle group; the rest of the girls are up there.'

'Dinah and Sally?'

'Yes, Martha. Your mammy has gone into hospital to have the new baby, and we have them all here. They will only stay for a short while, to give the poor creature a rest, God help her!' Sister

Eleanor was saying as I flew out the door making for the stairs with Agnes in me arms.

'Are ye takin me te Dinna? Are ye goin te find everyone?' Agnes roared at me in her little aul granny voice with the high-pitched squeak, holding me face with her two little hands, lifting her eyebrows and looking straight inta me eyes. 'Are ye?' she whispered, looking hopeful.

'Yeah! Come on! We'll go and find them,' I giggled, jerking her up and down with excitement. Then it hit me! I stopped dead on the stairs. 'Are me brothers here? Charlie and the others?' I said te Eleanor, belting up behind me.

'Charlie? . . . No, Martha. We have Teddy and Harry. Why, is there another one?'

'Yeah,' I said, me heart sinking inta me belly. So the bastard kept Charlie back te mind him and cook his meals and do the messages. Then leave him stuck minding the house all on his own while he goes off drinking and comes back outa his mind drunk, reeling around the place and beating the shite outa poor Charlie. He's . . . what age is he now? Gawd, he's ten. If he's anything like me, he'll start te fuck off and leave them to it any day soon in the future. Gawd! I wish I could see him, get him here. Me heart felt very heavy as I took the rest of the stairs, thinking his suffering is still going on while I'm well out of it. God! Please, please watch over me poor little Charlie, and don't let any harm come te him. Please, God! He has had a very hard life.

I walked quickly down the passage and inta the middle group playroom, me eyes flying around the room and settling on the two little girls with the long fair hair and the blue eyes sitting together on the sofa, looking lost and staring around them, afraid te move with the young ones flying around each other messing and shouting and slapping each other. All having great gas! They look like twins, I thought, staring at them with me mouth open, trying te take it in. They're here! With me! Dinah! Sally!

'Lookit! Dem's me sistas, Bar ta!' roared Agnes inta me face, pointing and jerking herself, slipping outa me arms. I let her go and she flew, throwing herself at them, screaming at Dinah and Sally, looking from one te the other inta their faces. 'It's Bar ta! Me big sista! Lookit, Dinna! Will ye lookit, Saleh!'

They lifted their heads, smiling shyly at me, their eyes lighting up.

'Look at you two!' I screamed at them, grabbing them and kissing them and sitting down between them, pulling them inta me arms.

'They're lovely children,' Miss beamed at me, her mouth twitching, and throwing her long grey hair back from her face te get a better look, then looking te Sister Eleanor, beaming at her, seeing Sister smiling and staring, nodding her head in agreement.

'Dat is me big sista, Bar ta,' roared Agnes, looking up at the two women and pulling the nylons offa Miss te get her te take a better look at me, and then roaring back te Eleanor, 'Dat's my big sista dere!' She pointed te me. 'De ye know da, Missus?' she said, roaring up at Sister Eleanor, who bent down and scooped her up inta her arms, roaring laughing, getting great enjoyment outa Agnes.

'When did ye all get here?' I whispered te the girls, looking from one te the other.

'Today, yeah,' little Sally whispered. Then she dropped her head, looking up at the two women, making sure they couldn't hear, saying, 'They gave us a wash!'

'Yeah! In a big bath,' whispered Dinah.

'Yeah!' slurped Sally with her tongue. 'An we nearly got drownded, so we did!'

'Yeah! It was terrible altogether,' moaned Dinah.

I kept looking from one te the other. 'Tsk, tsk. Ye must have got an awful shock altogether!' I whispered, shaking me head at them.

'Yeah! We did an all!' Dinah sighed, getting herself inta shock at the memory of it all over again.

'We were cryin for ye, an tha aul one there, her!' Sally said, pointing at Miss.

'Shush!' I laughed. 'Don't let her hear ye call her that,' I said, taking her finger.

'Well, the aul one there! She gave us the wash, an we kept roarin an cryin our eyes out an sayin we wanted ye!'

'Yeah!' Dinah sniffed. 'But she wouldn't get ye! She kept sayin ye'd be comin in a minute!'

'They have lovely table manners,' gushed Miss. 'They use their knife and fork beautifully. Do you know, Sister, they have much more refinement than our own lot,' she breathed te Sister, who kept smiling and shaking her head saying, 'Oh, they are beautiful girls. You have lovely sisters, Martha.'

I was busy thinking how they learned te use a knife and fork when they never even saw a fork up until now! It's instinctive, I thought te meself, looking at them, me heart bursting with contentment and feeling really proud of them. Delighted at the praise they were getting. How did ye's all get here without me seeing ye's? I wondered. They must have come in the back door, and nobody said a word te me about the fact that they would be coming here. Nuns! They tell nothing!

'Where are the boys, Sister Eleanor?'

She leaned inta me, whispering, 'They are in the nursery, Martha. They were having their bath when we arrived.'

'Let's go and see them,' I said, standing up and taking the girls' hands.

'Lift me up, Bar ta!' roared Agnes, getting worried we might leave her behind in a strange place again.

'Come on, ye little fairy,' I laughed, swinging her up inta me arms and taking Sally by the hand. 'Come on, quickly! Let's go down and see Teddy and Harry! I can't wait te see them.'

We walked back inta the nursery, seeing Teddy and Harry straight away sitting at a little table with their hands on their chins taking in everything around them. I recognised them straight away. Gawd! They've grown. Teddy's brown coppery hair was gleaming and silky-looking. They must have cut it, I thought, looking at how clean they looked in their matching wine jumpers and grey long trousers. Harry's strawberry blond hair and white little face stared out at me through a gorgeous pair of navy-blue eyes. Teddy has gorgeous eyes, too; they're sky-blue with the whites dazzling-looking. They look very thin and tired, I thought, me heart melting at the sight of them.

Teddy jerked his head, dropping his hands when he saw me. 'Marta! Marta! We're here!' he shouted, pushing back his chair and lifting his foot, getting caught in his hurry. 'Lookit, Harry! It's Marta! Come on will ya, quick!'

I flew over, grabbing Teddy, mashing him te me, and he pulled away, lifting his head te talk te me, breathing heavily trying te get out everything at once. 'Me ma's gone te the hospital te get a new babby, an we were all taken in the car be the woman an brought te ye!'

I looked over at Harry smiling with a crooked grin, wrapping his fingers through the top of his hair, smiling shyly and swinging himself slowly away from me, letting Teddy do all the talking and shaking his head agreeing with everything Teddy said.

'We're sleepin over here! Lookit! That's my bed, an the one next te it is Harry's.'

I looked over at the two beds in the corner. 'An we gorra wash, an he wouldn't let the nun wash him, an I got me hair washed,' he said, all in one big breath, stopping te swallow his spits, slurpin on them.

'I did! It was you tha wouldn't let the woman wash yer hair,' Harry said, finding his voice at the lies Teddy was telling.

'No! You were the one tha tried te gerouta the bath!' Teddy said, leaning over te Harry, keeping his voice reasonable.

'Fuck off!' Harry roared. 'I'm not speakin te you no more!'

'Oh, boys! Language!' screamed Sister Eleanor.

'Come here and stop fighting, you two,' I said, grabbing a hold of Harry and squeezing him in a hug, feeling his ribs sticking out.

'We missed ye, Marta!' roared Teddy, flinging his arms around me neck and strangling me.

'Yeah! I missed all youse,' I murmured inta their faces, squatting down on the floor and holding them against me cheeks. 'I always kept thinking about youse! I never left ye outa me mind,' I whispered.

'Yeah! An we missed ye, too!' they murmured.

'I think it's time to get that little one into bed,' Sister Eleanor muttered, looking at me and nodding her head at Agnes, who was busying herself examining Dinah and Sally's new frocks.

'Lookit! I got a new pah a shoes!' she was saying te the girls, stepping back and pulling up her Little Bo Peep frock, sticking out her tiny little black patent shoe with a black bow on the top. 'In dey luverley?' she shouted in a squeak.

We all started laughing at the way she can speak like a blue-arse fly.

'Goodness! Isn't she marvellous the way she can speak so well?' breathed Sister Eleanor, her eyes out on stalks, absolutely besotted with Agnes.

I couldn't get over her and the rest of them. They're lovely, I thought te meself, looking around at them, still finding it hard te believe they are here with me. God! They look terribly thin, though, and their faces are very pasty, with dark circles under their eyes. But good food and a clean bed with warm clothes would soon have them looking a lot healthier. But they may not be staying long enough for that.

'I better get over to the convent, Martha,' Sister Eleanor whispered te me, seeing the nursery nun, Sister James Teresa flying out the door. 'Get them into bed. I will be late for the chapel.'

'Yes, Sister.'

'I better get these two little girls off to bed, too,' said Miss. She made te take their hands and all the children started getting anxious.

The boys moved closer te me, looking up at me with fear in

their eyes, and Teddy muttered, 'Don't go, Marta! We don't want te be left here.'

Harry started wringing his hands, moving from one foot te the other, and the girls were whimpering, moving closer te me, grabbing hold of me skirt. Agnes let a piercing scream outa her. 'No! I wan te go wit you, Bar ta. No!' and she started dancing up and down with the fright.

'Listen, boys! I'm going up te put the girls te bed, and . . . come on, ye! Little light of me life!' I whipped Agnes up in me arms, saying, 'I'm going te take her with me, and when I get back I'll read ye a story. Will that be all right?'

'Yeah! Ye mean tha?' Teddy asked me, looking inta me eyes with the eyes of an old man.

'Of course I will, darling. I would never let ye down. If I say I am going te do something, then I will do it,' I said, grabbing their heads and giving them a quick kiss. 'Now, look! Everyone else is in the bed; you two get inta yer pyjamas and get nice and snug in yer new beds. Go on! Hurry!'

'Yeah!' they shouted, delighted.

I watched them race off, the two of them watching each other te see who would be first. 'Will yeh read us a story, too?' a little voice came from over by the wall.

I looked over, seeing a little fella of three lifting his head and asking me with a very serious look on his face, like this was the most serious thing in the world!

'Yeah! Of course I will, Arthur! I'll read ye's all a story,' I said, laughing.

'Naw! She's naw yer sista!' roared Agnes, leaning outa me arms, waving her hand over at the little fella, sounding like a real little aul one!

'Ah, be nice te the other babbies,' I said, shaking her up and down in me arms.

'Martha! Wake up!'

I struggled te lift me head, not knowing what was happening.

'Wha . . . what's wrong?' I said, looking up inta the face of Sister Eleanor leaning over me.

'It's Agnes. She's roaring her head off, screaming for you! Quickly! Run down to the nursery and lie with her until she goes back to sleep.'

I rubbed me eyes, seeing it was the middle of the night and everyone sound asleep and snoring their heads off, all snugly dug under their blankets.

I spent hours last night trying te get her te sleep, and eventually she dropped off! 'Sister Eleanor, I'm very tired,' I moaned, still not awake, hoping she'd leave me alone.

'I can imagine!' she muttered. 'Go down quickly, for the love of God. She has the whole nursery in uproar.'

I dived outa the bed, throwing me cardigan over me nightdress, and put on me shoes, heading off te the nursery while Sister Eleanor headed off te her room te catch up on a bit of sleep in whatever was left of the night. I shivered in the cold. The house was freezing and a draught hit me as I rounded the passage heading down te the nursery. Only night lights flickered along the passage, and I could hear the wind howling out through the television room door, screaming up from the end passages, sounding like the Banshee, threatening te freeze the legs off me. I pulled the nightdress tighter around me legs and gripped hold of me cardigan, sinking me neck down inta it.

'Bar ta,' she sobbed, sitting up in the bed. Poor Vanessa Andrewson was sitting on her bed looking shell-shocked, rubbing her eyes, and collapsed down inta it as soon as I arrived.

'I wanted ye te come! Don't go away, will ye?'

'No, darling,' I said, grabbing hold of her and tucking her under the blankets; her little arms are icy cold. 'Come on, baby! Cuddle inta me.' I lay on the bed, wrapping the blankets around her, and snuggled her in beside me as I lay on top of the bed with her wrapped under me arm and stroked her head, murmuring a quiet Brahms lullaby. 'Shush! Go to sleep, Go to sleep . . . Deh Deh Dah Deh!'

Her eyes kept flickering open and shut. She was exhausted but terrified I would go and leave her. 'Ye won't go on me, will ye, Bar ta?' she murmured.

'No, baby. I'll stay with ye.'

I dozed, aware of the cold, then opened me eyes, hearing her breathing. It's quite even. She's out for the count. I stirred meself, holding me breath and trying te float off the bed, not daring te wake her. I stood up, staring down at her. I've seen bigger dolls! She's so tiny. I watched te see if she would stir, then she suddenly turned her head on the pillow, giving a little whimper. I held me breath, waiting. No! She's inta a deep sleep now. Thank God! I let me breath out slowly without making a sound and crept outa the nursery, dragging meself along the dimly lit passage, hearing the winter winds howling in a fury, rattling the heavy window frames, and rain pelted the glass while the wind whistled around the passages. I listened as a door banged open and shut somewhere along the top passages, the wind finding an opening and tearing in from the outside playing fields. I took the stairs one at a time, feeling drained after the week that was in it. Christmas is just around the corner! I could smell the faint aroma of baking coming from Mercy's kitchen still lingering in the air. Please God me little family will have a good Christmas for the first time in their life; they got here just in time.

CHAPTER 13

I rushed up, heading for the convent passage, when I heard the children coming back from the Christmas party. Me heart was flying. I was dying te know how they got on; the poor kids never even heard of a party, never mind go te one. I had only been te two. Then it was over for me because I started working. But I will never forget it! Me first time ever te get to go te a party! Gawd, it was magic! The fuss they made of us from the moment we set foot in the place. It was factory workers, clubbing their money together and saving up for the orphans' party. That's what this place is seen as, an orphanage! It drives the kids here mad. 'We're not orphans!' they roar at the local village people who look and shake their heads, saying with pity, 'Ah, look! There go the poor orphans on their Sunday afternoon walk.' Jaysus! I could live with that. These orphans are not doing too bad.

But that first party I went te! They handed us out party hats and balloons, and bags of sweets, and played party games. Some of the men, the workers, were getting up and singing all the songs the kids wanted te hear. 'Jingle Bells', 'Ye better watch out! Santa's on his way'. We roared our heads off, then jumped around the place dancing te the music!

It still haunts me when I hear the words of a song being played: 'Train whistle blowing . . . all along the bay'. I stood listening te the words, me hands full of sweets, and me jaws working up and down lorrying sweets down me neck. Then as the words

hit me, and the music seeped inta the core of me, I suddenly
stopped chewing and looked around at all the children laughing
happily and the decorations and the different-coloured lights and
the people running te make children happy. It hit me. A terrible
feeling of sadness came over me. People doing so much for the
children, because it's Christmas, and they have no mammies. But
I had a mammy, and this is the first time I've ever seen people
all standing around watching and rushing te see if we are having
a good time, and I felt like a child for the first time I can ever
remember. I was feeling all this while the music was playing, and
I wanted te be on that train all along the bay . . . 'and underneath
the blankets go all the girls and boys'. I had a picture of children
being safe and happy, and I wanted te be one of them. I was a
child, an ye get minded when ye're a child! I was feeling happy,
and special, but even as I felt it, it was slipping away from me,
and I knew then me time was running out. Because soon I would
be big. And I'd never get te find out what it was really like te be
a child for long. Yeah! The Christmas party. I will remember that
day te me dying day. And that music! That song brings it all back.
Magic! I'm a child again, feeling the happiness and the sadness
all mixed together. I'd get te meet Santa! The man I gave up on
a long time ago, knowing some things never happen. But it was
all happening for me! I'm having me first Christmas. And it's like
stepping inta one of the fairy-tale books I used te rob for meself.
Yeah! It was the most precious time of me life . . . I was a child
and I felt like a child, even as it slipped away from me.

I felt tears spilling down me cheeks and I smiled, wiping them
away. Now me little sisters and brothers are getting their turn.

I heard the stampede of feet running along the convent passage
and I whipped open the door as a gang of happy children ran
through me, knocking me te one side. I looked at the faces, seeing
Dinah and Sally walking through the crowd, getting bumped.
They looked lovely, wearing hats with pom-poms, and their long
fair hair hanging over their lovely warm coats. They had long
scarves wrapped around their neck, and boots with red tights;

little Sally's was white. Dinah was holding onto a big doll, and Sally had a Rupert the Bear; she carried it like a baby.

I pushed me way through, shouting, 'Dinah! Sally!'

They looked up, seeing me, then I noticed Dinah was crying.

'I'm here! What happened? Why are ye crying? Come on!' I grabbed the two of them, taking their hands, and looked around for Teddy and Harry. Agnes's nursery group was not back yet. They'll probably be back soon; they went in a separate bus.

'What's wrong with ye?' I said, kneeling down te them, pulling them outa the way inta the corner of the landing.

'A big one punched her in the stomach, Marta!' Sally whispered, looking like she wanted te cry as well.

'Who? Where? Why?' I asked in shock. They were terrified. Afraid te lift their eyes and look around.

I looked around at the group standing and waiting for the Miss te arrive and herd them off te bed. A big young one stood staring and smirking at us.

'She did!' Dinah said, holding her stomach and sobbing.

I jumped up, whirling around, and flew at the young one. 'Did you hit me little baby sister?' I asked her, feeling the colour drain outa me.

'Yeah! So what?'

'Ye whore's melt!' I landed her such a smack on the side of her face, sending her flying. 'Ye big fucking eejit. What age are ye? Twelve?' Then I felt an electric bolt going through me head as I turned around seeing her big fat friend, a big young one from my group, come steaming at me.

'Bitch! Long! Don't you dare hit my friend again or I'll kill you.'

I took a flying kick at the young one again, sending her flying backwards and smacking her back inta the stairs. 'That's for a start,' I snorted, as Fatty came flying at me again with both claws out, ready te grab me hair and claw me eyes out. I ducked, grabbing her by the back of the hair, tearing her towards the banisters, and keeping well back I swung her head over, jerking her down, then dived in, pressing her neck up as far as I could get it with the palm of me right hand and holding her hair tightly gripped in me fists with me left hand, pulling her head down. I tugged for all I was worth, forcing her te arch her back, sending her nearly flying over the staircase and, jumping back, landed an unmerciful kick in her stomach.

I was icy cold! First it was only me. Now they pick on me helpless little sister, and they'll pick them off one by one unless they learn a lesson. 'Don't you or yer bitch of a friend ever mess with me or my family again,' I snorted, outa breath. 'Or next time ye will be needin a bleedin hospital.'

The door flew open and Sister Eleanor came flying in looking from me te the fat cow holding her stomach, and roaring, 'What's happening here? What's been happening? Come on, children, go up to your dormitories. In front of the children, Martha! How could you?'

I looked at Dinah and Sally; they were white as sheets. 'Come on, girls, I'll take ye up te yer beds and I want te hear everything about yer party. Did ye have a great time?' I whispered te the two of them. 'Did ye see Santa Claus?'

'Yeah! We got a dolly an a teddy bear,' they whispered, still in shock at seeing their sister get inta a terrible fight after being attacked themselves.

I was feeling like me heart was breaking; the whole fucking thing ruined. Them bastards are animals. I couldn't let it go when the bastard threw down the challenge! Otherwise they would all turn on the babies later on in the dormitory. That fucker needed te know she can't look crooked at me babies! Yeah! I did what I had te do. Or it would be worse again for them next time. 'Listen, Dinah! That big young one won't come near ye again. She knows I'm watching her, so ye won't be afraid, will ye?'

'No!' They shook their heads, a faraway look in their eyes, thinking about this. Then Dinah's face lit up in a smile. 'She knows ye will kill her, Marta.'

'Yeah! I'd only kill her, so don't mind them.'

'OK! Yeah, OK!' they smiled, Dinah letting her neck slip inside her coat, giggling. Enjoying the thought she was safe because I was around te protect them.

'Martha! Wake up!'

I shot up in the bed looking inta Sister Eleanor's face.

'Quickly, get up to the parlour. Jesus help us! The young couple who took Agnes for Christmas have had to bring her back. She's up there now, screaming her head off, waking the whole convent up! It's twelve o'clock at night. Hurry! Get dressed like a good girl,' she said, humping me outa the bed while I was still sitting staring at her, trying te get me senses back.

I jumped outa bed, diving inta me clothes, and followed her quickly outa the dormitory.

'Jesus wept!' Sister Eleanor wailed. 'They are a lovely couple. She left with them earlier this evening.'

'Yeah, I missed her when I went down te the nursery. They said she'd left already; that was just after tea.'

'Yes, the couple were delighted with her, but she screamed the house down when they got her to their home! They had to ring the convent, Martha!' she whispered, shocked at the idea. 'And take her all the way back. She wouldn't settle. They said she kept screaming for you.'

'Oh hell, that really is a shame. What an awful pity, Sister.'

'Yes, but it can't be helped. She's back now. I had to hurry down to get you. She took one look at me and went hysterical! I couldn't get near her. Come on! Hurry! Can you hear the screams?'

I could hear the screams from here as we hit the chapel passage. 'Gawd! The nuns will go mad in the morning, Sister,' I puffed, getting outa breath, 'with all the goings on!'

I didn't know whether I was coming or going, flying between the children and sleeping beside the baby every night te get her te sleep. Then rushing in the morning te get me work done, and thinking and worrying about them when I wasn't with them.

Sister Eleanor threw open the door te the convent parlour, and me eyes peeled down te a little fairy in a white fur coat and matching fur hat, standing looking like she was only a few inches off the ground. Agnes stood screaming in a continuous pitch, her tongue hanging out and her eyes keeping a watch, flying around at any movement and belting out at anyone who came near her.

I looked up at the lovely young couple standing beside each other, both of them stooping down te Agnes. The young wife had her hands out, and she was telling Agnes everything was fine. 'Look who's here to see you.'

And the husband was bending down with his hands on his knees and his eyebrows turned up, staring at her like he was going te cry because the baby was having nothing te do with them.

'Agnes! What's wrong with ye?' I stooped down te look at her and she flew at me, diving inta me lap.

'Tha buckers are tryin te rob me!' she complained in a high squeak, pointing at them and staring back. 'Now me big sista is goin te kill youse!' she suddenly roared.

'Shush!' I put her face inta me chest. 'No, no, Agnes! Ye can't say that! They only wanted te take ye te see Santa Claus, and buy ye a big dolly, and mind ye until me ma comes outa hospital,' I said, looking inta her face.

'Naw! I want te stay wit you!' she started te roar.

'Shush! OK!'

The couple were looking sad and fascinated with the size of her and the stuff coming outa her mouth. 'Oh, she's gorgeous,' the woman said sadly, shaking her head at her, feeling the loss at not being able te take her for the Christmas.

'Where did ye get the lovely coat, Agnes?'

'She pur it on a me!' Agnes said, pulling the two sides together and hanging onta it as if the woman was going te take it back.

'Oh! And look at yer lovely white fur muff te put yer two hands through,' I said, feeling it.

'Yeah! Dat's mine too!' she said, throwing her eyes, giving a warning look over at the couple.

They roared laughing. 'Yes, of course it belongs to you, Agnes,' the lady said. 'We bought it specially for you! Remember? We took you to the shop.'

Agnes just stared with a suspicious look on her face, still thinking she'd have te lose the coat if she let go of the two sides.

I picked her up, saying, 'I'm very sorry, she just made strange. Say goodbye, Agnes, te the nice people.'

'See ye,' she squeaked.

'Will we give them a kiss?' I whispered. 'They are going te miss ye!'

'Naw!'

'Why?' I whispered.

'Cos she might take me coat!' she whispered, leaning her face inta me and locking her eyes on mine, raising her little eyebrows.

'Ah, she won't! Come on, let's get ye down te bed. Say bye, bye!'

'Wha abou me Winkey?' she suddenly roared.

'Oh, yes! We can't forget him,' the man laughed, picking up a white furry cat with a red ribbon tied around his neck and coal-black eyes that glittered.

She grabbed Winkey, holding him tight te her chest, and snuggled inta me arms, then lifted one hand, waving happily at them, feeling safe again as we went out the door heading down te the nursery.

'Ye won't leave me, Marta?'

'No, darling. I'm staying right here with ye,' I said, snuggling her closer te me.

She closed her eyes, and I felt me eyelids getting heavy. I flicked them open, feeling them a dead weight. I can't stay awake!

I must have dozed again, because suddenly I opened me eyes feeling the cold stiffening me. I lifted me head, gently looking at Agnes. She's out for the count. I slipped off the bed gently, making out the door and headed down the passage, and took off taking the stairs two at a time, me legs feeling a dead weight.

Christ! I'm freezing and bloody exhausted. I didn't get te sit down once today; the time just flies. Oh, I'm dying te get te me own bed. Jaysus! I bet it's nearly three o'clock in the morning. I have te be up at seven. These days I go te Mass in the mornings, mostly te impress the nuns. It's better te keep in with them, seeing as the kids hate me guts. I can't be getting meself slammed in the middle like I used te, with the nuns trying te get rid of me on one side, and the kids trying te kill me on the other. It's working, because I've made meself useful te the nuns, and that gives me an advantage over the kids. Now at least I know where I stand, and I can keep outa trouble. Te hell with the kids; I know where me bread is buttered! Yeah, but I'm going te have me work cut out for me trying te get up in another few hours.

I slid inta the bed, going out like a light.

'Go forth in peace, the Mass has ended.'

I watched the priest give his blessing then leave the altar, taking off for the sacristy. I waited, holding me breath, then looked around at the nuns leaving their prie-dieux. The ones in charge of the children anyway, while the Reverend Mother and the rest of the Community stayed on for a bit of contemplation.

I quietly made me way outa the bench and genuflected, then opened the side door, closing it quietly, and tore off like the hammers of hell making me way down te the nursery.

'Buck off!'

Oops. That's my Agnes, I thought, pushing in the door, laughing te meself.

'Come on, Agnes! Don't you want to use your potty? Do wee wee!'

'Naw!'

Poor Vanessa was standing there with a potty in her hand, scratching her head, getting nowhere with her, trying te persuade her te go out with the other babies te the toilets and sit on the potty.

'Who's making all the noise?' I laughed, creeping up te her and grabbing her inta the air.

'Ye left me!'

'Aaaahhhh!' I nuzzled her neck, hearing her screaming laughing, me saying, 'Ah, stop yer aul giving out. Thanks, Vanessa. I'll look after her. Come on! Let's go out te the toilets and see all the other babies.'

'Naw! I don't want te sit on tha!' she screamed, waving at the pot.

'Course ye don't. Ye're too big for tha. We'll go and use the big toilets! Wouldn't ye like that, Agnes?'

'Yeah!' she said happily as I scooped her up.

'Marta! Harry, lookit! Marta's here.'

'Look at you two in yer lovely pyjamas!' I said, rushing over, picking up Teddy and leaving Agnes sitting on the bed. 'Give us a kiss, Harry!'

He giggled, his eyes lighting up and showing his lovely little white teeth.

'Are ye OK?' I said, sitting down on the bed with Agnes on me lap.

'Yeah! But we don't like it on our own, do we Harry?'

'No! We don't like it on our own,' Harry agreed, listening te Teddy and smiling at me.

'Listen! Get dressed, darlings, and ye'll be getting yer lovely breakfast! Won't that be nice? And I'll see ye at lunchtime when I come back from work for me dinner. Is that OK with ye? Now! I want te sort out this little fairy here. Isn't that right?' I said, giving her a tickle.

'Aaaahhh! More! More, Bar ta,' she roared.

'Tickle me!' shouted Teddy.

'And me!' said, Harry, slapping his chest.

I looked around, seeing the nursery nun coming in. 'Oooh! Too late, boys! All outa tickles until dinner time. Ye have te get dressed now. Go on, boys,' I whispered, 'put yer clothes on.'

'OK, Marta! Do ye mean it tha ye'll come back te see us at the dinner time, Marta?'

'Of course I will. I would never let ye down,' I said earnestly te them, bending down te look inta their eyes. 'Now, hurry up and go and get yer breakfast. Come on, you! Me little fairy.' I carried her out te the toilets. 'Look at you lot!' I laughed te the babies all lined up sitting on their potties.

'Will yeh read me anodder story?' Arthur shouted up te me from his potty.

'Yeah! Course I will, Arthur darling! Oh, ye're all such good babies! Aren't they, Agnes?'

'Naw!' she moaned, looking at them, not too sure.

'Aaahhh! They are! Don't be mean,' I laughed, grabbing her tight and sinking me mouth inta her neck, hearing her little tinkly laugh.

'Now! Finished. Good girl! Ye used the toilet like a big girl!'

'Yeah!' she laughed, delighted at being one up on the other babies after using the baby toilet.

'Hurry! Quick!' I whispered. 'We have te get ye dressed then we can rush down and see Dinah and Sally before ye get yer breakfast.'

I hurried down the passage wanting te see the girls, anxious te make sure they were OK. 'Naw!' Agnes was screaming in me arms. 'I wan me cooaat! An me haaat!'

'Ye can't wear that, ye silly! That's te keep ye warm when ye go outside in the cold!'

'Naw!'

I stopped dead with her in me arms, looking at her with me eyes wide. 'Oh no! It's terrible,' I said, looking at her.

'Wha?' She suddenly stopped roaring, staring at me wondering what I was going te say.

'If we run back for yer coat' – sob! – 'we won't get te see the girls. What will we do? Will we not see them?'

'Naw! Hurry, Bar ta. I want te see me sistas!'

'Right! We better hurry!' I said, faking me breath, puffing along like mad.

I flew outa the convent taking the stairs two at a time and charged inta Ma Pius, nearly knocking her sideways.

'Where on earth are you running to? Where is the fire?' she barked, fixing her veil and steadying herself.

'Sorry, Ma . . . Mother Pius. I was rushing for me . . . my tea.'

'Walk! Please walk, a lady always walks.'

'Yes, Mother Pius,' and fuck off outa me way! I'm thinking te meself as she stared at me, deliberately making me take me time. I stared at her, trying te take the sulky look off me face and smile. Only then she stepped outa me way, making me stand back and hold the door open for her. Then she sailed past, muttering, 'Energy is wasted on the youth!'

I let the door go and tore up the passage, flying down te the nursery. Jaysus! I hope Agnes is all right. I didn't get te see her at lunchtime. I had te go on a message down te the village for one of the nuns. I was bleeding raging. By the time I got back, it was too late te see them. I had te get back te work.

I puffed me way along the passage, seeing Sister Eleanor hounding a load of young ones in front of her. 'Martha! Where are you going?' she moaned, looking like she wanted te cry, run or kill someone.

'I'm just going te see Agnes, Sister, before she goes down for the night, and read her a quick story,' I gasped, slowing te a gentle run.

'No! Wait!'

'What?'

'You can't see her! She's . . .'

'Sister Eleanor! Will you be giving out sweets after the tea? When you come down from the convent?' roared Lilian Wring, shaking the nun's arm with one hand and scratching her arse with the other.

'Will you leave me alone the lot of you for one minute.'

I flew off.

'Wait! Martha!'

'What?' I stopped just inside the door.

'Come back here when I am speaking to you!' Sister Eleanor roared, losing her rag.

'What, Sister? What are ye saying?' I asked her, beginning te get worried. Me heart went inta me mouth. 'What's wrong?'

'Nothing! There's nothing wrong. I am sick of the lot of you! Nobody listens to me. You are all so selfish!'

'Jaysus, Sister!' I roared, losing me temper.

'Don't you dare take the name of the good Lord in vain!' she screamed, running at me and waving her finger in me face.

'I just want te go in and see me baby sister and Teddy and Harry! Have me tea, then see Dinah and Sally. What's wrong with that?' I stared with me mouth open, feeling me temper rise.

She dropped the pained look in her face suddenly and relaxed, trying te pacify me. 'Listen, Martha, I was trying to tell you they have all gone home.' She stared at me, and I stared back, trying te take it in.

'Why? When? I thought they were going te be here until after the Christmas. Go out with families . . . and have a . . . lovely Christmas . . .' I trailed off, staring at the floor, trying te take it in. I felt like bursting inta tears.

'Why? Because we had to take little Agnes home; she wasn't settling, you know that yourself!' she said, softening her voice.

'So why did the others go?'

'Because their father insisted. "If one comes," he said, "they all come." So they all left this morning. So there you are, they've all gone home,' she said, waving her hands.

'OK, thanks, Sister.'

Then she went heading off te the refectory after the other lot and I headed out te the toilets in the playing fields, where no one would bother me.

The grounds are deserted; everyone's in having their tea, I

thought, looking around at the open fields and the bare trees all along the Cloistered Walk. It's too cold te go down there and it's too dark anyway, and this biting cold would cut through ye, but I don't care. I just want te feel miles away from everyone.

I went inta the toilets and sat meself down on top of the toilet seat and listened te the quiet, the wind blowing through the bare trees and along the high stone walls the only sound te be heard, and the wind and the cold and the air blowing inta the open entrance te the toilets was lovely. Fresh and wild, giving me a sense of being free in the wide open spaces. The suffocating feeling I had when she said they were all gone. The people around me shouting, screaming, demanding, jeering, laughing, unfriendly, treacherous – all coming from the same scream, all wanting what I wanted. Someone for their very own. Te be special in someone's heart. The constant beat of the tom-tom drums, the fight for territorial rights, te be heard, noticed, wanted, loved, with the only adult who cared: Sister Eleanor! She was the coveted prize. Nothing and nobody stood in the way of survival, nothing could be too vicious, everyone must look out for themselves, for when ye have a full belly, a roof over yer head and a warm bed, then comes the pain again, the gnawing need for the warmth of a pair of loving arms te take away the cold and emptiness that pains yer heart.

The noise made me feel trapped, afraid, lonely, alone, like I'll never be wanted. I thought I was in hell for those few minutes. Jackser and the ma and the old ways were inside me and all around me. The children are gone! I've nothing, nobody, and I was drowning in Jackser and the ma, with the thought of the children not even having even one Christmas but having te go back now te that hell of the ma and him!

I took in a deep breath, standing up, and walked outside, looking up at the dark sky and feeling it is a big wide world beyond here. I can get lost out there, travel far and wide, and away from here, and everything that came before it, and live somewhere where I have peace and space and time te meself, and people around me who like me . . . and there's no more violence.

I took in a deep lungful of air, letting out the hot breath te mist in the cold night frost, seeing it curl around me head, warming me face, and looking out as far as I could see inta the dark night sky with the stars twinkling in their heavens. They're all the souls of people gone before me, I thought. Then me gaze lowered, resting on the trees throwing their shadows inta the light thrown down by the lamps at the top of the avenue, and slowly walked back towards the kitchen door, making me way in for a drop of tea, feeling more at peace, and a quiet feeling of stillness.

CHAPTER 14

I flew along the convent passage, yanking open the heavy door with the stiff springs behind it, letting it shut by itself. Still running, I barrelled inta a gang of kids all milling around on the landing, shouting te each other. The noise of bags and suitcases getting clattered up the stairs, and more coming down from the top, and all the time screaming up te the ones on the landing, 'Did you find my coat? Who took my bag?' was overwhelming. The roars and banging coming from all directions, and others screaming out te each other from one end of the house te the other in the panic of leaving something behind, and the nervous excited laughter hit me as I slid inta a group of young ones sorting out their suitcases. Jaysus! It's like O'Connell Street on a Sunday afternoon, when the culchies invade Dublin for a Gaelic football match.

'Excuse me!' I shouted. 'Outa the way, please. Anyone see a nun around?' I asked, talking te the walls, as no one was listening. 'Sister Mary Ann Augusta! Mairead Causetello!' I shouted up the stairs, me eyes flying around the faces, looking for someone from the middle group. 'Sister Herod Mary? Poppy Ticks? Is anyone here from the Child of Prague group?' I shouted, wanting te hurry back te the convent, knowing any minute now the people are going te start piling up te the door.

I looked around, searching the faces. 'Me! I'm here!' shouted a little one with short fair curly hair wearing a navy-blue wool coat, with a long red-and-white hand-knitted scarf wrapped around her neck, rushing over on brown laced-up leather boots and red tights. 'That's me! Wait for me!' she panicked, dragging a little brown suitcase gripped in her two hands.

'Hi, little Poppy!' I said, bending down te her and looking inta her lovely sky-blue eyes. I could look at her for hours; she's gorgeous, I thought te meself. 'Where's yer nun, Poppy?'

She looked around, saying, 'Will I run down and find her, Martha?' showing me the gap where her two front teeth were missing.

'Ahh, no! I don't want ye going missing.' I lifted the silver gong, giving it one bang then four more, saying, 'Let's wait te see if she hears her gong. I bet I know what ye want from Santa Claus for Christmas!'

'What?' she giggled.

'Yer two front teeth!'

'No! I want a doll and pram!' she roared.

'Yeah! I'm only joking. Santa Claus has ye first on his list. Ye're his favourite.'

The door whirled open behind me and a roar blasted inta me ear. 'Is anyone minding the hall door? The convent is in uproar.'

I looked around at Sister Benedict standing in her black slippers, waving her arms through the crowd, trying te get over te me. 'Martha Long! Stop this fustering at once and get up to the hall door this minute and sort out those unfortunate people you've left standing around in the freezing cold with the hall door wide open!' she gasped out without stopping for a breath.

'Right, Sister Benedict. I'm just looking for the nuns.'

'What is it?' Sister Eleanor moaned, hurrying up the stairs with a gang of young ones rushing up behind her and another lot pushing and shoving their way in front of her, desperate te get up the stairs and out the door. The noise suddenly increased te a deafening roar as a gang of young ones came down from Sister Mary Ann Augusta's group, all excited, pushing their way onta the landing, and everyone was pressed up against the walls.

Sister Benedict screamed from the safety of the convent door, 'The hall door is in uproar!'

'What?' shouted Sister Eleanor, trying te hear over the noise, creasing her face inta a crying look.

'Uproar!' shouted Sister Benedict, then disappeared, letting the door bang shut.

'Are you there, Sister?' shouted Sister Mary Ann Augusta herding down another lot from the middle group.

'I'm here, Sister!' shouted Sister Eleanor nervously up at Sister Mary Ann Augusta, who is in charge of all the groups and their nuns.

'Sister Mary Ann Augusta!' I shouted over the crowd. 'The people are here for the children.'

'Take them over! Jesus Christ Almighty!' shouted Sister Herod Mary from the bottom of the stairs, looking up with her lot of little ones behind her.

'Sister! My lady is here!' shouted down Poppy te her nun.

'Get over to the hall door,' shouted Sister Mary Ann Augusta down te me, pushing her way down the stairs and flapping bodies outa the way with her arms out like she was swimming. 'Who is here?'

'People for Poppy, Sister, and one for you, Mairead Causetello!'

'Fine! One of yours, Sister! For Poppy!' she roared down.

Then Sister Herod Mary lowered her head and pulled up her habit and made a run inta the crowd of children stuck on the stairs in a bottleneck, screaming, 'Get that bag out of the way! Get back down those stairs!'

Sister Mary Ann Augusta grabbed a hold of Mairead Causetello, shouting te Sister Eleanor, who was trapped over by the window, trying te sort out a mix-up with the suitcases, 'Get them all off the stairs, please!' and ran with Mairead, who was trying te keep up, dragging her suitcase with a nightie sticking out, and looking like she was going for good with the amount of teddies and a long ragged cloth doll trailing its blonde plaited wool hair along the floor.

Sister Herod Mary pushed past me, muttering, 'God give me patience!' and grabbed a hold of Poppy, making herself look like a bull about te do battle, with steam coming outa her nose. I could hear the air coming out through her nostrils. Her brown eyes looked inta the distance as she made a run for the convent passage. I took off running up behind her, trying te get past by running from side te side, but she blocked the passage and I had te slow down. The noise of chatter and laughter hit us as we rounded the corner going through the door inta the inner hallway.

The Reverend Mother was smiling and oohing and aahing, saying, 'Yes! It is lovely to see you, too! Oh, how are you! Hello! You are very welcome!' swinging her head from side te side with her arms hidden under her cloak, getting herself buried with the mound of people all crushed inta the hall and more outside on the top porch and down the steps. I could hear more cars whirring up the drive and doors slamming.

The Reverend Mother lifted her head above the crowd, trying te make room for the nuns pushing through with the two girls. 'Have a lovely time! And be very good, won't you do that?' she said, lowering her head and keeping her back straight, talking te the two girls. Then she straightened her head up, her eyes landing on me with the smile still stuck te her face. I watched as it dropped suddenly inta a glare, with her eyes narrowing and her head shaking slightly, telling me I was in for it. 'Martha!' she shouted out, sounding very nice as her face curled inta a smile again. 'Tell the Sisters to bring the children along.'

I raced off back down through the passages and on te the children's landing, roaring at Sister Eleanor, who was roaring at everyone else te get back te their playrooms and wait until they were called.

'No, Sister! The Reverend Mother said ye are te send them up now!'

There was a silence for a few seconds, then a stampede started.

'We're going! Hurry!' And I was sent flying as bodies steamed inta me and charged down the passages.

'Stop!' screamed Sister Eleanor.

Nobody listened! There was a crush for a few minutes as they all got stuck in the heavy door with the springs, and kids heaved in and out, their faces getting red with all the effort. Then it gave, and a few bodies got through, and the rest spilled after them. They were off!

'Really, Martha! How could you be so silly?'

'What did I do?' I roared, hating te get inta trouble with Sister Eleanor and always roaring back when she roars at me.

'Jesus!' she said, looking down the passage. 'Someone is going to break their necks before we can even get them out the door!'

She took off like a giant bat, with her two hands grabbing a hold of her habit te stop herself tripping over the hem, with her black veil flapping out behind her, flying te catch up after the herd of kids hell-bent on getting up te the convent and getting outa here for their Christmas holidays.

I took off after her, hearing Sister James Teresa breathing heavily up behind me, dragging a load of babies and shouting after me te come and hold the door open.

'Sorry, Sister!' I grabbed hold of the door, watching as she rushed past carrying baby Louisa Ellen in her little red coat and matching hat with the black velvet rim around the edges.

'Hello, sweetie sugar plum!' I crooned, making a grab for her, trying te tickle her chin.

'Come on! I haven't got time,' Sister James Teresa complained, huffing up the passage with a load of little legs trailing after her.

'Me goin t'see Santy!' little Alfie stopped te tell me.

I looked down at him standing in his little fisherman's hat and his laced-up little brown boots, and laughed, 'Yeah, Alfie! When ye go te sleep tonight, then when ye wake up, Santa Claus will have left loads and loads a toys and sweets for ye!'

'Yeah!' he said, listening te everything I had te say. Then he shook his head up and down, saying, 'An I no wet me bed!' looking very serious.

I took in a deep breath, looking down at him, saying, 'Oh, I don't know. But I think ye have te be the best, bestest boy in the whole wide world!' widening me eyes and putting out me arms, showing him the world. 'Aren't ye?'

'Yeah, Oi am!' he said, shaking his head up and down.

'Now hurry! Everyone will be waiting on ye. Let's go!' And I grabbed his hand and we set off with Alfie moving his little legs like propellers, but we were hardly moving at all; it was mostly the noise of me jumping up and down making it look like we were flying. Alfie looked up at me, laughing, his neck swinging back on his head, thinking this was great.

'We're here!' I puffed, leaving him with Sister James Teresa as she came outa the parlour, seeing a young couple off with Louisa Ellen and grabbing Alfie, holding onta his hand and waving out the door at the people taking off with the babies.

I watched as the baby was carried over te a big black old-fashioned car and the husband held the door open while the lady stooped down with Louisa Ellen in her arms, then slid in along the green plush-looking leather seats, and the husband checked te make sure she was sitting in comfortably, then slammed the door shut. He rushed te the front of the car, grabbing hold of his long dark coat with a velvet collar flapping around his legs with the wind blowing up from the avenue, and wrapped it around his legs, whipping himself inta the driver's seat, then started up the engine. The blonde lady gave a little wave back te the nuns, then turned her attention te the baby, smiling and holding her close te her chest and patting her back. Then the car turned slowly around the big entrance and purred off, gliding down the avenue.

There goes a happy lady, I thought, staring after the car. Poor Sister Mercy! She's going te miss the baby. She lives for her. Every day after her dinner is over she comes tearing over from the convent te spend her recreation with Louisa Ellen down in the kitchen, staring and fussing and laughing with the baby at the slightest thing she does. Louisa Ellen's face lights up at the sight of Mercy. Gawd! Poor thing! No, Martha! Don't be mean.

I wandered over te the gong, hanging up the little silver one in its place on the little rope attached, and headed for the convent stairs, looking back as the last of the children went out the door and the group of nuns stood on the steps waving them off. 'Goodbye now! Yes! Thank you,' the Reverend Mother said, 'and a very happy and peaceful Christmas to you, too!'

The place had grown quiet, and I felt meself feeling a bit flat. The children and the people had taken all the excitement with them. So! What now? I asked meself, wondering where I will fit meself in for the Christmas.

Sister Benedict came outa the chapel and rolled herself off te the convent. 'Now we shall enjoy a lovely time of peace! Isn't it wonderful?' she stopped te say te me.

'Yeah! Happy Christmas, Sister Benedict!'

'And a Happy Christmas to you, too, Martha. Enjoy yourself! You earned it. My goodness, you worked very hard! Look at all the shine on everything. All the credit is due to you,' she whispered, leaning inta me. 'So go off and relax for yourself!' Then she took off.

I turned, heading down the stairs and through the convent door inta the kitchen passage. The lovely smell of cooking and baking hit me straight away. Ah! Sister Mercy is helping out Sister Thomas by doing a bit of cooking in our kitchen. I wonder what's te eat.

I hurried in, seeing Mercy pouring honey over a huge ham with cloves stuck inside the lumps of fat cut in crosses, and the whole thing was covered in brown sugar. She looked up, smiling at me! Yeah, I'm in luck!

'Hello, Sister Mercy! Happy Christmas te ye!'

'Ah, and a happy Christmas to you too, Martha. Go on! Your dinner is warming in the oven.'

'Oh thanks, Sister. I'm starving!'

'Was dere a big crowd up dere?' she asked me, nodding her head te the convent.

'Oh, indeed there was, Sister! It was like Amiens Street train station, the amount of coming and going.'

'Ah, I hope everyone has a good Christmas,' she said, smiling te herself, thinking as she wrapped the ham in tinfoil.

'Yeah,' I said, bending meself in two and sticking me head inta the oven.

I lifted out a big white plate covered with a pie dish and took off the cover looking at lovely roast meat with roast potatoes and cabbage and carrots and gravy – lovely! – the steam going up me nose, driving me mad with the hunger.

'Dat's a lovely bit of beef! Enjoy dat.'

'Thanks, Sister!' I said, heading outa the kitchen and up te the refectory. Then I turned back and headed inta the kitchen again. 'Sister, can I take a jug of milk?'

'Yeah! Take a jug and go out to the dairy and help yourself. Make sure yeh cover it with the muslin. Oh! You can help yourself to some a dem buns dere.' She nodded over te the windowsill.

Me eyes whipped over te where she was pointing, landing on the tray with the mound of little buns with cherries. Cakes! And the steam is still coming outa them! Ah, gawd! All the birthdays I missed are coming in one day!

'Dere's some custard simmering warm over on the stove; pour some of dat over them.'

'Thanks, Sister, this is fine,' I said, struggling off with the hot plate in one hand and six cakes on a plate in the other, taking off quickly out the door before me luck runs out.

I hurried up te the refectory, dying te get me teeth inta the grub, and back again for a whole jug of milk, for meself, I hope. A body flew past me in a blur out the door as I walked in. 'Sorry!' it said, making me cakes wobble on the plate. I looked after her as she whirled around, swinging a brown leather suitcase. 'Bye, Martha! Happy Christmas to you! Have a great time!'

Oh! She's talking to me! 'And a happy Christmas te you, too, Dilly! Be seeing ye after the holidays!'

'Not if I see you first,' she shouted, laughing her head off with the excitement of going away for the Christmas.

I rushed inta the empty refectory, having the whole place te meself. Ah! This is going te be lovely, I muttered, grabbing a knife and fork, me eyes never leaving the plate. I polished off the lot of the cakes and two glasses of creamy milk. Oh, I could polish off another dinner! That just got me started. I wonder if she needs any help down in the kitchen. Then I could help meself . . . Hm! Maybe I should quit while I'm ahead. Yeah! Better not chance me luck too far. Still, she's not a bad aul soul when she has a mind te be.

I stood up, stretching, feeling the tiredness hitting me after the Christmas rush of all the cleaning and polishing and fussing. Gawd! It's great having the Christmas. Nothing te do and all day te do it! I washed up me plates and glass and dried them, putting them back in their place on the long table, and wandered out, moseying up the passage and heading out the back door.

I looked over at the white frost still sitting on the playing fields and not a movement te be seen. It looked pretty desolate, and I wandered back in te the bit of heat. What heat? Compared te outside that is! The wind whipping up these passages would blow ye off yer feet sometimes. It's pretty chilly now. Think I'll look for somewhere warm and cosy te roast me arse. 'Get off them heaters! You'll give yourself chilblains!' the big ones scream at ye when we sit on them. Then when ye move off, they jump on. Well, there's not one going te complain now! I have the whole place te meself, by the looks of it, I thought, staring inta the middle group's refectory. Gawd! It's so empty. The room looks like it's waiting; there's a feeling of stillness, then it seems te collapse in on itself and go te sleep. The place is so different with all the kids gone. There's nothing te look at and nowhere te go. Just empty rooms and silent passages, and yet I can still hear the voices of the children echoing in me head.

I wandered on, feeling a buzzing running through me, expecting something lovely te all happen. It's Christmas Eve! And tomorrow will be Christmas Day! It's still new te me, having a Christmas and a birthday. People wishing ye a happy birthday and knowing this is the day ye were born on! And knowing exactly what age ye are, instead of hearing outa the blue from the ma, when she'd say, 'Eh, yeah . . . she's goin on ten', or, 'She's eleven now.' An ye'd be left wondering when that happened! It wouldn't occur te ye te say, 'When's me birthday, Ma?' because dates didn't come inta it. No, for the first time I was able te wake up and roar at everyone, 'It's me birthday today! I'm fourteen!' And smile and listen te people wish me a happy birthday. I made sure te do the same thing this year. And stand in the refectory at teatime while everyone sings 'Happy Birthday' te ye, and end with: 'You live in the zoo! You act like a monkey . . . And you look like one, too!' And Sister Eleanor lowered her head, half laughing and half disgusted, saying, 'Ahh, stop, girls! That's not very nice.' And listen te everyone laughing, including meself, because everyone gets a dose of that.

Yeah! And now it's Christmas. And everyone is being very nice, and making huge preparations, and getting all excited, and wearing good clothes, and going off with people, and no work, and I'm wondering if I'll get te go out te someone! That's what I'm afraid te ask. Sister Eleanor hasn't said anything yet. She said she'll try, but I wonder if she doesn't manage te get me someone, what will happen then? All the others kids are sorted, because they've been going te the same people for years. They call them their 'ladies', or their 'godparents'. The problem is I'm just a blow-in, and I have me family . . . they think! So they don't really feel bothered about me, and I don't push it . . . in case! I have the terrible feeling in the bottom of me heart that Sister Eleanor will send me back te them for Christmas! Especially after me little brothers and sisters have just gone home. That Reverend Mother wouldn't think twice of sending me back te that aul bastard and the ma if she could get away with it! I think that's what Sister

Eleanor could be banking on. I could feel a rage starting up in me chest. They can go and fuck themself! I would rather walk the streets and be happy about it than even give a second thought te having anything te do with them two bastards! So whatever happens, they have two hopes of getting me te go with them: Bob Hope and no fucking hope at all! Yeah! Fuck that! I snorted te meself, walking on, me blood boiling with the thought of it. Because there's no such thing as Christmas in that fucking kip with Jackser! I know it only too well. The sights, sounds and, above all, the smell of fear in everyone as we wait for it te end.

It's just wakin up te the sound of footsteps passin the window, an the sound of new leather soles slappin along the pavement, or the clickin of new high heels, the woman takin little steps cos she's afraid of breakin her neck as she minces her way along the footpath, disturbin the quiet of the empty Christmas streets, wit no traffic an everythin closed up. Everyone gettin up, wakin te the new day, ready te dive inta the result of their big preparations – their shoppin an their savin the money, an moanin about all the hard work it is, an . . . here they are! On the move te Mass in their new clothes, the first few early birds, wantin te make an early start. Then doors open an kids' voices are heard, an they come flyin outa the house te try out their new little three-wheeler bikes with the flags hangin outa the handlebars, an ringin their new shiny bells. An young ones come staggerin down the path of their house, their legs goin in different directions, splittin themself in half on their new roller skates, tryin te balance themselves, the mammies and daddies shoutin at them te, 'Come in an have yer breakfast! It's gettin cold. And shut tha front door! Ye're lettin out all the heat,' an laughin, cos it's great, an everyone is excited, an no one is gettin annoyed, cos there's too much te look forward te.

Maybe the fightin will start later on tonight, when the dinner's over an the relations arrive, bringin the drink with them te add te their own drink, an the arguments will start when they sit sprawled, lookin cross-eyed at each other with the too much

drink taken, an start goin down memory lane. Then someone
will remember who threw the last dig in a previous row one
Christmas, when the argument got outa control. 'And tha was
the Christmas before last, I distinctly member tha! An you
were the one tha started tha! An me poor brudder had te get
six stitches at the back a his head! An we never forgot abou
tha!' Then the row will start all over again. The front door will
fly open, an men will spill outa the house an onta the street
in their stockin feet, staggerin aroun the road, shoutin, 'Come
on! Come on! Show ye're a man! Put yer fists up,' an the other
fella roarin, 'Hold me back! Let me at him! Mind me fuckin
coat!' An throwin his coat te the ground after whippin it off,
cos he was goin te go in the first place, cos he wouldn't stay
where he wasn't welcome!

And meanwhile Jackser spent the day from the early mornin
walkin up an down wit his fists clenched, an runnin back te the
winda, lookin out, an throwin the head back te us sittin on the
manky floorboards feelin very afraid, cos he wouldn't stay easy.
'Fuck them! Fuck them! We don't need any a tha stuff! Fuck them
an their showin off,' then puttin his fist te his chest sayin, 'Ah!
It's only one day! It'll soon be over.' An we stare at the winda,
watchin the light fade an the night creep in, an the lights go on
in the houses across the road. We watch as they draw the curtains
te just meet wit the Christmas tree in the middle, showin the
Christmas lights blinkin on an off. An we begin te feel we can
move now, soon. Outa this room an up the stairs, an inta the
safety of our beds, cos the night has taken away the terrible time
of Christmas.

Dear God! I don't have te go through that again. No! Never
again will I have te face that. I'm on me own now, and I can look
after meself. I'm fifteen years old. I can get a job. I'm working
here anyway. So I'm not going te even bother meself worrying
about that! They can always tell me te go te them. But they can't
bleeding make me go!

Maybe they might bring me over te the convent refectory te

have dinner with them! Ye never know! They might be feeling full a goodwill, especially if I'm the only one left. I wonder if I am? Then the picture of sitting with them eating the Christmas dinner started te hit me! Jaysus! I could see it all. I could be sitting with Ma Pius on one side a me and the Reverend Mother on the other! With Sister Benedict on the far side opposite, watching and passing remarks on me table manners. 'Martha Long! Would you mind not putting me off me dinner with your disgraceful manners at the table!'

'Pass the salt, please, dear Sister Mary Innocent,' Sister Thomas might mutter in her quiet little voice.

'Certainly!' says Duck Egg, handing over the salt.

'Isn't the turkey just lovely! And the roast potatoes browned to a crisp and just the right colour,' gasps Mercy on a mouthful of grub.

'Oh, indeed they are! Thank God!' whispers Sister Thomas. 'Now what sort of fat did you use?'

'Oh! The dripping from yesterday's lovely bit of beef dat nice new butcher sent me up. Old Joseph is dead, you know.'

'No! God rest his soul! Was it sudden? No one told me!' Sister Thomas moans.

'Oh, it was very sudden. He died on the job while serving poor Mrs Lamb from two doors up!'

'No!' gasps Sister Thomas.

'Yes! He was handing over a parcel of black and white pudding, sausages and rashers for the weekend breakfast last Saturday . . . the week gone, I mean! I know all dis because Johnny Mack is a friend of our Larry the farmer, and he told me when he brought in the milk last Monday, I think it was. I was doing sausages for the tea, so it had to be Monday! Now, where was I? Oh yes! And he collapsed over a tray of sheep's belly sitting in the glass case in front of him!'

'Tut, tut!' everyone gasps, all listening now.

'Yes!' pants Mercy, getting carried away now with all eyes on her. 'And dat wasn't the last of it!'

'What! There's more?' the Reverend Mother gasps, grasping her chest, looking at Mother Pius, shell-shocked.

'Shocking!' agrees Ma Pius. 'Utterly shocking!'

'Go on!' Mother Immaculate breathes, holding both hands te her chest now.

'Yes! Poor Mrs Lamb . . .' and she pauses te look around the table te make sure everyone is getting this, 'collapsed inta a heap on top of the seasoned and spiced beef sitting on the counter waiting to be hung up, and had to be carried away in an ambulance with a suspected heart attack.'

A shocked silence hit the room, and then they all started talking about the terrible things that can happen so unexpectedly, it is sooo frightening.

'Anyway, Sister Thomas, as I was saying! It works wonders for giving the taste and the colour.'

'Hm! You're a marvel, Sister Mercy,' mumbles Sister Thomas. 'I must give that a try with my Sunday dinners. For the potatoes, I mean.'

Then it would be silent again, except for the gnashing a teeth on the Brussels sprouts. Yuk! I hate them. Meanwhile, Sister Eleanor is at the other end of the table, keeping well outa the way, hoping the Reverend Mother doesn't come down on her hot and heavy for letting me stay here in the first place and ruining the nuns' Christmas dinner. They couldn't have a proper gossip with me sitting there earwigging, ready te take everything back te the institution and let the world and his wife know their business. 'No! It's just not good enough now, Sister Eleanor!'

Hm! I have two hopes of sitting meself down with them for me Christmas dinner: Bob Hope and no hope at all! Ha! Thank God for that! Yeah, and if the worst comes te the worst, I can always enjoy meself sitting down te eating me Christmas dinner all on me own. Aaahh! Poor me. Ha, ha! I can enjoy meself no end tormenting the nuns about what a terrible Christmas I had. Yeah! After the Christmas, when they smile sweetly at me, enquiring, 'Did you have a nice Christmas, Martha?'

'Ah, it was all right, Sister. Lovely and peaceful.'

'Oh, that's wonderful,' they'll say ready te move on.

'If ye can call sitting in the freezing cold eating yer dinner with no one te talk te except Tibbles, Sister Mercy's cat. And the worst of it was, I don't like cats. But I shared me turkey with her, because she was on her own, too.' Sniff! Ha, ha, ha! That should be a great laugh!

Right! But come on, Martha, they might just turn around and say, 'Well, wasn't it a pity you didn't go home to your poor mother, and she with a houseful of children. How did she manage without you?' Ah, fuck that! I'm keeping me mouth shut.

Right! Enough of that! It's time te enjoy yerself. Whatever happens, happens. It will be grand. Now! What am I doing? I looked around, finding meself on the children's landing next te the convent passage. How did I get here with all me thinking? Will I go over and see if Sister Eleanor has any news about what's going on? No, leave it for a bit. I'll head off upstairs te the dormitory.

I took the stairs two at a time, wondering if anyone was around the house. I sprinted up first te the top of the house te put me head inta the little ones' dormitory and looked around the room. All the beds were airing with the mattresses folded back and the blankets neatly folded on top, just leaving the wire springs exposed. Nope! Empty! Not a dickie bird. Right! I turned back down the stairs, taking them two at a time, and landed on me floor, rushing in through the dormitory, peeling me eyes around the little dormitory. Nope! Same here – beds all airing. Then flew inta the big one. I could hear music, and me heart lifted! I flew around by the little cubicles used for the big ones who are ready te gallop outa here and start living in the world, then stopped, clapping eyes on Ruthie lying sprawled on her belly listening te Sister Eleanor's little transistor radio. She uses that for the people sick in bed, te keep them company and cheer them up. How did she get that? I felt a rush of heat going through me belly, feeling meself getting jealous. Huh!

Eleanor wouldn't give me that if I asked her. Still, I'm delighted te see somebody anyway.

'How're ye, Ruthie? Are ye sick or what? What's happening? Are ye staying here for the Christmas?' I asked her hopefully.

'Oh, hiya, Martha. No, just taking it easy while I'm waiting for my godmother to collect me. She's on her way, Sister Eleanor said, so I better start moving.'

'Oh, so ye are going away for the Christmas?' I said with me heart dropping inta me belly.

'Yeah! Course I am! Who would want to stay in this place for Christmas? Why? Where are you going?'

'Dunno,' I said, collapsing me arse on the bed spring next to hers.

'Have you not got something sorted out?' she asked me, looking worried.

'No, Ruthie. Nothing's been said. Sister Eleanor said she will try te sort something out, but I'm still waiting.'

'Ah, don't worry yourself about it. You'll get fixed up! They won't let you stay here in the first place, because the nuns want the place cleared to give themselves a rest,' she laughed.

'Do ye think I'll get te go out with a family, Ruthie?' I asked her, feeling a bit of hope.

'Course you will! Well, I hope so,' she laughed again, then turned her head back to the magazine she was reading, looking very intent, not wanting to talk any more.

I sat staring around the room, listening te the song blasting out: 'Have Yourself a Merry Little Christmas'. I will if I get the chance! I moaned te meself, looking at all the empty black iron beds. Rows and rows of them, nobody needing them.

Everybody is all gone off somewhere te be with people who are happy te have them. With probably a warm house and lights and decorations and Christmas trees, and probably even a dog! I like dogs, but I'm a bit afraid of them. Me eyes swept around the empty room with the high windows looking out onta green fields. They are too high up te look out, unless you climb up onta the windowsill. But I could see the tall trees waving their naked branches in the wind, and it was really beginning te feel very desolate in here, and making me feel very empty.

I turned me head te Ruthie. 'How did ye get the transistor radio, Ruthie?' I said, throwing me eye on the radio, loving te get me hands on it! That would be great company! I thought te meself.

'I asked Sister Eleanor for it,' she said, making it sound so easy!

'And she just gave it te ye?'

'Yeah!'

'Listen, can I borrow it when ye go?' I asked, leaning inta her.

'Sorry! I said I would give it straight back,' she said, not looking at me, keeping her eyes on the magazine.

'How's school?' I asked, knowing she was going te the secondary school because she is very brainy. Only a few of them go. The rest all go te the technical school.

'Great! Great, Martha,' she said, looking up at me.

'What will ye be when ye leave school, Ruthie?'

'Oh, I haven't thought about it. I might try for secretarial college if the nuns keep me on. I will have to wait and see. Anyway, it's easy to get a good job when you have the education.'

'Yeah, I know! I'm hoping te do something, too, Ruthie! I've been working on me diction. And reading books.'

'Yeah, I've noticed,' she said, looking at me and smiling. 'Your speaking voice is improving well. You should practise your th's and always pronounce your endings. Ings and that kind of thing. There's no reason why you shouldn't do well, you're very clever, Martha. I can see that. Never mind what the others say.'

Me heart lifted. 'Ah, thanks, Ruthie! That's very nice of ye te say that about me.'

'No, it's true,' she said, shaking her head and going back to her reading.

'What are ye reading, Ruthie?'

'Oh, the problem page. The problems are very good. Listen to this one,' she said, moving over in the bed, making room for me. I sat next to her, dropping me head down beside hers, and we both read. 'Look at this one,' she said pointing to one.

Dear Mabel,

I am a married woman and a Catholic mother of six children. My husband is a very religious man. He had thought of going forward to the priesthood, but I got in the way, so his mother never tires of telling me at every opportunity. She is sorely disappointed and tells me all the time she had great hopes for him becoming a priest and one day a bishop! Every night of their family life, when they went down on their knees to say the family rosary, they always ended with a prayer that Colm would become a very holy priest and one day make it as a bishop. I don't think she has ever forgiven me for leading him astray, Mabel.

Now, Mabel, I have led myself astray. For the last four months I have been having an affair with another man! My husband knows nothing about this! I did not intend to let the affair get out of hand, but I found myself looking forward to our meetings. I told my husband I was attending the Countrywomen's Association; I have been a member for years. His mother, my mother-in-law, first took me to one of the meetings. I loved it because it was an escape from the house, a change you might say, and I got lots of tips on making little garments for the babies, and nice knitting patterns, and lots of cooking recipes. Now, of course, I have missed these meetings for several months, as I have been meeting my lover at his bedsitter in Harold's Cross.

Now, Mabel, I have just discovered to my mortal shame and horror I am pregnant. I know the baby is not my husband's, because we have not been intimate since I took up with my lover! I have been telling my husband I suffer with migraines and the doctor suggests we abstain for a while because the excitement was bringing on the migraines.

My parish priest was also in favour of this course of action, because my husband told me he discussed this with him and it was OK to abstain for a short while to let me recover, as our last baby, we called him Columbanus, was only four weeks old anyway. He said I should not be allowed to get away with this for too long, because it was my duty to give my husband his conjugal rights! So now you see my predicament, Mabel! Even if I could pass the baby off as my husband's, and there would be a remote possibility of that because as my mother-in-law proudly says, 'My son is so manly he only has to hang his trousers on the end of the bed and you are gone again!' I could cod him all right with the dates, say we must have gotten carried away at some stage, because here is the proof of the pudding! But unfortunately my lover is a student at the College of Surgeons; he is studying to be a doctor! And he is from Africa, a black man, so therefore the baby would be black. So now you see I can't pass him off as my husband's, as he has roaring red hair and very fair skin. He only has to look at the sun and his face burns bright red like a beetroot!

Please, Mabel, I hope you can solve my problem. Please tell me what to do! I am desperate. So much so, I keep looking out at the river. Our little cottage overlooks the river where my husband spends a lot of his free time fishing for trout with our two little boys. I have often thought of throwing myself in there, but the river is too low, and anyway I can swim. I have even thought about going to my mother-in-law's house – she lives four miles down the road – and sticking my head in the oven. I would have to go there because we don't have gas, only the Aga – I do all my cooking in that! The other problem about doing away with myself is that I might not get an opportunity of sticking my head in her oven and doing away with myself, because she wouldn't leave me long enough in her kitchen. She's very house-proud and watches you like a hawk in case you touch any of her things. So you see my predicament. I can't even do away with myself. Please help!

Desperate housewife and Catholic mother.

We screamed our heads laughing and didn't hear Sister Eleanor come creeping in the door. 'Ruth O'Brien! What have you got there? Give it to me this instant!' She sprang, whipping the magazine outa our hands, muttering, 'Where did you get this?' with her eyes flying along the page. Then turned and looked at us with her nostrils getting thinner as she took in deep breaths, sucking in her mouth and crossing her eyes te the floor, then looking up at the ceiling, shaking her head, looking more and more shocked by the minute. 'Oh, girls! This is absolutely disgraceful stuff to be reading!' she gasped, outa breath. 'I absolutely forbid you to read this dreadful magazine again. Are you listening to me, girls?'

'Yeah!' we muttered, feeling annoyed at the loss, wondering what else we missed, not getting a chance te see what the answer was!

'Now, come along quickly, Ruthie, the people are waiting for you up in the parlour. Ah, my God!' she said, looking and sounding like she was in pain, twisting her face. 'You are not even ready yet. Come on, come on!' she said, grabbing hold of Ruthie and pulling her offa the bed. 'You are not even ready, and look! You have not even prepared your bed! It has to be stripped and the mattress folded back to allow it to air.'

'I'm ready, Sister Eleanor! Don't fuss. Look,' she said, pointing beside her locker, 'my case and everything is ready. All I have to do is put on my coat.'

'Come on, then,' she said, picking up the suitcase and grabbing Ruthie and her coat and pulling her out the door. 'Martha!' she called te me over her shoulder. 'Would you be a good girl and strip Ruth's bed and bring the sheets down to the laundry. You will see the basket just inside the door. Drop them into that and don't forget to fold the mattress back.'

'OK,' I said, feeling the life go outa me watching Ruthie taking off. Then I raced after her. 'Sister! Sister Eleanor! What about me?' I called te her back as she flew out the door. I whipped after her, tearing out the door, and shouted down the stairs, 'Have ye found anyone for me?'

'Oh, what am I going to do about that child?' I heard her mumble te herself.

'Sister! What's happening?' I shouted, getting desperate.

She looked up at me just before going through the convent door. 'I'll be back,' she nodded up te me.

I dropped me shoulders, wandering back inta the dormitory, and headed over te strip Ruthie's bed. I put the sheets inta the pillowcase and folded the blankets onta the mattress, me eyes wandering over te me bed. I'll strip me own down; as Ruth said, there's not much chance of me being left here for the Christmas, and I felt meself lifting a bit with the thought.

I headed outa the dormitory, carrying the two pillowcases with the sheets, and down te the laundry te drop them in the basket. I didn't know what te do with meself next. So I wandered back along the empty passage feeling tired and restless. Me head was beginning te pain me. Jaysus! That's the last thing I need! It's all the worrying. I should take it easy and forget about everything, but I was beginning te feel very annoyed. Fuck them nuns! Especially that Eleanor one! She didn't bother her arse te even giving me one thought, but she's not too busy te fuss about the rest of them. I wanted te scream at someone . . . her! . . . and cry, because even though I'm big I still want someone te take me out. All the rest of them have gone! And the ones in me group, most of them are a lot older than fucking me! And they're not sitting here keeping me company, wondering if they're going te go somewhere.

My eyes flew around, looking for something te give a kick, and landed on the coat rack holding all the coats. I gave it an unmerciful kick, sending it flying against the sports stuff sitting in a big bin. All the racquets and tennis balls and hockey sticks and everything else went flying in all directions, the balls rolling down the passage! 'Now! Hmph! Fuck you, Ellie baby! Fucking fucker!'

I stared at the mess, snorting and flapping me shoulders up and down, feeling a vicious sense of satisfaction, making te walk away. Ah, fuck! Now look what I've done! 'Martha, ye're a right eejit. A complete gobshite,' I muttered, as I went after the rolling balls and picked up the coat rack, standing it up and putting the coats back.

Right! Me eyes peeled around, making sure everything was back in its place. Anyway, she would have known ye did it, so take it easy, I thought te meself as I took in a deep breath through me nose. I feel like shouting just for the fun of it. There's no one here te hear me. That's not a good idea. Sister Eleanor might come up behind ye and get ye carted off te have yer head examined.

I could hear noises coming from our playroom as I passed. I turned the handle wondering if there was someone still here. No – empty! It's the big radio! Sister Eleanor must have forgotten te take it away. She never leaves it here! That's used te bring the music lovers te their knees, getting them promising best behaviour for the next ten years! Then she rations the loan. 'You may have it for one hour! And if I hear it outside this room . . .' she says, wagging her finger warning them. 'Don't touch those knobs. I want it left at that sound!'

'Is she gone?' they ask each other, then turn it up full blast, while one half of the girls start dancing with each other cheek te cheek.

Sister Eleanor goes mad when she sees that! 'You couldn't get a pin between you!' she roars, separating them, puffing out her annoyance, looking very shocked. While the other half stand in here hugging the radio, swearing undying love for whoever happens te be singing.

Well, it's all mine now. I rushed in, flopping meself down on the sofa, then swung me legs around with me shoes still on, slapping them down on her sofa, because we're not allowed te do that. She'd go mad if she saw me! Pity she's not here. I could drive her mad!

I felt meself going off inta a doze, with Bing Crosby singing, 'I'm dreaming of a white Christmas. Just like the ones I used to know.' I hummed along, dreaming of someone coming te collect me in a big car, with a white fur coat and white leather boots te match. Telling me, 'I just knew you would look lovely in this, my dear! My husband and I wanted to buy a nice gift for an orphan this Christmas, and we especially wanted an older girl, because, frankly, my dear, we couldn't be doing with a small baby! Well, our children are all grown up now, and we want to share our Christmas, but not that much!' Then she looks up at her husband and smiles sweetly, 'Isn't that right, Frankie, darling?'

'Whatever you say, my sweet,' he croons back at her. Then they rush me out the door te spend the Christmas in some big swanky house with an avenue up te it! Amen! That's me prayer, God! But I'll settle for an old lady from the village coming up on her bicycle, telling me, 'We'll have a lovely Christmas, dear, you, me and the cat. I'm so glad I found you, now I won't be alone for Christmas, and neither will you!'

Yeah, there's only too many lonely people out there; it's just a question of one of us making the first move and we'll find each other! Anyone want . . . sniff . . . an orphan for Christmas? Well, not really an orphan. I have a ma. Well, sort of . . . I had a picture of meself walking up and down the village with a placard swinging around me neck. 'Get yer orphan for Christmas; only one left!' I could shout, sounding like the aul dealers on Moore Street around Christmas time, shouting their lungs out: 'Get yer Cheeky Charlies! Only the one left! D'ye want it, love?' Shaking it hopping up and down on a string in yer face. Not te me, though! They knew I was a robber. One look at the state a me told them that.

'Aaaah!' I started te roar, wanting te hear the sound of me own voice. Jaysus! I'm not sitting around any more. I jumped up, heading for the door, shouting, 'Sister Eleanor!' knowing she couldn't hear me, but I wanted te feel I was doing something.

'Martha! Are you there?' Sister Eleanor breathed, suddenly appearing in the door.

'Aahh! Jaysus! Sister Eleanor! Ye gave me the fright of me life,' I puffed, outa breath.

'Oh, really,' she said, squinting her face at me in a half laugh, and the other half in pain. 'Don't take the name of the Lord in vain.'

'No, sorry, Sister! Whadid ye want me for?' I asked in a rush, getting meself all excited.

She breathed, swallowing down her spit, and put her hand te her chest trying te get a breath.

I waited, watching her, holding me breath!

'I got a call! A last-minute call just came in now! A family want an older girl; they have a young girl your age, and I'm delighted! To be honest, Martha,' she said, whispering inta me and holding her chest, 'I didn't hold out much hope of getting anyone at this late stage. All the calls coming in were for younger children, mostly tots. So you must be blessed!'

'Yipppppppeeeeeeee! Oh thanks, Sister! Ye're the best in the world! When am I going?' I flew out the door then back in again. 'Where am I going? When are they coming? Where do they live?' I couldn't get a breath; me head is flying!

'Take it easy! Now go and pack, and be ready. They won't be here for an hour or so.'

'Pack! Pack what, Sister Eleanor? I only have me one set a good clothes.'

'Yes, of course! Pack them, and don't forget to pack your night things.'

'Me nightdress, right!' I took off, flying up te the dormitory, then flew back down again, catching her making it out the convent passage. 'Sister! I need a suitcase!'

'Oh, darling! Find something to put your stuff into. I don't think we have any suitcases left.'

'What?' I shouted.

'Shush! You will disturb the nuns in the chapel.'

'I have te have a suitcase, Sister. I'm going away on me holidays, amn't I?'

'Yes.'

'Well, I have te have a suitcase, then!'

'Oh dear God!' she moaned. 'I'll see what I can find.'

'Thanks, Sister.'

Then I took off again, dying te put me stuff inta a suitcase. It makes me feel I'm really going somewhere! I always wanted te feel respectable. That's what ye bring on yer holidays when ye go away. Anyway, everybody else got te bring one; I'm not going te be left out! I snorted te meself. Even if I have te rob one. From where? There's none left! Fuck! I hope she manages te find me one.

I rushed up te the dormitory and went flying in and threw open me locker, looking in. Right! Me best clothes. I took out me new maroon wool skirt with the wide belt, and the pink polo neck jumper te match. I lifted them gently onta the bed and folded the skirt the way Sister Eleanor taught me te; it stops the clothes getting creased. The first things I ever bought meself with my own hard-earned money! I didn't have te rob it! That still makes me happy, the thought of it. I got more satisfaction outa that than if I had managed te rob the whole shop! Yeah!

I only wear them on Sunday, going te Mass, when everyone shows off their good clothes. The fuckers snigger behind their hands when I arrive in the chapel. They say I have no taste! 'Psst! Look at that gom! The big eejit Martha Long! You can't wear pink with maroon!' they spit.

I spent ages, week after week, every Sunday after Mass, running te Sister Eleanor, asking her did me clothes look well on me or not.

'Yes, of course they do!'

'And do they match, Sister Eleanor?'

'Yes! Why wouldn't they?' she said the first time. Until finally she lost her rag and didn't want te hear any more about it! 'Yes! Yes! Yes!' she roared, waving her head up and down. 'You look very nice, very nice! Don't be minding what those girls say to you. They are very bold, and they can be very nasty!' she said, squinting her eyes.

So now I don't bother. That was months ago. She was right. They got fed up tormenting me, and now I can enjoy wearing me lovely best Sunday clothes, the first things I ever bought meself!

I sighed happily, thinking about all that as I packed them nicely on the bed, putting me nightdress on top. I wonder if she has any more of them new pyjamas left? The Reverend Mother ordered them from Clerys for us, and there was a huge run on them when Sister Eleanor went te her press that she keeps locked up and started handing them out. Jaysus! The news flew around the group in no time. The big ones – overgrown eejits! – came barrelling in, getting themselves two and three pairs, confusing Sister Eleanor, whose eyes were swinging around in her head, trying te keep track of who got what and who didn't get any. As usual, I was trying te be on me best behaviour and stand back waiting patiently. Until she said that was the last of them, and the rest of us went mad. With me shouting the loudest!

'I am not going to get into a row now this minute with anyone,' she said, locking her press, giving us a quick look at the top shelf where she keeps her big cardboard box of sweets, and rations one or two out every now and then. 'I have to run to the convent. I am late, but I will see to the end of it when I come down! Now please move out of my way.'

We screamed after her all the way te the convent, not caring we were going te be punished. Telling her she only gives stuff te her favourites and we hate this place! Later on, when she couldn't get the stuff back – the big eejits had hidden them – Sister Eleanor informed us that when they turn up at the laundry she will count them and put them back in her press and give them out fairly te everyone. So we have te be satisfied with that. Yeah, well, I am going te rush over te the convent and look for her when I'm ready, or ask her when she brings me suitcase. I'm entitled te a pair of them pyjamas. Especially now I'm going away on me holidays. Gawd! I hope she manages te find me one of them suitcases. It would really make me Christmas, seeing meself going off in style!

'Are you ready, Martha?'

I jumped up off the side of me bed, after being sitting on the bed springs waiting patiently. Me bed was folded and me face washed, and I had put on me Pond's cold cream that I keep for special occasions, and I'd brushed me teeth and even brushed down me wool grey skirt and navy-blue jumper. I was wearing me second set of good white knee socks and gave me brown flat shoes a good polish. I'd love high heels, but I'll have te wait for them. Maybe sometime when I get more money. But I certainly gave these shoes a good polish, I thought, looking down, admiring the shine. I even had a look around for something nicer when I was in the shoe room. But no fear of that! If there was, they didn't stay there long. The big eejits would have got their hands on them straight away.

'Where are you, Martha?' Sister Eleanor was muttering even before she laid eyes on me coming through the small dormitory. I picked up my green gabardine coat with the belt. It looks a bit worn for wear now, greasy along the sleeves, I thought, looking at it. I was the first te grab it when Sister Eleanor held it up, asking if anyone wanted it. 'It's in perfect condition,' she said, telling the others all laughing their heads off at the idea of wearing a school coat.

'I want it, Sister Eleanor!' I said, grabbing it and holding it up te meself. It fitted grand. I always wanted te wear a school uniform. People might think I'm going te the secondary school wearing that. Yeah, I loved it; it has a belt. I still like it. I wonder if I can get it cleaned?

I put my coat on and grabbed up my suitcase. Suitcase? I looked down at it still wondering. 'This is all I could find, Martha,' she said, rushing in with an old battered case tied up with a brown leather belt.

I stared at it.

'It came over from the convent, Martha,' she whispered, watching me staring at it. 'It belonged to one of the nuns.'

The leather was long worn away and what was left was peeling off. It looks like a box more than a suitcase. But it has lots of stickers on it, saying, 'White Star Shipping Lines', and places it travelled te, like China, Zambia, the Far East! Gawd! It's been all around the world!

'I'll take it,' I said happily. I hope no one laughs at me. Fuck them. I like it!

'Oh, there you are! Come along, Martha. The people are waiting up in the parlour for you,' she said, taking my arm and rushing me out the door, smiling and sounding very happy.

Me heart was going mad with the excitement. I'm going te be staying with a family! Getting outa here! Oh, God! Thank you for looking after me!

I rushed along the convent passage with Sister Eleanor flying ahead of me. Her leather belt hanging on her hip, with her rosary beads tied te it, was clacking like mad, and her habit was swinging out and her veil flying, and I'm thinking she's rushing te do something for me. Normally she's rushing about on someone else's behalf and wouldn't have much te be doing for me. But now it's my turn. I'm getting fussed over! And someone is waiting for me in the parlour. Little ole me! They just want me! I can't believe it!

I slowed down when I got just outside the door, feeling a bit shy. Maybe they might be disappointed! They might not like me . . .

CHAPTER 15

'Come in,' Sister Eleanor said, smiling and waving me in the door.

I crept around the door, putting me head in and bringing me suitcase after me.

'This is the girl I was telling you about, Mrs Daly! This is Martha,' she said, holding her arm out for me te come closer and say hello.

'Hello,' I said, looking at the woman's black tight perm that she must have just got done for the Christmas. It looked like a little woolly hat. I stared up at the sort of granny hat sitting on top of her head, a bluey grey one that puffed up at one side and sat flat on the other, looking like someone had let the air out. She kept it sitting there with a big knobby pin pushed through inta her scalp and coming up again out through the hat. Me eyes travelled te the red-and-brown headscarf with horses jumping over bars, folded around her neck, and the brown wool figured-in coat that the women used te wear when I was small. It looks a bit short for her. I'd say she's been wearing that for years. Her high heels were a bit hickey, too! They're not really high heels, more the type grannies wear when they want te look glamorous. Brown with a square toe and a bow on the front, with wedge heels. Very hickey! She looks like a country woman, not glamorous at all, I thought, staring at her, feeling disappointed. I was hoping for someone with a bit of style.

'Martha is fifteen, Mrs Daly,' Sister Eleanor breathed, leaning towards the woman and smiling from her te me.

'Ah, Martha! It's really good to meet you,' she smiled, saying in a big country voice, putting out both arms, coming towards me and leaning over te grab me te her and smother me in her coat, and put her hand on me back and the other one on me head. I held meself tight, feeling a bit afraid she might not be really like this; she might just be acting nice. Then she turned me around, still holding me, saying, 'This is Thelma, my daughter; she's fifteen, too. Say hello, Thelma.'

I could smell lovely perfume and powder from the woman, and she smelt fresh and clean. She kept rubbing me back and squeezing me shoulder without thinking, and I started te let go me breath, feeling a bit easier in meself.

'Hello!' Thelma said from across the room, staring at me from head te toe.

I stared back at her short mousey-brown wiry hair, chopped around her ears. She must have cut it herself, I thought, gaping at her with me mouth open. Or maybe her ma cut it. Sister Eleanor is always chasing me with the scissors, but I wouldn't let her near me. No fear! I'm letting me hair grow down te me toes. Even if it does look like rats' tails, that's what Sister Eleanor calls it.

She stared out at me through black horn-rimmed glasses, wondering what she was going te make of me or whether she'd even like me or not. I could see it in her eyes; they flew up and down me, not looking too sure.

I was thinking the same. She's not exactly what I had in mind for someone te have a great time with! Her face looks the colour of raw dough, and she's covered in big pimples all around her chin. She must squeeze them! I've seen the big gobshites do that, and you end up looking like Thelma, covered in big spots and boils.

'Hello, Thelma,' I said, giving a little wave.

She took her time answering me and just stood taking me in,

this time from me toes te me head. I watched her standing straight with her arms down by her sides. I bet she does everything her mammy tells her! She's a bit stupid-looking. Gawd! She's very plain. I'd hate te look like her!

Ah, gawd help her! I bet she doesn't have many friends. Now I think I know why they took me out for the Christmas! I suddenly felt sorry for her and the poor mammy, gawd help her. She wants te make Thelma happy, give her a nice Christmas, that's probably what she asked for. She's probably lonely. I felt meself cheering up. So, that's grand with me. And I get te spend Christmas with them. Fair exchange is no robbery! Then everyone's happy.

'I'm really happy te meet ye, Thelma!' I said, reaching over with me hand te shake hers.

She gave me her hand, holding it out in a limp, and smiled shyly, showing me her big buck teeth. She had te rest them on her lower lip, they're that big. Ah, she's shy, I thought, looking at her face turning bright red as she looked over at her mammy, smiling.

'Now!' the mammy was muttering te the two of us. 'I can see you two will get on like a house on fire,' then started te roar laughing, letting out her breath with the relief of it all, getting that over, delighted at the sight of us smiling at each other.

'Martha is a lovely girl,' Sister Eleanor said, smiling and nodding at the mammy and patting me on the back, and rushing over te Thelma, putting her arm around her shoulder, saying, 'She's a very big and grand girl for fifteen, isn't she?'

'God bless her, she is, Sister,' the mammy nodded, smiling at the fuss over Thelma. 'She takes after my side of the family. My brothers are all tall, and Thelma takes after them.'

'Is she your only girl?' asked Sister Eleanor, stroking Thelma's back.

I watched, wondering why we never got that treatment. I suppose it's because she's a visitor!

'Oh, the one and only girl,' the mammy said, 'and one boy, Joseph! He's eight. I lost a few in between,' she said, 'still births.

One girl managed to struggle for three days. Then we lost her, too,' she said, sounding very sad, nodding her head and lowering it at the sudden memory, letting the light go outa her eyes.

I felt terribly sorry for her, the poor woman. Thinking the ma can't get them fast enough inta the world. Jaysus! Life is very peculiar.

'Ah, God is good,' smiled Sister Eleanor, trying te buck up the mammy quick, before she starts getting down and out in herself, and Sister Eleanor started it. 'Now you have this beauty!' she shouted, laughing and slapping Thelma on the back, then rubbing it te take out the sting. Sister Eleanor can send ye flying inta tomorrow with one a them slaps. I should know, after I pushed her too far inta losing her rag.

Then it hit me, what she just said. Beauty! Thelma? I looked at Thelma, delighted with being called a beauty, puffing herself up, an nearly erupted inside meself. I suddenly wanted te burst out laughing. Beauty! Thelma? No! I'm not laughing at Thelma; it's just the way Sister Eleanor comes out with things. I could feel me face getting red and coming out in a sweat. I'm not going te be able te stop meself. It's me nerves. The effort of trying not te snort out through me nose and make a show of meself and end up hurting the people and spoil everything. They'll think I'm laughing at them! Dear God! Don't let me make a fool of meself and have them run out the door, leaving me standing here, because they think I'm insulting them.

'Could I go te the toilet, Sister Eleanor?' I wheezed out, holding me breath, me face getting redder by the minute, ready te burst, and rushing past her, out the door. I flew down te the nuns' toilet, knowing they will go mad if they catch me in there. Fuck them! I shot in and put the catch across and turned on the tap, snorting me heart out inta me hands, laughing at nothing. Right! OK. I'm grand now, just take it easy. I'll wash me face and hands in cold water. I need te make meself go easy. It's just nerves! I'm not used te going te people's houses; that's all that's wrong with me. I only went the once and that

was a few years ago when I stayed with Flo . . . Flo! Oh, I
still miss her! One day I'm going te go back and visit her . . .
Yeah, that's definite.

Right! I took in a breath, easing me heart; I could feel it
hammering away in me chest. I felt it! Jaysus! It's going like the
clappers. Now, take it easy; ye'll be fine. She's a lovely woman,
and Thelma is grand; we'll get along fine. They really do want me
te go te their house. They're not feeling sorry for me, or making
me feel I owe them something. Or making themself feel better
by looking down on me. No! She's a nice woman, and she is a
real mammy. I like her. Right! Get going!

I opened the door, making me way up the stairs, and they were
standing in the hall waiting for me.

'Are you all right now, dear?' the mammy asked, looking
concerned. 'Ah, she'll be fine, it's just the excitement,' the mammy
smiled te Sister Eleanor, who didn't look too happy, thinking I
was making a joke outa people. 'Sure they're all the same!' she
said, laughing in Thelma's direction.

Gawd! The mammy understands I'm just excited. I think they
all knew I wanted te laugh. Gawd! Behave yerself, ye gobshite,
I muttered te meself.

'Goodbye now!' Sister Eleanor said, opening the hall door and
watching as we all trailed out. 'Happy Christmas to you all, and
may it be a peaceful one filled with joy,' she shouted te the mammy,
looking from them te me, giving me a warning look, squinting
her left eye at me and twisting her face. Then she beamed back
te the mammy, saying, 'Thank you so much for taking Martha.
She really is all excited.'

'Yeah, I am,' I laughed happily, rushing over behind them.

I stood back, waiting behind the others as a grey-haired man
wearing a cap pulled down over his eyes hopped outa a little beige
Baby Austin car. He pulled the back seat up te let the mammy
bend herself in half, trying te get in without knocking herself out
on the roof. She squeezed herself inta the corner te make room
for Thelma getting in next. I stopped, looking down at me case,

wondering what te do with it, because there was barely enough room for me.

'I'll take dat for yeh,' the man said, grabbing it and heading off te the back of the car and opening the boot. The mammy gave a big sigh, lifting her big black leather handbag up from underneath Thelma's arse and slapped it on her lap. She laughed happily and looked around, saying, 'We should make good time if Daddy gets his skates on,' and then looked out the back window, saying, 'Where's Grandad got to?'

'He's over looking at the cows, Mammy.'

'I declare to God! It's a pity we couldn't talk him into staying at home with Granny. She'll be giving out lingo now about Scrapper. They're not too fond of each other,' she said, looking at me.

'That's the dog,' Thelma said, lifting her eyebrows and dropping her mouth, letting a big sigh outa her.

The mammy rolled down the window, shouting, 'Daddy! Will yeh ever get Grandad moving? He'll stand there all night gaping at them cows!'

Thelma gave another big sigh, dropping her shoulders, and muttered te the mammy, 'Mammy, shush!' and gave me a sidelong glance te see if I heard her.

I pretended te look out the other side of the window, taking no notice of the carryings on.

'Dem's lovely heifers,' the grandad muttered te the mammy, slowly passing her window and hauling himself inta the front seat of the car.

'Ah, Daddy, can we get moving now?' the mammy puffed with impatience, slapping the shoulder of the grey-haired man, who was sitting himself inta the driver's seat with all the time in the world on him, and looking around at the dashboard te make sure everything was still there.

'Dem's lovely milkers,' the old man said, turning around te the mammy.

'Tsk, tsk,' sigh, sob. The mammy grunted, ignoring him and

looking more impatient by the minute, staring daggers at the back of the daddy's head. He was still staring around the front of his car and testing the window wipers, sending the water flying in all directions.

'Look at the lovely udders on dem!' the grandad muttered, eyeing the cows. 'I'd say now dey give buckets a milk.'

'Oh, holy be!' the mammy muttered, beginning te lose her patience.

'What de yeh tink yerself, Tom?' he asked, looking over at the driver turning the key in the engine, trying te get it started.

'I would!' Tom said, staring at the key, waiting for the engine te start.

It went, Neh . . . neh . . . neh! And he turned the key again. Neh . . . neh . . . and he pumped the pedal like mad and the engine danced inta life and went, Brum, brum, then faded away with a load a smoke pouring out the back. 'I'll get it this time,' he said quickly.

We all stayed quiet, holding our breath and watching the key. Brum, brum . . . it started, and the daddy's leg pumped up and down like mad, and his head with it, and the engine screamed but kept going, and we took off with the car jumping forward, and holding that for a minute, then he pulled back the gear lever and we shot back inta the seat again. We were moving, with a load of blue smoke pouring out the back.

'Close the windows!' the mammy shouted, twisting the handle like mad, looking around te see if there was any other windows open. 'Or we'll all be suffocated!' she puffed, then sat herself back, gripping onta her handbag, waiting te get home.

'Take her easy now,' muttered the grandad, staring straight at the gates miles ahead and throwing his voice te the daddy, who was not taking his eyes off the avenue. 'Mind dem trees! Dem branches is leaning dangerously close to the car,' muttered the grandad.

The engine was screaming, and me neck was straining, but we weren't moving any faster. Then he pulled the gear handle down again, and the engine went amump! and took off, and we were pushed back in the seat again. I lifted meself forward a bit te take a look at the clock te see how fast we were going. It's nearly tipping ten miles an hour! And the grandad said, sitting back in his seat, 'Dat's right, Tom! Keep her going at dat! Let her take it nice 'n easy! Dem's lovely fields the nuns have here,' he said contentedly, looking over at the fields and sitting himself back for more comfort, knowing everything was under control and Tom was taking it nice 'n easy. 'Dey have lovely grazing for dem milkers! I wonder how much milk dey'd get outa one a dem cows,' he asked, throwing his head at the daddy.

'Begad! I'd say they do well! And the land's lovely all right! Haven't dey got dem animals out an managing to get the winter grazing? Ah, leave it to dem nuns! Dey do know what it's all about, right enough,' the daddy said, dropping his neck and shaking his head, looking like he was trying te get rid of a bluebottle fly whipping around his neck.

'T'is fierce cold,' he said, puffing out his breath.

'Ah t'is not! T'is not at all! T'is spoilt yeh all are since yeh started moving into yure fancy house wit yure fancy heaters in every room. Den yeh go blocking all the doors and windas to keep the God-given fresh air out! Sure, t'is suffocating yeh all are!' the grandad said, looking around at the lot of us one by one and rattling his false teeth up and down.

I stared at his rubbery face with folds a skin hanging down and his big nose covered with blackheads. I wonder why he doesn't squeeze them? I thought te meself, taking in the white hair sticking outa his two nostrils. He even has hair growing outa his ears! I'd love te get me hands on him and use the tweezers the other big eejits are always messing with. I could get rid of that hair in no time!

'How are the new teeth, Grandad?' asked the mammy, leaning inta him.

'Ah! Don't start me off about dem,' he shouted. 'Dese ones are worse dan the last lot!' and he whipped them out, sticking them in the mammy's face. 'Gluck! Dey don't flit!' he mouthed, showing her his gums.

'Grandad!' roared Thelma. 'That is disgusting. Mammy! Tell him to put back his teeth,' she said, waving her head in the air, trying te look everywhere but at him.

I burst out laughing. 'Grandad!' whispered the mammy. 'Put your teeth back in, you'll make a show of us,' she said, looking at me laughing, trying te laugh herself, but snorting instead, looking out the window, muttering, 'I'm mortified! What will people think of us at all, at all?'

'Here we are, thank God we finally made it. Home at last,' the mammy suddenly said, stirring herself and lifting her handbag.

I woke up from me doze, looking around at the line of old houses with lovely trees, and porches that ye can stand in te keep outa the elements. All the footpaths were lined with trees as well. We drove in a gate and swung around a little bend, stopping the car, and the daddy shouted, 'Take it easy now, everyone. Give me time to switch off the engine.'

'Oh!' said the mammy, grabbing her handbag and gloves. 'Move out there, Grandad, and let us all get into the comfort of the house.'

'God! But dere's no doubt about it! You women are always in a hurry!' Grandad muttered, not shifting himself.

'Come on, Grandad, let us out! I have more to be doing than gabbing with you all night!' she snorted, losing her rag.

We all sat patiently while the daddy turned off the engine and slowly pulled out the key and looked te make sure everything was all right. 'Have I switched off me headlights, Paidir?'

'Oh, I'll go and take a look,' Grandad said, heaving himself outa the front seat.

The mammy was half sitting up with her arse balanced over the seat, and as soon as the grandad emptied himself outa the seat she was up and trying te squeeze herself out through the door. 'We'll have to get a bigger car, Daddy,' she huffed, trying te get her breath. 'The lot of us won't fit in that thing. The children are getting too big.'

'Dere's nothing wrong with my car,' he muttered under his breath. 'It's more like yourself is getting too big!'

'What was that I heard you say?' roared the mammy.

'I said you're right, love! We ought teh be thinking in dat direction right enough,' he said, taking the cap off his head and slapping it back down again.

'Oh, Daddy! You shouldn't be going and upsetting Mammy like that,' Thelma moaned, giving him a little slap on his arm.

The daddy pretended te fall, and laughed, saying, 'I said nothing at all to Mammy; I was just codding!'

'Yesh! The lights are off right enough!' Grandad said, looking from one light te the other, flapping his teeth up and down and sucking them onta his chin and back up te his mouth again.

'Come on into the heat,' the daddy said, 'before yure mammy has a chance to give yure poor aul daddy another roasting,' and he ran at her, grabbing hold of her waist and running her inta the house.

The mammy had put the key inta the door and pushed it in. I followed behind them, and a white streak came flying outa nowhere, barking its head off and making straight for me. 'Aah!' I moaned, getting a fright, looking down at a little white dog trying te take the toes off me. He was biting and growling, and standing back te look at me.

'Stop, Scrapper!' roared Thelma, making a grab for him. 'He's our little demon,' she said, squeezing him and rubbing her head on him. 'He's a Jack Russell,' she said, trying te keep a hold of him, the dog watching me like a hawk, wriggling and trying te get loose te run at me again.

'Get outa dat!' roared the daddy. 'Don't worry he won't touch yeh,' he said, patting me on my shoulder.

'Take that bloody thing to hell outa here!' roared a voice from the kitchen.

I walked backwards towards the kitchen, not taking me eyes off the dog.

Thelma stooped down, grabbing him, and he twisted and turned in her arms, spinning around, and landed himself on the floor again and took off, flying along the hall, slipping and sliding on the shiny floor cloth, and making straight for me again.

I lost me nerve, forgetting te stand still when a dog is after ye, and ran straight inta the mammy hanging up her coat. 'Aaah!' I moaned.

'Stop, Scrapper!' screeched Thelma.

'Come here teh me, you!' growled the daddy. 'Enough of yure aul carry-on,' and he grabbed hold of the dog, running with him te the hall and banging the door shut.

I let me breath out, me heart going like mad. I'm frightened outa me life of dogs when they bark at me, I thought te meself, trying te get me breath back.

'We picked up the orphan!' shouted the grandad te the granny sitting in the armchair beside the roaring red fire, staring at me and looking at him te hear what he said. 'The nuns!' he pointed at me.

'Wha?' shouted the granny, holding her hand te her ear. 'Wha nuns? She's not a nun!' she said, pointing her finger at me.

'No! I didn't say she was,' roared the grandad, leaning down and screaming inta her ear.

'Ah! Stop talking like that!' shouted the mammy folding her scarf and getting very annoyed.

I was annoyed, too, and about te tell him I had a mammy, and brothers and sisters!

'This is Martha, Granny. She's come to stay over the Christmas with us!' said the mammy, with her arm around my waist, pulling me over te the granny and leaning down smiling.

'Oh, right!' Granny said, looking at me, then looking at the mammy te make sure she was hearing right. 'Martha, did yeh say?' roared the granny.

'Yes!'

'Oh, dat's lovely,' the granny said, pulling down her long black old frock, stretching it nearly te her ankles. 'And wha part of the country are yeh from?' shouted the granny te me. 'Who did yeh say she belongs teh? What side a the family do yeh belong teh? Do I know yeh? Are yeh on Tom's side a the family?'

'No, Granny! She's a friend of Thelma's,' shouted the mammy, shaking her head and looking at the ceiling. 'Take no notice, Martha, pet! The poor thing is deaf as a post.' Then she whirled around, shouting, 'Are ye wearing your hearing aid, Granny?'

'Wha?' screeched the granny, holding her hand te her ear, getting very annoyed. 'I can't hear yeh! Speak up, for the love of God!'

'Oh, Thelma, pet, would you ever go and see if Granny has her hearing aid switched off.'

Thelma bounced on Granny, checking her, and shouted, 'Now, leave your hearing aid on, Granny. She had it switched off, Mammy!'

'As if I didn't know,' clucked the mammy. 'She hears what she wants te hear.'

The dog was making an awful racket, crying and whining and jumping on the handle; eventually it slipped down and he was in like lightning, making straight for the granny's slipper.

'Get dat thing outa here!' she roared, rolling up a newspaper and belting him with it. He came flying back at her, trying te get the slipper off her foot. 'Me bunions!' she roared, slapping the dog harder with the newspaper. 'Oh, the curse a blazes on yeh!' she whined, watching the dog take off with her slipper as she stuck out her right foot te get a look at the big knob sitting on her big toe.

'DADDY!' screamed the mammy, giving an unmerciful roar.

I jumped with the fright and moved meself outa the way, and edged over te the far side of the kitchen, sitting down at the table. 'Daddy,' the mammy said quietly, dropping her head in her hands and lifting her face up again, looking mortified, with her face turning red and throwing the eye at me, then looking away quickly.

The daddy was pouring himself out a drink from a whiskey bottle and spilt some with the fright, saying, 'Oh! Be the Holy Moses!' And looked up at the mammy shouting, 'What? What is it? What's wrong wit yeh? I'm afther spilling a good drop a me poteen here yure father brought me up special from home. Now look at wha she made me go an do!'

'Never mind your aul poteen, Daddy, would you ever take Scrapper and his bed and put him outside in the hall, this minute! I want him to know he's banished!'

'I have a quicker solution to dat!' roared the grandad, glaring at the dog, bending down te wait for the dog te pass, then snatch him! 'Give him a good kick up the arse for himself!'

'You'll do no such thing!' the mammy said, raising her voice, her eyes travelling around after the dog, who was sitting in the corner, growling and tearing lumps outa the slipper.

'Dere's no peace for the wicked!' moaned Daddy, leaving down his bottle a poteen and moving slowly after the dog with his hands out ready te catch him.

Poteen, did he say? I heard a tha stuff! One whiff a tha stuff and it's supposed te blow the top of yer head clean offa yer shoulders. The aul fellas in the country do make it, and they're always on the run because the police are tormented running after them trying te catch them at it! That's gas, I thought to meself, looking over at the aul grandad slurping away on his jungle juice – that's what some people call it. And they only get their hands on it if they know somebody coming up from the country. Then they're not real Dubliners at all; it means they were only born there, but their mas and das are probably culchies. Or maybe they are married te one, like the one I met!

'You are miles away!' said Thelma, jumping inta the seat beside me, giving me a fright.

'Yeah! I was just thinking about that poteen stuff yer da is drinking.'

'Yeah!' she laughed, looking over at him wrestling with the dog. 'That's his special Christmas treat,' she laughed.

'But it would blow the head off ye!' I said.

'Yeah, I know,' she laughed, looking at me. 'Why? Have you had some?'

'No! Never! I wouldn't touch drink, not on yer nelly!' I snorted, disgusted at even the idea. 'No, how I know all about that stuff, Thelma, is because I heard two aul ones talking about it, telling each other how they got on over the Christmas,' I said, moving me chair over closer te her and staring inta her face.

'Yeah?' Thelma said, nodding her head up and down, smiling and listening.

'Well,' I said, 'one aul one said she hoped she'd never have another Christmas like the last one. They all, the whole family, all ten of them ended up without any Christmas dinner at all.'

Thelma burst out laughing, and I laughed. 'Yeah!' I said, shaking me head and going on with me story. 'It all started when one aul one stopped te talk te a neighbour. "How're ye, Maggie?" said the blonde aul one with the husband who delivers the bread for Golden Crust – that's a good job, so it is.'

'Yeah!' said Thelma, her eyes shining with the laugh, her mouth open, waiting.

'Anyway! She asked the grey-haired aul one who lives up the road – this was in Finglas, and the blonde one lives at the other end of the road te her – "How did ye get on over the Christmas?" asked the blonde one, leaning herself against a garden wall, and fixing her shopping bag on her arm, and settling herself in for a bit a news.

'"Ah, Jaysus! Don't be askin! I'll only tell ye, Missus!"

'"Why? Wha happened te ye?" screamed the blonde, the eyes hanging outa her head from shock and excitement at getting a bit a great news.

'"Well!" the grey-haired one said, planting herself in fronta the blonde and leaning herself back and rocking on her feet, then folding her arms, wit her purse a money in one arm and the shopping bag in the other. "The relations in the country sent me up a lovely big turkey. Right?"

"'Right! Go on,'" said the blonde, encouraging her.

"'Well! . . . Oh, them's the relations on his side, not mine be the way! He's a country man from Connemara, a finer-lookin man ye couldn't meet, Missus! I fell for him straight away. Jaysus! If ye only saw the state a him now. He's gone te seed!'" I said, looking over at the mammy, screaming her head laughing, standing and listening. "'But anyway, back then he was a lovely-lookin man altogether,'" she said, her eyes wandering back te them days. Then she straightened her eyes, flickin them back on the blonde one again, saying, "So, anyway! Where was I? What was I just saying? Oh, yeah!" she went on. "So they are his relations, ye see, not mine," she said, staring at the blonde, making sure she understood that important fact. "No! Mine are all from the city centre, Dominick Street. We're all born and bred Dubliners, and them tha came before me," she insisted te the blonde, making sure the woman understood she was no bog woman.

"'Oh God, yes!'" said the blonde, tightening her face and shaking her head like mad. "Oh, I know that."

"'Well, anyways, they sent the turkey up by the post, and when it arrived it was really only a lovely-lookin turkey, Missus! Ye shoulda seen the size of it. Jaysus! It was only massive! I kept wonderin if it would fit in me oven. Anyways! Te cut a long story short, I stuck it in the way it was, straight inta the oven, te let it cook, after lighting the gas, and put loads a newspapers around the floor te catch the grease. Are ye wit me?'" she said, slapping the hand offa the blond one.

"'Oh, yes! Indeed I am,'" said the blonde, dying te get te the end a the story te know what happened.

"'So anyway!'" the grey-haired one said, continuing her story. "I was blind, bothered an bewildered tryin te keep them kids a mine from slopping all over me papers, then!" she said, holding her forehead wit one hand and the woman's shoulder with the other. "Missus! I am still not the better of it. Outa nowhere there was an unmerciful explosion that sent the cooker door flyin off its hinges, straight across the room! Jaysus, Mary an Joseph! It's a mercy no one was kilt stone dead, an me lovely turkey went flying in another direction, splattering itself all over me ceilin!"'

Thelma screamed her head off laughing, rocking back in the chair, and the mammy grabbed a hold of the mantlepiece after giving an unmerciful roar outa her, laughing hysterically, and the daddy slammed down his poteen, throwing his head back with the laugh, and slapping the grandad, who nearly swallowed his false teeth. I laughed me head off at them laughing, trying te say, 'Wait! I'm not finished.'

'Oh God almighty,' said the daddy, wiping his eyes with the back of his hand and sniffing. 'Dat's the best story yet!'

'Go on! Go on!' said the mammy, waving them quiet, leaning herself over te me, her mouth open ready, with a big red nose and watery eyes from all the laughing.

'Right!' I said, continuing me story, taking in a big breath. 'Then she waited te see wha the other woman thought of tha. By leaning herself in on top a the woman an staring inta her face, then folding her arms, with her mouth drawn straight across, clamped tight shut. "Go way! Isn't tha terrible?" the other woman said, this time slapping the hand a the grey woman, her eyes bulging, hanging outa her head. "An wha caused tha may I ask ye?" the blonde woman said, dropping her jaw, staring at the other woman.

"'I was waitin for ye te ask me tha," the grey-haired one said, looking very serious an shaking her head up an down slowly, like she knew when the world was going te end and was just about te tell the blonde one. "Yes! May well ye ask," said the explosion woman, slapping her friend on the hand. "Do ye know what it was?" she shouted, slapping her again.

"'No!" said the friend, her eyes in the back of her head trying te picture it and work out wha mighta happened.

"'Well, I'll tell ye now, it was them relations in the country. They stuck a bottle a tha bleedin poteen stuff up the bird's arse, te hide it from the post office, ye see!"' I kept talking over the screams and roars of laughing coming from everyone; they coughed and sniffed, trying te keep themself quiet while I went on with the story.

"'The bleedin poteen," she roared, slapping her pal on the hand with every word coming outa her mouth. "And the bleedin bottle exploded in the oven. They couldn't tell me te look for it, or it woulda given the game away. And we woulda all been arrested."

"'Oh holy Mother a Jaysus," said the pal, her jaw droppin down te her chest. "So after all tha ye's got nothin te eat?"

"'No! We had no oven, did we? An we ended up with the sausages an black an white puddin an the eggs they sent us up, because their ones do be lovely an fresh. Anyway, tha was supposed te be for the breakfasts all over the Christmas, an we ended up eatin the whole lot in one day. Leavin us nothin much te eat for the rest a the Christmas."

"'Ah, Jaysus, Mary an Joseph! That's terrible altogether! No! Tha was very unfortunate altogether, wasn't it?" the woman said with a half laugh on her face, her eyes shining, looking like she wanted te go mad and laugh her head off. "Well, goodbye now! An I hope ye have better luck next time."

"'I'll see ye! Look after yerself!" An they flew off, taking themselves off in different directions. Yeah, I remember tha all right! I kept picturing the turkey flying in all directions, getting splattered,' I said te the air, because no one could hear me. The place was erupted with the noise of them laughing.

'Oh God almighty! I've never laughed like dat in me whole life!' the daddy sniffed, trying te wipe the tears outa his eyes.

The mammy was trying te get up off the chair, complaining she'd wet her knickers. And rushed out the door holding her knees together, still laughing, desperate te get te the toilet.

'Oh, jeepers! I'll have to go to the bathroom upstairs,' moaned Thelma, laughing and jigging out the door after the mammy.

CHAPTER 16

'I'm going to get the tea, girls! You must be starved, you poor thing, Martha, pet,' the mammy said, looking hot and tired, yet still and all worrying her head about me.

Ah, she really is a lovely woman, I thought, looking over at her with her head flying around the kitchen, thinking how much she has te do and where she should start first.

'God! What you must be thinking of us, I don't know,' the mammy said, looking like she had the weight of the world on her shoulders.

I smiled, mumbling, 'No, everything's grand thanks,' but really feeling I'm in the way.

'Do you want to go up to your room and see where you're sleeping?' she suddenly asked me, filling the kettle for the tea, her eyes softening in hope the family will look better if she can get me settled.

I stood up smiling happily, 'Yeah! Thanks, Missus!'

'No! Call me Mam if ye like, but not that. It's too formal,' she laughed. 'And you're part of the family as long as you are staying in this house.'

'Thank you, Mam,' I said, shyly.

'Daddy!'

'Wha now?' he barked, looking up as he tried te pour himself another drink without spilling it.

'Bring Martha's case in from the back of the car.'

'I did!' he roared. 'It's sitting out in the hall waiting for ye's. Now let a man have an honest drink, for the love a God!'

'Honest drink, me eye!' muttered the mammy, laughing te us.

'Will yeh have one yerself, Granny?' roared the daddy.

'Wha is it?'

'Give her no such thing!' roared the grandad! 'Dat stuff is not to be wasted on the likes of her,' he snorted, waving his glass in the granny's direction.

'Come on!' Thelma laughed. 'Let's get out of here!' Then the doorbell rang and the dog leapt up, going demented, barking his head off, forgetting about his slipper and tearing for the door, following the daddy out te open it.

'Get in!' roared the daddy, and I could hear a pause and a mutter then the dog came flying back in, not stopping te look behind him, and carrying his two back legs like he was trying te protect his arse. Then he whirled around and stood his ground in the middle of the kitchen, waiting and watching te see who's coming in the door, moaning an keening because he couldn't get out at them.

'Mammy! I'm home!' shouted a little fella with short brown curly hair and a little white face with a button nose, and lovely grey eyes that shone outa his head as he whipped it around the room, taking in everything at once, and landing them on me, staring with his mouth open. Then he shouted, 'Did yeh get the orphan, Mammy? Is that the one?' pointing at me.

'Oh holy God!' the mammy said, turning bright red and burying her face in her hands laughing, then shaking her head at me, saying, 'Take no notice, Martha. He's just excited to see you.'

'Mammy!' he shouted, forgetting about me. 'Look what Uncle Seamus bought me!' He held up a little box with a Dinky car inside. 'It's a Roadster sports car,' he roared, his eyes rolling outa his head with the excitement as he dropped down onta his knees, trying te get the box opened in an awful hurry, while the mammy bent herself looking down.

'God bless all here!' laughed a man coming in and standing at the door with his hands in his pockets and smiling, showing the whitest set of gnashers I ever saw, and laughing outa the brightest pair of blue eyes I ever laid eyes on. I stared at him. He had straw fair hair that stood up even though he tried te flatten it down with Brylcreem. I could smell it from the other end of the kitchen.

'Uncle Seamus!' screamed Thelma, running and throwing herself inta his arms. 'You're back! What did you buy me?'

'Easy now! Uff! Ye're a strong girl,' he panted, getting the wind knocked outa him. 'Yeh nearly knocked me sideways,' he said, tumbling backwards with her and steadying himself and her.

'What did you get me? Did you buy me something nice?' she said, looking up inta his face, smiling.

'Ha, ha, yeh'll have to wait for Santa Claus teh find dat out,' he roared, laughing.

'I know what he bought you!' screamed Joseph.

'No! Shush! Mustn't spoil the game,' Seamus said, putting his finger te his mouth and nodding slowly te Joseph.

'Oh, yeh're right! It's our men's secrets from the women!' he said, shaking his head up and down slowly, whispering like it was the most sacred thing in the whole world.

'Yours is sitting under the Christmas tree in the front room,' the uncle whispered, leaning over te her ear.

'Oh, what is it? Will you not tell me now? Is it big?' she said, hopping up and down, wriggling herself around the place like a two year old.

Jaysus! She's a bit childish for her age all the same, I thought, looking at her. I suppose she's like that because she got an awful lot a minding.

'Oh, Daddy! I can't wait to open all my presents!' she squealed, flying over te the daddy and swinging her arms around his neck.

The daddy's eyes went crosswise with the sudden shock of his drink swinging around in his hand as he watched a splash go inta the air. He held it steady, away from him in the air, saying, 'Ah, dotie! Go easy on yure aul daddy, I'm not as young as I used teh be, and mind me aul drink. This stuff is like gold dust!' he said, swinging her around te the other side of him and grabbing her under his left arm, nursing the drink well away from her in the other. She sat on his left knee with her arm around his shoulder and his arm around her waist, watching contentedly with a little smile on her face, sucking on her thumb while the daddy talked away te everyone.

Gawd! Sucking her thumb at her age! I stared at her, not believing me eyes. There must be something wrong with her, I said te meself slowly, watching her drop her head on his shoulder, stroking her nose with her fingers and sucking like mad, her lips getting pushed out over her thumb, and her eyes half closing. She'd never get te go off on her own next year like the rest of us in the convent when we're sixteen. No! I really wouldn't have too much te say te her; we'd have nothing te talk about. I'm thinking about different things, while her mind is on school and what she's going te get for Christmas. Yeah! Just as well for her, because with looks like hers ye'd need all the help ye can get! Still an all, there was a bit of me that wouldn't mind getting meself minded like that. I could feel the sour humming of jealousy flying up and down me chest as I turned me head away in disgust.

'Will yeh have a drop a the hard stuff?' Daddy said, holding the bottle up and looking at it te see how much was left.

'Ah, begad! Grandad is at it again,' Seamus roared, laughing his head off. 'One of these days,' he said, laughing and wagging his head at the grandad.

'Well! We won't be the only ones teh suffer, begad! The sergeant would be crying inta his socks this Christmas for the want of the drop a the craythur, the hard stuff, if it wasn't for me,' he said, sending his false teeth flying up and down in his head, giving a sour look around the room, then taking a big slurp of his drink and smacking his big lips together, pressing them out and tasting them.

'Yeh mean you're bribing the local sergeant back home is it?' roared the mammy, looking shocked.

'Ah, go on outa dat! Bribing me arse!' growled the grandad, making te spit, looking around him but finding nowhere te land it, so swallowing it.

Gawd! The mammy is going back te her fierce culchie accent, I thought, seeing her staring at the grandad, full of interest at what was being said. I've never been with real culchies before, not this close up anyway, and they're gas! They spend all their time shouting, but they don't mean a word of it. There's nothing vicious at all about the way they carry on! I took in a deep breath, letting me chest drop, feeling easier in meself, getting used te them.

'Will a mixed grill do you all?' the mammy said, lifting up the heavy frying pan outa the press and lighting the gas. Then she took out stuff from the fridge and slapped a load of lamb chops on the pan and started te fry them, and put a pile of sausages under the grill with black and white pudding sliced with a big knife and stuck them on and started washing tomatoes and slicing them up. Then she put sugar on the tomatoes cut in half and put them beside the sausages, and started cutting up slices of brown soda bread. I could see it was fresh and wanted te ask if she made it herself. But there was talk going backwards and forwards between everyone, and I didn't want te hear me own voice talking te them, because I'm the odd one out with me real Dublin way of talking, and I'd stick out too much. So I kept meself quiet.

I'm feeling a bit tired now with all the excitement and trying te fit in, not be in the way. But I'd like te take it easy now on me own where I wouldn't feel I'm on show. I wonder where me case is sitting and where I'm going te sleep. Wonder how many bedrooms they have. It's a lovely house, I thought te meself, looking around at the kitchen with the wooden overmantle going from the fireplace te nearly the top of the wall with the high ceiling. I looked up at all her little ornaments lined up on the mantle, and the photographs of her and the husband getting married. I could see the granny standing beside the mammy, and the two of them looked a lot younger. She's wearing a long white frock down te just above the ankles, and white wedge sandals they look like, and a white veil, holding up a big bunch of flowers and smiling with a big mop of curly hair. And the daddy is wearing a black suit with a white tie, and he has a white carnation in his lapel. They all look very happy; there's a big crowd of them. I leaned over te get a look at the other grandaddy and granny. She's wearing a big hat with a scarf tied in a bow at the front. Showing up this granny here, who only has a little hat on, and it's collapsed over the side of her head; she looks drunk! Her husband, this grandad here, is giving a big toothpaste smile, showing off all his own teeth. Lovely, I thought, taking a big sigh, wishing I could ask her who's who, and what did they get te eat at the wedding, and where they went for their honeymoon.

I could smell the lovely fry, and me belly started te rumble and me mouth water. I'm dying te get me teeth inta that fry.

'Well, glory be teh God!' roared the granny, lifting her head outa the newspaper and turning around te the grandad. 'Paidir! Looka dis! Do yeh know who is just gone and passed away?' she said, swinging her head back te squint at the newspaper, her eyes moving along the death column page, looking through a spying glass and reading the words te herself, her lips moving and her voice mumbling. 'Well I never!' she roared. 'Do yeh know who's just gone and died? Yeh never will guess!'

'Who?' mumbled the grandad, not really interested, examining the floor like there was better things happening there.

'Do yeh know who it is?' she roared again, lifting her head quickly and swinging it at him then back te the paper.

'WHO?' roared the grandad. 'I'll be dead meself by the time yeh get around teh telling me at dis rate a going!'

Everyone roared laughing, looking at them and waiting te hear what the granny was going te say.

'Aul Finnigan himself, begad! Would yeh credit that now?' she roared, still not lifting her head off the newspaper.

'What Finnigan are yeh talking about?' roared the grandad,

looking like he was going te cry with temper. 'Who? There must be twenty a dem Finnigans! Which one are yeh talking about, Maeve? Will yeh tell me outa that and stop yure aul codding. Is it a mind reader yeh think I am?'

'For the love a God! I'm telling yeh, yeh cantankerous old man!' she roared, shaking the newspaper and shaking herself in a rage! 'Aul Mattie Finnigan himself! The undertaker!'

'Ah, he's well past his time! Sure, he's no loss teh anyone. Dat fella was so mean he wouldn't give yeh the steam offa his piss!' the grandad muttered te the floor, taking another slurp of his drink.

'Removal to the local parish church, Wednesday,' she read, muttering te herself, holding the newspaper close te her face and running the spyglass over the words. 'Ah! Dat will be a big affair!' she keened, beginning te raise her voice. 'T'is an awful pity we'll miss dat. I'd a loving teh be at that one. The world and his wife won't miss dat funeral!' she said te herself, looking very woebegone, shaking her head in disappointment. 'I do love a good funeral! Dat's why I do keep me eye on the death columns in the newspaper,' she said, looking over at the mammy, who wasn't minding her but trying te stop the sausages burning, and flapping away all the smoke with her dishcloth.

The telephone started te ring, and the dog leapt up, making for the handle of the door, jumping up and down on it trying te open it.

'Get away outa dat!' said the daddy, jumping up and flapping his hand at the dog, missing him. 'It's for you, Granny,' he roared.

'Me! Why would anyone want teh call me here?' she roared, looking shocked.

'It's yure neighbour, Mrs Hennesey. She wants teh talk teh yeh.'

'From down yonder is it?'

'Go and find out,' shouted the grandad, 'and stop yure fustering, woman! T'is calling yeh long distance dey are! The people will be getting a phone bill as long as yure arm! We may end up paying for it, or I'll have teh be paying for it, more like.' Then he jumped up, saying, 'I'll speak teh dem,' making for the door.

'PAIDIR MURPHY! Yeh'll do no such thing! It's me they want teh talk teh! Not the likes a you!' She was up in a flash, moving on her bunions, and out the door while he was still thinking about it, and shutting the door with an unmerciful bang, nearly taking the face off him.

'Begad! Dat woman can move when she wants teh!' he said, looking at the room, getting a shock for himself.

'What would that be about, Grandad?' said the mammy, looking worried.

'I don't rightly know,' he said, thinking, his false teeth flying in and outa his mouth, looking worried. 'Begad! I hope the house hasn't burnt down teh the ground,' he said. 'Listen! I want teh hear what she's saying,' he said, leaning his head te the door.

'Ohh! Is that right now? Yes, it is a great loss teh the locals right enough! Indeed we all are. I was just saying only this minute how we'll miss him greatly . . .'

'Who is she talking about?' the grandad muttered te the room.

'All right so! We'll be back down soon, and we'll be seeing yeh then. Goodbye now! And a very happy Christmas teh them all.'

'Tea's ready!' shouted the mammy just as the granny came dragging herself back inta the room.

'Who was yeh talking about?' asked the grandad. 'What loss were yeh on about?'

'Whist! Hold yerself back and let me sit down,' said the granny, making for her chair.

'Over here, Granny! We're going to have the tea,' said the mammy, landing plates a mixed grill, she called it, down in front of everyone rushing te the table. 'You stay where you are, Martha,' she said, putting a plate a sausages and rashers and black and white pudding with tomatoes and a lamb chop down in front of me.

I waited for everyone te get themself settled and then started on me grub. Oh, the smell was tormenting me, and I lashed inta the chop straight away, not bothering te see if they were noticing me flying through the sausages, and dipping me hand inta the basket and taking a thick slice a home-made soda bread and lathering on the butter. Oh, the taste is outa this world. We never get grub like this in the convent! They keep that for the nuns.

'Well! Out with the news!' barked the grandad, taking out his teeth and landing them beside him on the table.

'Ah, t'was only the neighbour Mary Hennessey phoning teh say tha auld Mattie Finnigan has gone an died!'

'WE KNOW DAT!' roared Grandad, shoving his teeth back in, trying te chew on the chop. 'Is that all she had teh say?'

'Yes! What more do yeh want?'

'If yeh let me speak, yeh might hear more!'

'She said the talk is he'll be getting a hero's funeral, if yeh wouldn't be minding!'

'A what?' roared the grandad.

'Yes! He fought in the war of independence.'

'WAR!' roared the grandad, grabbing a lump a fat from the chop outa his mouth and landing it on the plate, nearly choking with the news he was getting. 'What war a independence did he fight in? Sure, as soon as he even heard the mention a the Black and Tans, he took teh his heels an hid in Dinny MacSweeney's hayshed! It took a whole month before dey could tear him down, screaming he's not a well man. Up in the bloody hayloft, he'd been hiding himself out. Buried under the hay, he was! That was the nearest he got teh any war!' shouted the grandad, looking very disgusted, slapping more half-chewed meat onta the plate.

'Well now! I'm only relaying the news back to yeh! He's going to be lying in state in our local church from tonight, an getting the flag wrapped around his coffin. So I know nothing more than dat!' said the granny, attacking the fry, making short work a the sausages and grabbing two cuts a soda bread.

I made another grab for the last one left, giving up trying te be polite by waiting for someone te ask me if I wanted more. I polished that off in seconds and looked at me plate, clean except for the bones. Gawd! I'm still starving. That was lovely. They don't give us anything like this in the convent. Ye nearly have te share the two little sausages they give ye. I wonder if I should ask for more bread? And a drop a tea. I looked around at the table; everyone is still gabbing.

'Would you like something else, Martha?' the mammy asked, looking at me, ready te give me whatever I want. 'Would you like some mince pies?'

'Yeah, please, eh, sorry! Are they the things with currants in them?'

'Yes!' she said, smiling, ready te jump up, heading over te the oven. 'Oh, my mince pies! I forgot to take them out of the oven!' She grabbed a cloth, taking out the burnt pies, flapping the dishcloth te get rid a the smoke. 'Oh, they're ruined! I only meant to heat them.'

'Yeah, never mind, Missus. I'm not really hungry anyway,' I heard meself saying. Ah, fuck! What did I go and say that for? I'm still starving!

'Are you finished?' Thelma asked me, jumping up from the table.

'Eh, yeah.'

'Come on, then! Let's go to the front room and see the Christmas tree!'

I took out after her, hoping there might be mention of another bit a grub later on. I followed her inta a big sitting room with a brown three-piece leather suite arranged in front of a big open fire. The red-hot coal was settled down te an orange glow, sending lovely warm heat blasting inta the room. 'This is lovely, Thelma,' I said, sitting meself down in the armchair beside the fire and looking around, admiring the room. The two armchairs sat each side of the fireplace, and the sofa in the middle, with a coffee table sitting in front. I looked behind me at the alcove with the lovely shiny mahogany table holding a big lamp.

'That's called a Tiffany lamp,' Thelma said, seeing me staring at it.

'All the different-coloured glass is gorgeous, Thelma, isn't it?'

'Yeah! We got that passed down from my great-grandmother on Daddy's side.'

'Lovely,' I murmured, staring at the silver photographs sitting on the table. One of the mammy and daddy: she's holding a baby on her lap and the daddy has Thelma wrapped te him. She's half standing and the rest of her is under the daddy's arms. She looks about six or seven. I looked at the other one in silver of the mammy with a child on her lap and Thelma standing beside her, holding the baby's hand. That must be Joseph when he was a baby, sitting in a white linen suit with his little fat legs kicking out.

I looked at the bookcase, wondering who reads all the books.

'Daddy and Mammy read a lot. She likes the romances, and Daddy likes history. Mostly on Ireland,' she said, seeing me looking at the bookcase. It's a lovely old-fashioned mahogany one with glass doors, and gorgeous panels in the door at the bottom.

'Come on! What do you think of our Christmas tree?' shouted Thelma.

'Yeah, it's outa this world,' I said, bringing meself across. 'I was saving that for last, Thelma. I wanted te see the books first,' I said, throwing meself on the smashing thick rugs.

'This is a Chinese rug. Mammy made Daddy buy it in Switzers last January, during the sales. Isn't it fabulous?'

'Yeah,' I said, stroking it, feeling the thick pile a wool. It's lovely and soft. 'Ye're a lucky girl, Thelma, I hope ye know that,' I said, thinking what a lovely mammy she has, and a daddy who dotes on her.

'Yeah, I know,' she said, looking at me. 'Have you parents?'

'Yes and no! I suppose no,' I said, thinking about it. Getting a picture of the ma in me head, feeling sad and annoyed, and wanting te leave her behind. 'No! I have no family,' I said, meaning it. I'm not going te think about them any more. Fuck it! What's a family anyway? I don't think it means what I want it te. People who take care of their children. 'No, Thelma. No family.'

'Gawd! That's awful! I can't imagine not having Mammy and Daddy,' she said, looking very worried.

'That won't happen te you, Thelma. Look how old yer grandparents are.'

'Yeah,' she said, giving a big sigh of contentment.

'So anyway! Where's yer present?' I said, looking at the Christmas tree with the pink fairy standing on the top branch, and Santa Claus holding onta a present and holding out his other hand, dangling from the tree! The lights stayed on, and they were like little carriages, ones the horses used to pull in the old days.

'Mammy bought them lights in Switzers. She waits until after the Christmas to get our real presents, like winter coats or shoes, or something for the house. But this year I'm not waiting. I'm dying for a new coat. Hope she gets me one.'

'That's a very dear shop, isn't it, Thelma?'

'Yeah. That's why we wait for the sales. These are the presents Joseph and me bought,' she said, pointing under the tree te parcels wrapped in Christmas paper. 'The rest are hidden away for Santa to bring,' she laughed, 'for Joseph!'

'Yeah,' I said, thinking I never believed in him. 'Did ye ever believe in Santa Claus, Thelma?'

'Yeah, of course! Didn't you?'

'No!' I laughed.

'I didn't stop believing in him until I was about nine! Then I heard Daddy and Mammy coming down from the guest bedrooms – they kept that locked. Daddy dropped my two-wheeler bicycle down the stairs; he was drunk! And the roars outa him and the mammy woke us up! That was hilarious,' she screamed, laughing her head off. 'I came charging down the stairs when I heard the noise, thinking it was Santa at first! Oh, you should have seen their faces. Mammy was fit to be tied, raging she was with Daddy, and Daddy was blaming the poteen that Grandad brought up. He makes it himself and brings up bottles of the stuff every Christmas for as long as I can remember.'

'Jaysus, Thelma! Them two are a scream! They never stop shouting at each other.'

'No! But Grandad is devoted to Granny, he wouldn't go anywhere without her.'

'That's lovely,' I said, feeling like crying and not knowing bleeding why. What more could I want? Here I am with a lovely family, they can't be nice enough te me, and I feel like I'm on the outside looking in. Jaysus! Be satisfied. What's wrong with me? I stood up going over te try out the other armchair, and the door opened.

'Ah! Are yeh all right, girls?' the uncle said, laughing and showing his snow-white teeth, and waving a hand behind him. 'Come on, men! The girls have beaten us teh the chairs,' he shouted, watching Thelma race and bounce herself inta the armchair, screeching, 'We got here first! Dere's no one taking my seat!'

'Ah! We'll see about dat now,' growled the uncle, making a run at her.

She screamed, 'No! Stop! No tickles; you're not getting me out. Daddy!'

'I'm coming,' muttered the daddy, making a move for the other side of her, and the two men lifted her under the arms, bouncing her onta the floor, and the daddy sat down.

'Yeh're next,' the uncle said, pointing his finger and coming at me.

'Ha! Ye'll have two hopes of getting me outa this chair, Mister!'

'What? Begad! Is dat a challenge the little whipper snapper is throwing out?' he shouted, whipping his head at the grandad.

'Yeah!' screamed Thelma, tearing over te throw herself in beside me, and the uncle stood sizing us up with his arms on his hips.

'Begad! I think they have me beat, right enough! I could get one a dem out, but the other would hop back in. Aaah! The floor'll do me!'

'Get up outa dat, the pair a yeh's, or I'll take me boot to yure arses if yeh's don't let me sit down!' roared the grandad.

I went stiff as a poker! 'Don't mind Grandad!' Thelma muttered, nudging me. 'His bark is worse than his bite. He's only an aul pussycat. One word from Granny, and he shuts up!'

I stared at his eyes twinkling, trying te make himself look serious. I knew he wanted a chair, because he was looking from the daddy and back te us. 'I'm not putting me arse on that thing,' he said, looking at the sofa. 'Come on, girls! Be nice teh an old man and move yerselves over dere,' he said, pointing with his glass.

'Ah, will we let him sit down?' I said, hopping up feeling sorry for the poor aul man getting tormented.

'Yeah, let's go up to my room.'

'Have ye yer own room, Thelma?'

'Yeah! Course! I'd hardly share with that shrimp of a brother of mine! Aaah! Perish the thought.'

'Gawd! It's big, isn't it?' I said, looking around at the big single bed with the lovely mahogany bed ends and the lovely white candlewick bedspread with pink roses and patterns in the middle. 'Ye have loads a stuffed toys, and books, and dolls, and posters, Thelma!' I stared at one with Elvis buckling his knees with the tight trousers crippling him and looking like he was enjoying himself with his eyes closed. But I think he's really dying with the pain a them trousers! 'Ye have everything,' I said, swinging me head around the room, looking at the dressing table with the three mirrors and three big drawers, and a jewellery box sitting on top. 'Can I open it?'

'Yeah, look! It's a musical box.' She opened it and a ballerina popped up with a mirror underneath, and little compartments for rings and bracelets and gold chains, and even a watch! I listened te the music, me mouth dropping open at the lovely sound. 'That's *The Nutcracker Suite*, by Tchaikovsky,' Thelma said, seeing me delight.

'That's lovely,' I said, hearing the music and watching the ballerina whirl around and around on top of the mirror with the red velvet box and the shiny gold and silver bracelets. 'Where did ye get all this?' I said, lifting up a silver bracelet with little charms of dogs and all different little miniature bikes and a woman in a long fur hat and coat. 'This is lovely.'

'Yes! I really like that. Daddy bought me that for my twelfth birthday, and aunts and uncles always buy me a present of a little piece of jewellery when they come to visit or we go to visit them.'

I looked at her, seeing how nice and kind she really is. She's very gentle and calm. Not a bit like the kids in the convent. Or me either! I'm not quiet the way she is. There's a stillness inside her that comes from the inside out. There's no fear or worry in her. She has her place here, with her mammy doing all the worrying for her from the day she was born. And the daddy looking after the lot of them. She's more like a child, really, and will probably just grow old, that childishness staying with her most of her life. She'll have a husband te take care of her, and bring her children up the way she was reared. Coming from a long line of respectable people. I want te be like that. Respectable. I wonder if I should become a nun! That might not be a bad idea. Ye get well fed, a roof over yer head, no money worries, what more could a body want? Hm! I might look inta that.

'Thelma, come on! Show me where I'm going te be sleeping. Do I have te share with someone?' Me heart leapt. Jaysus! They could put me in with the granny, or have me sleep in the front room with the dog scratching te get in. 'Am I on my own?'

'Yeah! Course you are, we have five bedrooms!'

'Ye have? Gawd! Ye have a big house.'

'I suppose so. Let's go.'

I followed her out onta a big landing and down onta a smaller one and up some steps inta a small bedroom. 'You're in here,' she said, flinging the door open and switching on the light.

My eyes flew around the room, taking in the rosy wine curtains with fancy rope pelmets. They were very heavy and hung down te the wooden floorboards that are black varnish. I made a move te the single bed with the carved wooden bed ends and the same matching bedspread as Thelma. I have a bedside locker with a shelf for putting yer book in or whatever ye like, and a pink lamp, with a dressing table and a wardrobe in the corner, with a mirror in the door. 'This is lovely, Thelma,' I said, smelling the lovely lavender polish, and opening the door te the wardrobe, smelling the mothballs. The smell of the room cheered me up, making me feel a sense of everything being clean and in its place, and that gives me a sense of peace. Makes me easy in meself.

'I am going down te the hall te get me bag.'

'OK! See you when you come downstairs.'

I ran down, picking up me case. It's light as a feather. I probably didn't need it, but still, it's nice te think I'm going somewhere, that I'm really on me holidays.

I flew up te me room, shutting the door quietly, and made for me bed, landing down the case and taking out me stuff. I'll just leave me nightdress here. Pity I couldn't get me hands on a pair of them new pyjamas. But Sister Eleanor said they are all given out. I wonder where I was when she was giving them out after they came back from the laundry. Probably in the convent. Anyway! I have a whole room te meself. This is more like it. Nobody will bother me, and I can come up here and read or do what I want.

I kept me good stuff in the case and put it in the wardrobe. Just so nobody will come in and maul them! I don't like me things being touched. The bleeding cows in the convent are always robbing me stuff. I've been dug outa many a pile a bodies, me usually at the bottom a them, ending up in threadbare order after a massive hair pulling. But it's never a fair fight! No! They all jump in te protect each other against me, the street kid! Well, the overgrown cows would need their cronies' back-up! Because when I lose me rag, then it's hair, teeth and bones that start flying! No! This is nice; no one will bother me here.

I lifted back the quilt, looking at the tan wool blankets with the gold satin on the edge, and the lovely white sheets with the embroidery on the pillowcase. They smelled of lavender. This is great! I sat meself down and just took in the room. I looked up at the brass light hanging down from the ceiling, and jumped up, putting the lamp on the locker on and switched off the big light. I could hear Christmas carols coming from the radio downstairs in the kitchen when the door opened, and the sound of laughing and the smell of cooking. She must be cooking for tomorrow! This is lovely.

I lay down on the blankets, pulling the bedspread back and throwing off me shoes and twisting me back and arse on the soft mattress. Bouncing up and down, getting comfortable and resting meself. I felt very nervous inside meself all day, and me head was feeling tight and hot. But now I don't have te be on my guard with being in me own lovely room. Ah, thank you, God! This is the life!

I woke up feeling icy cold and looked around wondering where I was. I couldn't see the line of black iron beds or hear the snoring coming from all directions. Me head flew around the room, trying te take in the new surroundings. Oh, I'm not in the convent. I went te a family! Gawd! I must have fallen asleep. I listened, not a sound, everybody must be gone te bed. I dived outa me clothes and inta me nightdress, and under the sheets and blankets, feeling the heat from lying on top of the bed, and snuggled down, wriggling and coughing and smelling the lavender. Oh, this is definitely the life, I tittered, having the lovely feeling of me eyes going very heavy, then felt meself sinking inta a world of peace and order with a smile on me face.

CHAPTER 17

'In the name of the Father and of the Son and of the Holy Spirit, Amen. Go in peace! And may I wish you all a Happy Christmas,' the priest said, blessing the congregation with his hands in the air and pointed sideways te us, then kneeling and bowing te the tabernacle and walking off the altar, heading in te the sacristy with the little altar boys, one on each side of him.

'The Mass is over,' Thelma said and smiled at me. 'Let's go quick!' And she was moving fast, trying te get going before all the grannies and the mammies and daddies with the small children started moving.

We were outa the church ahead of the rest and looked at each other's style. 'I like your hipster skirt. Pity you don't have black patent shoes to match,' she said, eyeing me from me pink polo neck jumper te me wine skirt with the matching thick belt and the gold buckle, down te me new white knee socks and me shoes. I looked down at me brown shoes with the strap across, and, yeah, somehow there's something missing. I never really thought about it before, because the other eejits just make a laugh of me. But Thelma is nice, and she's kind.

'Do ye think I would look better, Thelma?'

'Definitely! And a white jumper to match the white socks would be lovely. Or a black polo neck to match the shoes. But you're too young for black, that's only for older people.'

'Yeah! Pity I haven't got a white jumper,' I said, feeling very disappointed I'm not really looking smashing. 'Where did ye get yer kilt from, Thelma?' I said, eyeing her long red-and-green kilt, with the big Tara brooch and the off-white new Arran jumper, with the red knee socks and black patent shoes, like the ones I would like, with a little bow on the front.

'Oh, Mammy bought the kilt from a little shop back home in the country. Well, Mammy and Daddy are from Roscommon, so they call it back home.'

'Ye look lovely, Thelma, really nice,' I said, standing back te take in the style of her.

'Thanks!' she said, happily jigging up and down and tapping her new black patent shoes.

I stayed quiet, not really wanting te show off me style I thought I had in me suitcase. Still, they're nearly new. I only got them six months ago!

'There you are, girls,' the mammy said, with the breath coming outa her mouth and her nose looking red from the cold. She was wearing a lovely new long tan coat with a new white-and-gold scarf with a lovely glittering diamond brooch in the middle and a fur hat te match the coat, and black patent high-heel shoes. I looked at her lovely red lipstick and blue eyeshadow and powder on her face. She really looks lovely, all dolled up te the nines.

'Where's Daddy?' she said, looking around, seeing the granny and grandad moseying over te us, all done up in style, too.

'He'll be along shortly, he's gabbing teh John Joe O'Reilly from back home,' the granny shouted, seeing the mammy looking around for him.

'Where?' she whipped her head around, getting impatient. 'Thelma, go and find your father and tell him we have to get going straight away. My goose will be burnt to a cinder! Hurry! And bring Joseph.'

The car heaved up te the front door, and I lifted meself off the granny's lap, only managing a little, me head was stuck te the roof, and Thelma was squashed on the mammy's lap with the uncle buried in the middle, with Joseph sitting on the grandad's lap.

'Safe and sound, home again,' sang the daddy.

'Let us out! For the love a gawd! I can't breathe,' screamed the mammy, and Thelma screamed, 'Move, Grandad; get out, Joseph,' who was looking at her, laughing, with her head stuck out the window.

'Get a move on, Paidir Murphy!' shouted the granny.

The daddy heaved himself outa the car and pulled back the seat, and I was flying out the car all hunched up, and looking back at the granny standing and sitting, trying te get herself moving.

'The grandad is an awful torment,' muttered the mammy, giving the granny a push.

'Hurry! I want to get out and see my Christmas presents,' Thelma moaned.

'I'm getting there first,' roared Joseph, making for the door, pressing himself against it and turning his head, looking for someone te open the door.

'Don't you dare!' screamed Thelma. 'Mammy! Don't let him touch the presents without me!'

'Stop all the shouting, children. Nobody is opening any presents until we are all ready!' shouted the mammy.

'Are yeh right, Granny?' the daddy said, helping the granny outa the car.

'Dat's a crucifixion!' breathed the granny, trying te get her breath back.

I stood back, waiting for everyone te peel themselves outa the car, feeling the chilly wind without me green coat. It wouldn't go with me good clothes. I'd look foolish on a day like today. Everyone made a run for the front door, the mammy turning the key, and the rest galloped in behind her. Even the granny was trying te gallop in her new black granny laced-up high-heel boots, getting herself knocked sideways in the rush and shouting, 'Mind me! Yeh's will kill me yet, with the hurry on yeh's!'

They all made straight for the front room and the Christmas tree with the pile a presents wrapped around the floor underneath. The mammy flew down the hall, making for her goose, shouting,

'Don't open anything without me! I'll be along in a minute when I baste me bird.'

'What have we here? What did Santa Claus bring us?' said the daddy, walking in, slowly rubbing his hands together and bending himself te the floor looking at all the presents.

'What did I get?' screamed Thelma, dropping on her knees, grabbing up parcels.

'Where's mine?' screamed Joseph, diving on the lot of them, picking up armfuls, his head twisting and his eyes crossing trying te take everything in at once. Then dropping small ones and grabbing up the big parcels, and looking at the names. 'This is for me, and one for you! There's yours, Thelma,' and he threw it down beside her.

'Records! I got . . . Where's the record player, Daddy? Oh, did you get me the record player I asked for?' She was nearly crying with shock and excitement.

'Keep looking,' the daddy muttered, watching the two of them and reaching out for a present, looking at the name and handing it te the granny.

'Oh, what is it?' muttered the granny, squinting at the little card on it.

'And here's yours, Grandad.'

'Begad! One for me an all!' he said, eyeing the big soft parcel.

'Yeh started without me,' roared the mammy, laughing and rushing inta the room with a big red face on her from all the rushing.

I moved back, feeling a bit foolish. I might be in the way, and they wouldn't be easy, either, with me watching, maybe thinking they had te give me something when they weren't even expecting me, when I only got here last night. I wonder if it would look OK if I shift meself out. Would they think I'm being insulting?

I saw the mammy whisper te the granny and give me a sideways glance. Jaysus! They're talking about me! I made for the door, smiling, saying, 'I'll be back in a minute. Just going te the toilet,' I mumbled in the mammy's direction.

I rushed down the hall and up the stairs, making for me room. I flew in the door, shutting it quietly behind me, and walked over te the window. I stood looking out at the frost on the bare trees in the big back garden, me eyes landing on the swings, two of them together, and the see-saw. The dog was running around the garden trying te catch a white cat sitting on the high wall staring down at him.

Jaysus! I'm glad te be outa there until they get all their stuff. I was feeling a right gobshite! Yeah! It's nice of them te have me here, that's very good of them. But I'm not one of them, and I don't want te be reminded of that. Gawd! The more we get, the more we want. Here I am standing in a lovely room going te get a lovely Christmas dinner, and I feel like crying because Thelma has a mammy and daddy that think the world of her, and I feel left out in the cold. Yet, I could be with Jackser and the ma, having hell on earth now along with the other kids, and yet I'm still feeling a bit hard done by! If Charlie was here now, he'd be the happiest boy in the world! Stop yer carry-on and be grateful! Yeah! God is looking after ye, otherwise ye wouldn't be here now; ye could be still stuck with that bandy-legged aul bastard Jackser! On the other hand, there's no fucking way in hell I would be still there. I'd be living in England and working away, making a new life for meself. Right! I'm going down te enjoy meself. It's all in yer head. They won't be taking any notice of ye!

'Martha?' I rushed over te the door, opening it, and heard the mammy say, 'Where is she?'

'I'm coming!' I flew down the stairs, seeing her waiting for me.

'Come here to me, pet,' she said, holding out her hand and giving me a present. 'This is for you!'

'Me?'

I opened the red Christmas wrapping paper, taking me time not wanting te tear the paper, and took out a light-blue cardigan with buttons all down the front, feeling the soft wool. 'Ah, thanks, Mam, it's lovely,' I said, looking at her with the worried look in her face in case I didn't like it.

'Granny has the same one in white,' roared Joseph. 'Look!'

I looked at the granny grinding her false teeth and shaking her fist at Joseph. 'Oh, sorry! I was just saying,' Joseph mumbled, looking shifty and whipping his head around looking for more presents.

I laughed, seeing the poor mammy go bright beetroot in the face and the granny rolling her eyes te the ceiling, muttering, 'That child hasn't a pick a sense.'

'No! I really like it,' I said, feeling sorry for the poor mammy feeling she got caught out giving me one of the granny's presents.

I fitted it up te meself, seeing it was a bit long, but I'll grow inta it, and now I have something new te wear. No, it won't go with this skirt, pity! But I can wear it with me other skirt and frock; it will be lovely with me white blouse I have.

'Look what I got!' screamed Thelma, showing me her new record player that ye lift the lid and sit the record down and it plays. 'I got two new records, one of the Beatles singing 'A Hard Day's Night', and Elvis singing 'Heartbreak Hotel'. Ohhh! I can't wait to play them. And look what else I got! A new maxi coat.' She whipped it on, fastening the silver buttons with a big collar going up around her neck and tying the belt, whirling herself around te show it off. 'What do you think?'

'It's lovely, Thelma,' I said, admiring it, wishing I had one like that. Pity about me new one, but still, I'm happier letting me ma have it. I just have te be patient and save up te buy another one. I have everything ahead of me. 'Ye look lovely in that,' I said, looking at the mammy throwing her eye over Thelma, staring at the style of her and shaking her head, looking satisfied it suits her all right.

'Ohhh! Thanks, Mammy!' And she threw her arms around the mammy, making her laugh, saying, 'You look lovely in that coat, love! I'm delighted it looks so well on you. Now! I'd better get back to the kitchen or there will be no dinner this day.'

'Bang! Bang, bang! Got yeh all!' shouted Joseph, standing in his cowboy suit, with his hat on, waving two guns with smoke coming out.

'Take dem tings out teh the back garden,' roared the granny, getting a shock, jumping with the fright. 'Yeh will blow us all up with the smell a dem caps.'

'They're not real, Granny!' laughed Joseph, saying, 'I'm going out to play with Scrapper!'

He was gone, flying out the door, not listening te the daddy shouting, 'Don't scare the shite outa tha dog!'

'Tut, tut! Don't be using dat kind of language to the child,' said the granny, glaring at the daddy, who rubbed his hands, jumping up from the armchair and going over te the sideboard and opening a bottle of Paddy Irish Whiskey, pouring one for himself and saying, 'Will yeh all have a drop?' holding the bottle out te everyone.

'Yeh know I don't drink!' said the granny, throwing her eye at the bottle and fixing her new long frock over her legs and pulling off her boots. 'Ohhh! The pain in me bunions, dem new boots are crippling me altogether! I'll just have a drop teh deaden the pain in me corns,' she moaned, watching him pour out a drink for himself after handing one te the grandad, and pouring a little drop for her. 'Fill the glass!' she roared, watching him. 'It will do me for the rest of the day!'

'Oh, begad! She'll end up plastered teh the floor yet before the day is done,' laughed the grandad, lifting his shoulders te his neck and munching on his false teeth, smiling and guzzling down the drink.

'I'll have none of yure aul chat outa yeh now, Paidir Murphy! I'm just as entitled teh enjoy meself as you and the rest of yeh's,' Granny snorted, looking at the drink and flying it down her neck, saying, 'It does a body good all the same teh get a bit a the craythur comforts,' then smacking her lips and wiping them with the back of her hand, and slapping the nearly empty glass down on the table beside her armchair.

The daddy switched on the big Bush radio, and the green eye came on. Then the room lit up with the sound of the 'Little Drummer Boy' being sung on the radio. 'Ropa bom bom!' we all sang, joining in the song.

'Dinner!' shouted the uncle, and Thelma flew in shouting, 'Come on, everybody! Dinner is ready. Daddy! Mammy wants you to carve the goose. Where's Joseph?'

The granny stood up and flapped her arms out, getting dizzy. I grabbed her, holding her arm. 'Thanks, Martha, love! The heat a dat fire would send yeh flying on yure back,' she said, shaking her head and steadying herself.

I laughed, saying, 'Oh, yeah! The heat would kill ye all right if ye stand up too sudden.'

'Right! Yeh hang onto me arm like a good girl, and we'll make our way dere nice 'n easy,' she said, grabbing hold a me arm and staggering off in her nylon-stocking feet, with her toes sticking up, and she rocked backwards.

'Are yeh all right, Mammy?' said the uncle, coming in laughing and taking the granny's waist, letting her lean on him.

I followed the crowd inta a lovely big dining room with a long table covered in a heavy white embroidered tablecloth, with a glittering vase made of Waterford crystal sitting in the middle filled with flowers, and silver knives and forks and white linen napkins. I held me breath, letting it out in a gasp! My gawd! I never saw anything look so lovely, I thought, looking around at the mahogany sideboard with the wood shining from the lamps lighting on the wall overhead, and it's heaving with the amount of stuff sitting on top. Bowls of fruit, tins of biscuits, sweets, bowls a yellow trifle! Oh, I don't like that, nor custard, yuk! Makes me sick. But there's plenty more te eat.

The granny sat herself down, saying, 'You sit over dere, Grandad, opposite me, and put Joseph one side, and, Seamus, you sit next to yure daddy.'

We all sat down with Thelma sitting next te me, and the daddy came rushing in carrying two plates, saying, 'Come an give a hand to yure mammy, Thelma,' who was planting a Christmas hat on my head.

'Here, Granny! Let me put your hat on!' Joseph said, jumping up and racing around the table.

The granny sat still, her eyes crossing with too much a the drink taken and waited patiently for Joseph fixing the hat on her head. 'Now, Granny! Ye're ready for the Christmas party!' shouted Joseph, rushing off with his own hat on and sitting himself down just as the grandad muttered, 'Begad! She's well ahead a the rest of us with the party! Look at the state a yure mother, son!'

The uncle looked over, grinning like mad as the granny stared at the two of them, shouting, 'Yeh have some cheek on yeh, Paidir Murphy! An you dhree . . . three shifts . . . shits . . . sheets to the wind last night!'

The roars of laughing coming out a them, and even Joseph joined in, not really knowing what they were laughing at, because he wasn't minding what the granny was saying.

'Your dinner, Martha!' Thelma puffed, landing a big plate of dinner down in front of me and the other one in front of the uncle.

'Mine! Where's mine?' shouted Joseph, swinging his head around te the door, getting impatient and looking back te see what we got.

I looked at me plate a roast potatoes and mash and white goose meat and Brussels sprouts, that looked buttery and soft. I don't like Sister Mercy's. Hers are like stones and taste like piss. I have carrots and cauliflower, with gravy poured over the lot, and the steam rising outa the dinner, the plate is hot. Oooh! This is heaven.

I tasted the meat and the mash with a bit of roast potato, and it slid down me neck before I could really get te taste it. Jaysus! I never tasted anything like this in me whole life! People really do have a great time at Christmas! I dug inta the grub like there was no tomorrow, cleaning the plate and looking around the table, watching everyone take their time, still only half finished, drinking and talking and eating.

I sat wondering what we were going te get next. 'Would you like more?' the mammy asked, looking down at me seeing me empty plate.

'Eh . . .' I was afraid te say yes, in case they thought I was a glutton.

'Daddy! Jump up and carve the child another bit of meat, and there's more potatoes keeping warm in the oven.'

He leapt te his feet, grabbing my plate, anxious te get back te his eating and drinking. 'Now, get that down yeh,' he said, landing another dinner in fronta me and opening another bottle a wine.

'Gish a drop more a dash!' said the granny, waving her glass, with the hat hanging over her eye.

Thelma and me looked at each other and burst out laughing. And Joseph roared laughing at us, not knowing what the laugh was about. That made me laugh louder, because he laughs not wanting te be left out.

'What's tickled yeh, girls?' laughed the daddy.

Thelma pointed te the granny holding her left arm in the air, letting her wrist flop and trying te find her mouth te the glass and missing, nearly landing her head in the dinner plate. Everyone watched, roaring their heads off laughing. 'She gets plastered every year,' whispered Thelma, bending over te me an saying, 'but she always swears she doesn't drink!'

I dug inta me second dinner, and it was even nicer than the first. I finally put down me knife and fork, leaving a clean plate, feeling me belly full at last. Gawd! Ye'd sure know it was Christmas with a dinner like that. I smacked me lips, looking around at everyone, and they were all beginning te look dozy!

'Would yeh like me teh bring in the pudding, Mammy?' the daddy asked, throwing down his napkin, saying, 'Begad! Dat was a good dinner! Yeh can't beat the mammy's cooking. Isn't dat right, everyone?' he said, looking serious at everyone and shaking his head in wonder, giving a big belch and punching his stomach. 'Begad, it was an all,' he said, heading for the kitchen.

The mammy sat looking at everyone around the table with a smile on her face, feeling very contented in herself.

'Fire!' shouted the daddy, rushing in with a dark-brown Christmas pudding with blue flames coming outa it and landing it on the table, then grabbing the whiskey bottle and pouring whiskey over it and setting fire te it! The pudding went up in blue flames.

'That's the whiskey!' Thelma laughed te me, seeing me eyes hanging outa me head.

I never saw the like of that before. 'No, thanks, I'm grand,' I said, refusing the pudding.

'It's Granny's home-made recipe dat's been in the family for years! Go on, try a little,' said the daddy, pushing the plate at me, 'and have some brandy butter.'

'OK,' I said, not wanting te be a nuisance. I tasted a little bit with a bit a brandy butter, and it's gorgeous! I don't like currants, but this is heaven.

I had the lot polished off and was waiting for more. But the last of it went te Granny, who was snoring, and the mammy shook her, shouting, 'Wake up, Granny! It's your favourite part of the meal. The Christmas pudding!' she shouted.

'The what? Me pudding, did yeh say?' Her eyes flew open, trying te land on the pudding, then clapped on the big dollop of brandy butter getting slapped on.

'If she doesn't eat that,' I whispered te Thelma, 'grab it quick and pass it down te me.'

'Ha, ha! No chance in hell of getting your paws on Granny's pudding. I think it's the brandy butter she likes.'

'Yeah! Me, too,' I said, keeping me eyes peeled on the pudding.

She took her time but managed te clean the plate, and I was left wanting something else te eat. 'Oh, Daddy!' said the mammy. 'Bring in the mince pies. I have them warming on a low heat.'

'Right, Mammy,' said Daddy, stirring himself, looking red-eyed and sleepy. 'Do anyone else want dem mince pies sitting in the oven?'

'I do!' I roared up.

'Not at all! God bless us all, we will all burst!' moaned the grandad.

Me heart sank! I was planning te put some of that brandy butter stuff on them, I thought, looking up hopefully at the daddy.

'Right so! They don't want dem,' said the daddy, sitting himself down.

'Thelma!' I whispered, giving her a nudge.

'What! What's wrong?' she asked, looking at me.

'Tell yer daddy I want a few mince pies.'

'Daddy! Bring a few mince pies for Martha.'

Everyone looked at me, and the daddy looked shocked. 'Yeh mean yeh still have room in yure belly for more?' he shouted down, laughing at me.

I could feel meself going red-hot in the face, but I wanted te get me teeth inta more cakes. 'Yes, please!' I said, laughing.

'Begad! Yeh must have a hollow leg,' he said, getting himself te his feet, looking at me, saying, 'I don't know where else yeh put it, because dere's not a pick on yeh!'

Everyone laughed, and the mammy said, 'Let her alone. Good girl, Martha. Eat up! Sure you're growing at a great rate, and it's a compliment to me to see you eating all around you.'

They started te clear the table and clear around me, while I sat, lathering on the brandy butter, having a party all te meself. 'I'll help as soon as I'm finished this,' I said, trying te get it down me fast, helping meself te more brandy butter. I was feeling light in me head and heat in me belly and wondering if I was getting drunk on the brandy butter. Gawd! I won't forget this meal in a hurry, I thought, putting down the spoon on the plate, barely stopping meself from licking the last of the brandy butter and pudding streaking the plate. And te think I nearly deprived meself of all that! Hm! Lovely.

I stood up, making for the kitchen, seeing the men doing the washing up and Thelma and the grandad putting the dishes away. 'What would ye like me te do?' I whispered te Thelma.

'Nothing! You go and brush your teeth or something, or talk to Granny in the front room,' she laughed.

'Really?'

'No! I'm only joking, she's probably asleep!'

'Right! See ye later,' I said, flying upstairs te brush me teeth and wash me face and comb me hair. It's lovely and shiny; that must be the shampoo they have here. We use carbolic soap in the convent.

I bounced onta me bed, lying down for a minute, enjoying the luxury of having nothing te do and having a full belly. We would never get a full belly in the convent. There's too many people wanting more! And there's never more, unless ye're going out te work or something, and sitting on the big ones' table.

I woke up, looking around me. What happened? The light has gone; it must be evening. Jaysus! I must have conked out. I leapt outa the bed, taking meself off downstairs, wondering what they will think of me. Eating their grub then doing a vanishing act. I wonder what's for tea? I'm hungry again. I heard noise coming from the front room and opened the door.

'Here she is!' roared Thelma, looking around and smiling at me.

'Did yeh sleep off the big dinner?' laughed the daddy, sitting in the armchair by the fire.

'Come on!' shouted the granny, sitting in the other armchair by the fire with a table in front of her, playing a board game. 'Yeh're just in time teh see me squeeze the last penny outa dis lot,' she said, pointing te the game board and holding up cards and a load of play money.

'No, Granny, I'm not out yet,' shouted Joseph, making a grab for money outa a box.

'No yeh don't!' said the uncle, grabbing the money off him.

'I'm allowed! I can do that! I can borrow money from the bank!' roared Joseph.

'No you can't!' shouted Thelma. 'You've already lost all your houses to the bank. You have nothing left to mortgage!'

'No! Daddy! Tell them to stop cheating,' screamed Joseph, nearly losing his mind.

'Ah, begad! Yeh're now in the same boat as yure poor aul father,' laughed the daddy, shaking his head. 'The banks will give yeh nothing for nothing!'

'Come on! Hand over yure cards,' said the granny. 'I own dem houses now yeh have dere.'

'But they have mortgages on them!' screamed Joseph. 'They belong to the bank.'

'Not if I pay off the mortgages,' cackled the granny, taking all of Joseph's cards, rattling her false teeth up and down, laughing like a hyena. 'Come on! Who's next? Now just remember teh land on dis one,' she said, stabbing her finger on the board. 'I'm always very delighted teh see the lot of yeh! Dis is the best road in Ireland, Ailesbury Road, and I even have me hotel on top! So anyone dropping in teh see me will end up not even standing in the knickers dey're wearing! Because with the cost of dis place, I'll take every penny off yeh. I'll skin yeh alive, and yeh may make yure own way home, walking in yure pelt!' she screamed, laughing like a hyena.

'Begad! Don't say yeh're related teh me! I don't know yeh if the policeman comes knocking on my door,' roared the daddy, laughing his head off.

'No, it's not,' shouted Thelma. 'I have the best road; Shrewsbury Road is the poshest and most expensive road in Ireland, and I have it, look!'

'Yes! But a lot of good dat will do yeh; sure, it's empty! Yeh haven't even got a house on it, never mind a hotel like me,' the granny laughed, dropping her head down te admire her hotel, then her eyes peeled around the board, taking in what everyone else owned.

'I'm not playing!' screamed Joseph, starting te cry his heart out. 'Daddy! They cheated me!' he screamed, landing himself on the daddy's lap with a thump.

'Ouf!' moaned the daddy, lifting him outa the way while he grabbed himself between his knees, going red in the face. 'Ah, son! I think yeh may have damaged me for life,' he puffed. 'God! Take it easy.'

'Mammy!' screamed Joseph, flying out the door, screaming like a banshee, sobbing his heart out, holding his head like he'd been killed, roaring, 'They're all very mean teh me, and Granny robbed all me houses.'

'What's this game called?' I asked, dropping meself down on the floor next te Thelma.

'Monopoly!'

'How do ye play it?'

'Easy! You just . . .'

'Easy, she says!' said the granny, muttering as she counted up all her money.

'OK! We'll play a new game,' said Thelma, collecting up her houses and money and trying te put it back in the box quickly.

'Not on yure Aunt Biddy!' roared the granny. 'Yeh have teh wait until I'm finished winning dis game!'

'Ah, I don't mind waiting,' I said, getting nervous of the granny's dirty looks at the two of us.

'No! I'm fed up playing this game; let's start a new game!' shouted Thelma.

'Yeh can, but it will cost yeh,' said the granny, eyeing her.

'OK! There's all my money.'

'Yeh can keep that. I want real money. Yeh owe me ten bob if yeh want teh get out early.'

'What? We're not playing for real money.'

'No! But it's called a penalty clause!'

'You're talking rubbish, Granny!' screamed Thelma, getting red in the face.

'No! If yeh're intent of depriving me of me winnings, then cough up!'

'Where does it say that in the rules, Uncle Seamus?'

'Ah, yeh don't play with Granny without getting yerself scalped,' laughed the uncle.

'Oh, by all dat's true and holy,' the daddy agreed, nodding his head up and down like mad. 'Many's the man at home found dat to his cost. Begad! She's a fierce woman for the poker! Or any card game for dat matter.'

'Pay up!' said the granny, holding up her hand, looking very serious and giving me a look much as te say, ye're next!

'Ah, I don't know how te play,' I said, losing me nerve, not wanting te get meself skint. But still and all wanting te have a go. I never played any games like this before. Or any games for that matter.

'Teatime!' shouted the mammy, putting her head in the door and laughing at everyone shouting and fighting.

'Thank God!' mumbled the daddy. 'Dat will shut the lot of dem up for a while.'

The mammy poured out the tea and I sat meself down te help meself te a plate of sandwiches. 'Yum! These are lovely and tasty, Thelma.'

'What's in them?' she said, opening the bread te get a look.

'What's going on out dere?' the daddy said, looking out the kitchen window, hearing the dog roaring his head off. He opened the kitchen door and we could hear people's voices shouting, and it sounded like a baby crying. 'Are yeh all right?' he said, going out the kitchen door.

'What's happening?' said the mammy, following him.

We all jumped up and ran out the door, me following Thelma.

'We have a problem,' said a man looking over the wall from the next-door garden. 'Jasper is trapped up your tree.'

We all looked up, seeing a white cat sitting on a branch high up in the tree.

'That's very high up, isn't it, Thelma?'

'Yeah, it must be about forty feet.'

'How did he get up there?' said the mammy, holding a dishcloth, looking up very worried.

'Can you get a ladder and get up and get him down?' said an aul one with glasses on her nose and thin white hair, pointing her walking stick at the daddy, then up at the tree, sounding very snotty and staring at him, waiting for him te jump up and do her bidding. 'And stop that nasty dog from frightening my Jasper!' she shouted, waving her stick at the dog. 'He caused all this, you know!'

Scrapper was slipping and sliding, flying around the tree, going demented, looking for a way te get at the cat. 'Get in!' the daddy said, making a run at Scrapper, who tore up the garden then came flying back, headbutting the tree and knocking himself out.

'Well, can you get him down?' said the skinny man with the thin fair hair and the thick glasses, wearing a brown V-neck jersey with yellow bars on it. The kind grandads wear, not aul fellas like him in their forties.

'No! I can't do dat,' said the daddy, shaking his head, looking up at the cat. 'It's far too dangerous. But I would be willing teh lend yeh a ladder and yeh can have a go yerself. But I wouldn't advise it!'

'Don't you dare step up on that ladder, Frederick! I will not have it!' screamed the aul one. 'You might fall and hurt yourself.'

'So it's OK if I climb a ladder and break my neck! Is dat what yeh're saying, Mrs O'Brien?'

'Your dog is responsible for terrifying my Jasper in the first place and driving the poor boy up that tree. He lives in terror of that thing; it's totally out of control,' she roared, whipping her head te the dog, snorting at it, then folding her hands and leaning on her stick, looking mournfully up at the cat.

'Well! If dat's the case,' said the daddy, 'yeh can go and . . .'

'Maybe I should have a go,' said the skinny man, throwing his leg over the wall.

'Don't you dare go near that tree, Jonathan! If you fall and break your neck, who is going to take care of me?' she screamed, giving him a whack of the stick on the leg. He whipped it back quickly, rubbing it like mad. 'I am an invalid,' she barked at the daddy, 'and Jasper and I are devoted to each other. Now! It is your garden and your tree my poor Jasper is trapped in. What's wrong with you? Surely you are capable of getting on a ladder and lifting my poor Jasper to safety? A fine strong man like you,' she trailed off, while the daddy and the rest of us all stood looking up the tree, listening te the silence, with the stars shining and the frost on the grass, and the dog staggering over te lie on the grass beside the mammy, not knowing what hit him.

Suddenly we all jumped with the sound of explosions as Joseph came flying out in his cowboy suit, shooting his caps up at the cat, shouting, 'We can scare him outa the tree, Daddy! Bang, bang.'

The dog tore inta the house and the cat screamed, leaping up on the branch and arching his back, showing his teeth and clawing the branch.

'Help! He's going to be killed!' screamed the aul one, waving her stick at the cat then turning it on Joseph. 'Stop that racket! You horrible people! I'm going to go in and call the guards this minute!' And she turned on her stick, making for the house.

'Mammy!' shouted the aul fella. 'Wait! Don't leave, that will only make things worse,' he screamed, wringing his hands and shivering over at us.

'Come on!' shouted the daddy. 'Let's all go inside and leave the bloody cat alone. He can make his own way down. He got up, so he can come back down the same way.'

'I have the answer,' said the grandad, dragging out a long hosepipe and shooting water up at the cat.

'Stop! Stop that at once,' screamed the aul fella, throwing his leg over the wall. 'Mammy! Help! Poor Jasper! You'll send him flying out of the tree!'

'Dat's the idea,' said the grandad, trying te aim the water at the top branch, but it wasn't far enough and rained down on us.

'Aaah! We're getting soaked,' screamed Thelma and the mammy.

'Come on! No more of dis nonsense!' the daddy roared, waving the lot of us in the door. He put his hand on my back and grabbed hold of Thelma, while the mammy wrestled Joseph for the guns.

'Put the hose away, yeh old fool,' shouted the granny from the back door, standing in her stocking feet, glaring at the lot of us and waving her arms in disgust. 'Did yeh ever see the like of it in yure whole life?' she muttered te the air. 'All dis fuss and bother over a bloody aul cat.'

We all tramped back inta the house, with the mammy shouting at us te wipe our shoes on the mat outside the door. I went back out and shoved me feet up and down, laughing te Thelma, who was roaring her head laughing.

'I could have shot him outa that tree, Daddy!' said Joseph quietly, talking te the daddy.

'Yeah! And that aul hag would have the lot of us up for murder,' snorted the daddy, looking back over the wall te the aul fella shouting, 'Come back! What about Jasper?'

'Feck you! And yure bloody Jasper!' snorted the daddy, slamming the back door shut as Scrapper trailed in, holding his head te the ground, still feeling dazed. 'Come on, let's eat!' said the daddy, sitting down te the tea.

'Brrrr, it's brass-monkey weather out dere,' the grandad shivered, taking a bite of his sandwich and looking down at his wet trousers.

'Dere's no fool like an old fool!' barked the granny, throwing a dirty look over at him. 'Take dem trousers off yeh quick, before yeh catch yure death a cold, Paidir Murphy!'

'I will when I've finished me tea,' he mumbled, his jaws working up and down trying te chew a mouthful of meat. His teeth kept falling out, and he lost his patience, whipping them out with a load of bread stuck te them.

I looked away, feeling me stomach turn.

'Ah, stop that aul carry-on! Either get dem teeth fitted properly or go without,' shouted the granny, looking away in disgust.

Everyone laughed, looking at the grandad wiping the teeth with the sleeve of his jumper. Then we heard sirens and we were wondering where the fire was. 'It sounds very close,' said the mammy, looking at us, listening. Then the hall doorbell rang, and rang again. Someone was keeping their finger on the bell.

The daddy got a shock and moved slowly te the door, opening it, then seeing the lights flashing through the stained-glass door.

'Jesus! What's happening now?' he mumbled in fright.

'Go on! Open it and find out,' said the mammy, not moving herself, wanting him te go.

'We have a distress call from number eighty-three,' said a man's voice. 'You have a cat stuck up your tree. They're just passing a ladder across now and up to the tree, is that all right?'

'Oh, go ahead! By all means,' said the daddy, looking at the big fireman with the yellow hat on his head and the hatchet in his hand and the big boots with the black rubber suit. 'Do yeh need me for anything?' the daddy said.

'No, I think we can manage, thanks for the offer,' said the fireman, heading out te the truck, with the lights flashing and men running around, grabbing down the ladders.

'Right so,' said the daddy as we all rushed te the hall door te get a look. The woman stood outside, directing the men with the long ladders and pointing them with her stick te the back garden and giving us all a dirty look.

We rushed back in, making for the kitchen window, with me tearing in behind the granny in her bare feet, with her toes curled up, running on her heels, forgetting about her bunions in all the excitement. Scrapper was doing circles in the air with rage, wanting te get outa the kitchen te take lumps outa whoever was at the front door, then tearing for the back door with all the excitement going on there.

'Look! They've thrown a big light across,' shouted the mammy, and the tree was lit up like the middle of a summer's day! The cat was shivering up the top of the tree and showing his teeth and crying like mad. The ladder went up, and a fireman went climbing up and tried te grab hold of the cat, moving his arms out slowly, taking hold of it, just as it sprang through his closing arms, flying through the air and landed on the high back wall. It stood with its back arched, hissing, then took off flying inta the garden next door, and we could hear the firemen saying, 'There you go, Missus. Safe and sound.'

'I told yeh! I told dat aul hag next door! The bloody cat was in no danger whatsoever! Would yeh believe that? Wasting dem poor men's time bringing dem out on a night like tonight. Oh, she's a selfish bloody aul cow! Dere's no mistaking dat!' screamed the daddy, losing his head altogether, whipping down the curtain, while we laughed like hyenas.

'Calm down, Daddy, you'll give yourself a heart attack!' laughed the mammy, looking at the daddy's face turning purple with the rage.

'And teh boot, blaming our Scrapper!' he said, looking at the dog, who stopped headbutting the back door at the mention of his name.

CHAPTER 18

'Here we are,' said the daddy, slowing down as we hit the big black gates left wide open for people coming back after the Christmas holidays.

Me heart sank seeing the sight of the dark avenue, with the big old trees leaning over making me feel they were going te trap me back inside again.

'Did you enjoy yourself, Martha?' the mammy said, looking at me, her eyes turning sad.

'Yeah! More than I can tell ye!' I said, thinking happiness is grand, but it's always followed by a worse feeling of misery when it ends. Me stomach was feeling sick at the thought of facing back inta work and having no one te talk te. Not in the way I could talk with the family. I didn't need te say much, but when I did they all looked at me and listened, and they made me feel I was somebody who mattered. Here, the kids just ignore ye or give ye dirty looks, or keep snapping and tormenting each other. I spend me days with the nuns, getting on with me work, watching them creep past me, lost in their own world and only smiling at ye if ye do something for them. Most of the time they look haunted and hunted. Fucking Jaysus! This place would put years on ye!

A car whirled around in front of us, the tyres skidding and making a crunching noise on the gravel, then slowed down, pulling te a stop outside the door. 'There's the Reverend Mother,' smiled the mammy, looking up at the aul biddy holding open the front door. Me heart missed a beat watching her letting the young one pass through with her suitcase, smiling down at her and waving over at the people in the big black car, looking like butter wouldn't melt in her mouth.

'I better go in,' I said, taking the suitcase from the daddy, not knowing what else te say te them.

'You take care of yourself, pet,' the mammy waved. 'You were a pleasure to have. We're going to miss you,' she smiled, looking out the open window of the car.

'Yeah! I'm going te miss the lot of ye's, too,' I said, waving at Thelma, who was looking out the window with a half smile on her face.

'I'll miss you, Martha. It's a pity we're not sisters,' she said, making me want te cry.

'Thanks again for having me,' I mumbled te the daddy, keeping me head down and heading for the steps. I stopped and turned around, looking at them all waving out the car window at me, and waved back, giving them a big smile, keeping down the flood of tears wanting te erupt inside me. I turned away and headed in the front door, flicking me eyes up at the Reverend Mother, giving her a smile and rushing past her, saying, 'Thank you, Mother.'

'Yes! So did you have a nice Christmas, then?' she asked me, waving at the people and smiling.

'Yes, Mother, very nice, thank you,' I said, heading down the passage, wanting te make for the dormitory, not in the mood te talk te anyone.

'How're ye, Long? Did you get anything nice for Christmas?' asked Dilly Nugent, feasting her greedy eyes on me, looking down at me suitcase.

'Yeah, loads a things,' I said, flicking me eyes over her, seeing her eyes flash, hoping she'd get something offa me, or they'd rob it if ye don't give it te them. Bleeding robbers some of them are, I thought, thinking of me blue cardigan. I'm not saying a word about that. They would laugh their heads off, silly cows.

'Wait until you see what I got, girls,' she said, hiking her suitcase up onta the bed. She held up a long knitted scarf with loads of different colours that wrapped around her neck and went down te her legs. 'It's a maxi scarf; it will go with the new reefer jacket my godmother bought me. Wait until you see it, girls!'

'Oh, show us, and I can't wait until you see what my godmother bought me!' cackled Pasty-face, with the beady eyes jumping in her head, getting herself all excited over nothing.

'Loretta! Come on, come over here. Look! She's back, girls. Show us what you got.'

'Hi, yeah, girls! Oh, wait until you hear all about my Christmas holiday, girls,' gushed Loretta, throwing her suitcase on the bed, looking like the cat that got the cream. 'We went to the Shelbourne Hotel for our dinner one night. It was my godmother's birthday, and all the family turned up.'

'Ooh, wait until you see what they bought me. I had the time of my life,' screamed Olivia Ryan. 'You should have seen the amount of presents under the tree for me. Here! Look at this!' She held up a gorgeous cream sweater and a pink dressing gown with a matching nightdress the same colour and fluffy pink slippers.

'Ohhh! That's gorgeous,' they all screeched.

'No! That's not all! Wait until you see the rest of my stuff.'

'Girls! Look at mine!' screamed Dilly Nugent.

I had had enough. Not wanting te bother me head about what they got, I walked off, landing me suitcase on the bed and put everything folded carefully away in me locker, taking out me night things. I flew inta the dressing-room in me nightdress and brushed me teeth, wanting te get meself inta the bed and cover up me head, not wanting te think any more about being back in this place and having te get up early for Mass and start work again. That's what's on me mind, I thought te meself. Te hell with them and their fancy godmothers. I had me family, and they may be culchies, probably not good enough for the likes of them. But they suited me, and I'm not opening me mouth te give them ammunition te make a laugh of me. Especially if they find out about the granny's cardigan. Definitely not!

'What did you get, Long?' Loretta shouted up te me.

'Yeah! Show us what you got,' they all said, staring up at me bed, wondering where me stuff was.

'Ah, I'm not in the mood. Sorry, girls, I'm tired, I want te get te sleep.'

'Aah! Long got nothing! They probably gave her a box of talcum powder if she was lucky!' Dilly Nugent shouted, laughing at the rest of them.

'Yeah! She's a right gom! Sister Eleanor probably got her an old-age pensioner to keep her company for the Christmas,' cackled Olivia Ryan. 'She knows Long is a right eejit.'

Fuck you all! I'm not rising te the bait, I thought, jumping inta me bed and ignoring them. They forgot about me as more came slamming through the door, shouting about what they got and the great time they had. So did I! If I had gone with the President of Ireland, they would have still found fault with me, and I couldn't have had a better time than I did. So fuck them, I'm saying nothing.

Everyone stood around Sister Eleanor all shouting at the same time. 'Sister! Can you give me another shilling out of my holiday money you're holding for me?' shouted Dilly Nugent.

'Stop shouting,' said Sister Eleanor, screwing her face up at the noise.

I stood back, quietly waiting, wearing me green coat, and not wanting te get left behind. This is the first time she let me out for a whole year since the first and last time I got te go te the Legion of Mary club in the city centre. The last time I went I got so excited at being let loose I hung out the window of the bus shouting me head off at all the passers-by. The big young ones said I made such a holy show of them, the nun wouldn't let me out until now. So I'm staying very quiet and keeping well outa trouble.

'You look a right eejit in that coat!' muttered Dilly Nugent, swinging her head around and landing her eyes on me coat. 'Look at the state of her, girls,' she whispered, with her hand over her mouth so Sister Eleanor wouldn't hear.

'Fuck off, Nugent! If I looked as ugly as you, I would drown meself,' I muttered through me teeth. 'You look like the hunchback of Notre Dame! Fucking Quasimodo!'

'Who're you calling a hunchback?' screamed Nugent, giving me a push.

I landed a kick on her arse as she turned back te roar at Sister Eleanor, 'Did you hear what she just called me, Sister Eleanor?' Then she turned back te try and land a punch at me.

'Keep yer hands te yerself!' I roared.

'Stop, the pair of you!' screamed Sister Eleanor, landing a clatter on me shoulder and glaring at me. 'One more word out of you, madam, and you will go straight to bed!' she roared, pointing her finger in me face.

Nugent shook her head at me behind the nun's back and stuck her tongue out, crossing her eyes and laughing.

'Stop it, Dilly, like a good girl,' said Sister Eleanor, twisting her face and looking like she had eaten something sour.

Fuck Sister Eleanor, she makes a pet of her and a fool of me. 'Ye better tell that one te keep her hands te herself or I'll put manners on her, Sister Eleanor. I'm warning ye,' I snorted, feeling the heat a me rage race through me belly.

'Uhhhh,' they all screamed, laughing their heads off.

'She's going to put manners on you, Dilly, you should be shaking with the fear,' Olivia Ryan jeered.

'That's enough! This is your last warning, Martha Long! One more word,' she said, wagging her finger in me face, moving close enough for me te smell her breath and get the whiff of mothballs off her habit.

I moved back, looking away from her, deciding te keep quiet, and feeling meself go cold. There's more than one way te skin a cat! My turn will come, I thought te meself.

'Now, you must be back no later than nine forty-five. If you are back any later, you will all be punished and won't be going out to the club next week. Now remember, I will be waiting up for you, and please come up the avenue quietly. I don't want you making noise and waking the nuns in the convent.'

'No, Sister Eleanor,' they all shouted.

Then we were out the door and walking down the avenue. I trailed behind, keeping me distance, happy with me own company, just glad te be getting out. The bus landed us on O'Connell Street and we walked across te the Gresham Hotel, heading up te Parnell Street and turning right then left onta North Great George's Street. We passed the old Georgian houses with railings around them and steps up te a heavy door. We went down the steps te the basement, and fellas passing called out, 'How're ye, young ones?'

They all looked back up and Dilly Nugent shouted, 'How're you, Anto? Come on, girls!' and they all tittered and went back up the steps.

I looked up at the two skinny goughers with the shifty look in their eyes and the sneer on their ugly mugs, with their jaws hanging open, shaking their heads and giving each other the eye. Not believing anyone would even look at them, never mind run te talk te them! I kept going down the steps. Pair of chancers, I sniffed te meself. They're welcome te them! Fellas like that will suit them down te the ground: beat the shite outa them and won't work in a good fit! It takes one eejit te know another.

I pushed the door in, seeing the faces of the women all looking around at me, smiling and coming over te welcome me. 'Hello! How are you?' beamed an aul one with a long skirt and thick nylons like Matron Millington wears, and stone-grey hair clipped back behind her ears like a schoolgirl. I stared at the dandruff covering her black cardigan, getting a musty smell as she laid her hand on me shoulder and lowered her red face with purple veins so close te me I couldn't see her properly; me eyes were crossing.

I moved back, saying, 'Thanks for having us, Sister. I couldn't wait te get here!' And kept moving back, pretending I was looking around the place.

'Ohh!' she gushed, coming at me again and grabbing me shoulder, pulling me inta her. 'Oh, Sister Brigid! We have a new girl. Isn't she wonderful?'

'Ohh! Isn't that marvellous!' screamed Brigid. 'You are so welcome!' A tall skinny aul one wearing a greasy long frock with flat black shoes and a strap across that went outa fashion with the Indians back in the 1930s. Jaysus! The state of her, I thought, watching her flying over te grab me hands, saying, 'Now! You have been sent to us by our Holy Mother, Our Lady!' Then she blessed herself, saying, 'Sister! It is such a blessing Our Blessed Lady has bestowed on us. She is answering our special intentions for new recruits. Sending us lovely new young girls. We must say an extra decade of the rosary to give thanks!' Then she bent down and stared inta me face, showing me her yella teeth and a red-raw face that looked like she used a scrubbing brush on it.

That face never saw paint or powder in its life, I thought, staring at her. Even her lips are white for the want of a bit of colour.

'We will offer up our prayers also for your special intentions. Now, is that not a wonderful thing?'

'No,' I said, looking at her face, wondering why she is getting all confused. 'Eh, I can't wait te start praying, Sister!'

'Yes! Of course!' she breathed, the smile coming back to her face. 'Do you have any special intentions you would like us to mention?'

'Eh, yeah . . .' I was trying te think, 'I do,' I said, me face lighting up at the thought of praying fat Dilly Nugent and the rest of her gang would end up splattered under a bus on O'Connell Street.

'Well, we shall pray specially for your intentions,' she breathed, tapping me gently on me shoulder and shaking her head slowly, raising her eyes up te Holy Mary. 'Oh, now what is your name, dear? Are you from the convent?'

'Yeah.'

'Oh, I thought . . . Where are the rest of the girls?' she said, looking at the window, hearing them cackle with the fellas up on the footpath.

'They are up there talking te the fellas, the ones hanging around on the corners,' I sniffed, looking disgusted. 'The nuns wouldn't allow that,' I said. 'No! Especially as Dilly Nugent seems te know him very well. I heard her asking him when did he get outa the reformatory school! The other fella, the older one, laughed and said he just got outa Mountjoy Prison after robbing an old lady's handbag in the church . . . while she was praying!'

'No!' she gasped.

'They're not allowed te talk te fellas, never mind criminals like them,' I snorted, wondering what she was going te do about it.

'Indeed not!' said the woman, lifting her head and shaking her shoulders, making straight for the door.

'Hello! Are you a new girl?' a woman asked me, with black-and-grey straight hair cut te her ears and parted te the side, clipped back off her face, like another old-age pensioner who still thinks she's a girl. More bleeding 'nuns if they could be', so the next best thing is te live in the world but keep away from the men and pray all the time, and hit women with their rosary beads when they go astray, chasing after the men.

'Please come in and don't stay out there talking to those boys,' said the woman, sounding very annoyed but getting nowhere with the girls.

'Yeah! We'll be in any minute now,' shouted the girls, laughing and going back te their business of trying te get off with the fellas.

'They are acting like strumpets!' snorted the woman, coming back in holding her fists down by her sides then changing her face inta a smile and making for me.

'Yeah! Strumpets!' I said. 'But ye wouldn't catch me talking te any man.'

'No,' she breathed. 'You are a lovely girl; I can see that straight away,' she said, leaning her hand on me arm.

'I haven't told the nuns yet,' I whispered, breathing inta her and smelling mints off her breath.

'Yes?' she said, all ears, giving me one, cocking her head te the side.

'I am thinking of becoming a nun,' I breathed.

'Oh, how wonderful!' she said, holding her chest and her breath.

'Yes, Sister! But not just any order. I am thinking of entering the Brown Carmelites, an enclosed order. Naturally I will be taking a perpetual vow of silence.'

'Ohhhh, the beauty of it! You will devote your life entirely to prayer!'

'Yes, Sister. I have been practising by not speaking te the other girls. I came in te see you holy ladies in complete silence tonight!'

'Ohhhh!' she gasped, getting weak at the knees.

I stared at her watery faded-blue eyes misting over at the thought of me being so holy. 'Would you like a cup of tea and some biscuits?' she said, putting her arm on me shoulder, and I could even smell the mothballs coming off her, too. The black jumper had patches on the elbows. Jaysus! These aul ones would put years on ye, I thought, feeling I was dead and buried already.

'Yeah, thanks, Sister,' I said, heading over te the table with the plates of biscuits, while the pensioner with the sweetie-pie smile leaned her face inta me, handing me a white cup and saucer with strong-looking yellow tea.

'Would you like a biscuit?' she said, holding out a plate of mixed biscuits, with Kimberley and custard creams and plain Marietta.

'Yes, please!' I said, taking the plate, finding it too hard te choose and wanting the lot. Fuck them. They didn't bother their arse coming in, so I'm going te eat me way through the lot.

'Yes, em, we do have more,' she said, smiling at me, creasing her face up and leaning her head over at me.

I grinned back, saying, 'The girls are probably not in the mood

for biscuits anyway, Sister. They have more important things on
their mind.'

'Hm! We shall see about that,' said the woman, glaring at the
window, hearing the cows laughing their heads off at probably
nothing.

'We are ready to read the minutes of the last meeting,' said
one of the other women, coming over and whispering, wringing
her hands and looking very worried. 'The girls care not a jot for
what we say to them, Sister Brigid! What shall we do?' she said,
swinging her head around at all the women organising their prayer
books and rosary beads, and big books of the minutes probably,
and putting new religious pamphlets inta the bookshelves.

'Goodness! We shall be very late getting the rosary started,
Sister Maeve,' worried another grey-haired aul one, who was
probably only in her thirties but made Matron Millington
look more in the fashion compared with the get-up she was
wearing.

'Come in here right this minute, girls, or I shall ring the
convent and speak to the Reverend Mother.'

I listened te them shouting back they were coming and giving
out like mad, not wanting te leave the fellas. I looked up, seeing
more pairs a trousers, and said, 'It looks like a gang of young
fellas up there, Sister. I think ye should do something. I think
the girls may be in great danger!' I muffled through a mouthful
of biscuits, trying te make short work of the lot, not wanting te
leave any for the fat cows.

'Oh dear! You may be right,' shivered the Sister with the hair
plastered back with the clips.

'They are not used te being out in the world,' I said, shaking
me head in terrible fear for their souls. 'They could be lost, lose
their souls and end up like Saint Maria Goretti, getting themselves
killed trying te protect their virginity!'

'Oh my goodness! Go out at once and tell them to come in
here!'

'Who? Me?'

'Yes! You are one of them, they will listen to you, surely?'

'No, they can't stand me,' I said, looking very woebegone. 'They certainly won't, Sister. They laugh at me because I get up at the crack of dawn and go te Mass every morning. They jeer me for that, Sister,' I sniffed, looking very sad.

'Tut, tut! They are dreadful girls; look at them, Sisters. Brazen hussies! I intend to report them to the Reverend Mother at the first opportunity,' she huffed, looking out the window at their legs standing close te the trousers. That's all we could see, and hear the laughing and the pushing and shoving.

'Oh, brazen hussies, Sisters,' I said, shaking me head very sadly and looking at them piously. 'It might be a good idea if we go te a phone box and ring the Reverend Mother right away,' I said. 'You never know, they might just get it inta their head te go off with them dangerous-looking fellas! Ye could be doing them a great favour in the long run. Saving them from hellfire and damnation!'

I could get no good outa the aul ones. They stood staring at me after going inta shock. 'It is yer duty as a . . . Legion of Mary!'

'Ohhhh, what will we do?' they whispered, hardly any strength left in them, standing like planks, staring at me with me mouth open, getting no movement outa them.

'I know the phone number,' I said te the silence, looking from one te the other, hopeful of getting the fat cows inta trouble.

'No! If we make a complaint, then they would not be allowed out again, then we would lose them,' yer woman with the red face said, squinting her eyes, calculating the loss and profit te herself.

I went over te the table and put down the empty plate, picking up a full one and asking the woman staring at me helping meself te more biscuits off the last remaining plate and piling them on me own, 'Could I have another drop a tea, Sister, please, thanks!'

'Eh, yes,' she said, staring at me plate, wanting te tell me te put half of them back.

'I can't wait te start the rosary,' I said, leaning inta her with a big smile, me cheeks bulging with biscuits.

'Eh, yes!' she beamed, cheering up at the thought of all the prayers we were going te say.

'And two sugars, Sister, thanks,' I said, slipping the last of the biscuits off the plate onta me own.

CHAPTER 19

'Gawd! Do you think the Legion of Mary will report us to the nuns?' worried Dilly Nugent, biting her lip then examining her little finger, biting that, too.

'Oh gawd, we'll really be in for it,' moaned Pasty-face, staring with her beady eyes stretching outa her face. For once ye could actually see the colour of them. They're muddy grey.

'What will we say if they do, girls? Say it was one of the altar boys that come in to serve Mass in our place?' croaked the Jane Mary one, flicking her lovely long blonde hair back from her shoulders and throwing a look over te see if the fellas standing outside the Gresham Hotel hoping te pick themself up a young one were maybe giving her the eye.

'Look at him! He's a fine thing,' she muttered te the others, hoarse from all the laughing and shouting at what the gobshite good-for-nothing eejit young fellas were saying.

She has no sense. Otherwise she wouldn't even look at them wasters, I thought te meself, giving a look back and seeing the bus coming just as we passed the Gresham Hotel. 'Come on girls, run!' I said, flying past, hearing them say, 'No! We won't catch that, it's going too fast.'

'Come on! Run! We're nearly at the bus stop!' I shouted back, flying for the bus, seeing it pass me and hearing the young ones laughing.

Just as I got te the bus stop, it took off, and I dropped me head, steaming out me chest, throwing me shoulders back and taking off after the bus, running like the wind. The conductor watched me from the platform, seeing I was not going te give up, and belted the bell just as I lunged out te grab hold of the bar. The driver thought he meant they were off, and took up speed. I could hear the young ones going hysterical, laughing their guts out. I couldn't afford te let go now. I grabbed the bar, trying te settle meself te get me right leg up, but the bus went faster. I held onta the bar, hopping up and down, running on thin air now, me legs flying, hardly hitting the ground. Then he gave another four hard bongs and the bus spluttered and screeched and slowed down so suddenly I shot inta the bar, winding me. But I wouldn't let go. I was still running at the full speed and leapt onta the bus, flying across the platform. I couldn't stop meself running, and smacked against the end seat, and the bus stopped with a jerk, and I was flying back down the bus again te land sprawled at the feet of the conductor, with me head hanging off the platform.

'Jaysus! I dreamed about tha happenin te me! Havin women land at me feet. Were ye that excited te see me?' he breathed, looking down at me knees covered in blood and me white socks ripped and filthy. 'But ye didn't have te put life and limb at risk,' he said, bending down te put me standing on me feet. 'It's nice ye were so anxious te see me, but not this way!' he said, looking down at me and seeing the young ones wrapped around each other trying te stop themself from collapsing with all their laughing and seeing the conductor looking at the state a me.

'Here! Are ye all right?' he said, lifting me leg te get a look at me knees, looking at me lovely white socks covered in blood and dirt. He took a white hanky outa his pocket and started spitting on it, wiping me knees, while I held me leg up, holding onta the bars.

'Jaysus, you young ones are always in a hurry,' he muttered. I watched the gang getting closer and wished he'd bang the bell, not wanting te half kill meself for nothing.

'Hey, Conductor, wait for us,' they shouted just as the

conductor let me leg drop, telling me te go inside and take it easy. Then he banged the bell and we were off, leaving the others stranded.

I limped off down te sit at the back of the bus, not wanting people staring at me after making a holy show of meself.

I walked up the avenue in the pitch black, listening te the trees whispering in the wind and thought they were people hiding in the bushes. I stopped te listen, holding me breath. No! It's only the wind, I said te meself slowly, letting go of me breath and moving meself off. I hurried up the avenue, giving a shiver passing the old graveyard that's over beyond the high wall with ivy growing on it. The monks who had this place over two hundred years ago are buried in there. Once they came through them gates they never saw the world again and were locked up for good. Ye could only visit them by passing gifts in through a little grill in the door, and ring the bell first, te let them know someone was leaving something. Or ye could speak te them through a grill if ye got a special appointment, and that was only te the Abbot. I read about that in a book in the convent library. Me chest leapt with the jump me heart gave thinking about it. Now of all times. Jaysus! Some of them could be on the prowl! Who says the dead don't come back? I started running, working meself inta a terrible sweat by the time I banged on the back door.

'Yes! Who is that?' whispered Sister Eleanor.

'It's me! Martha! Let me in, Sister Eleanor,' I squealed, not wanting te be left out here in the dark with all them trees and bushes around, the January cold wind blowing around me legs.

'Where are the others?' she whispered, looking around behind me.

'They're not here, Sister.'

'What! Where are they?'

'In O'Connell Street,' I said, flying past her inta the light and the heat in the room.

She closed the door quietly, looking very annoyed. 'Why did they not come back with you?'

'Because I saw the bus coming and ran for it.'

'Well, really! How dare they?'

'But, Sister, I ran fast!'

'Exactly! And they could have done the same,' she snorted, getting very annoyed and picking up her sewing, getting back te her embroidery, saying, 'When they come back here, I will certainly have words with them.'

'Yeah! And they drove the poor Legion of Mary wom . . . Sisters mad!'

'What? What do you mean?' she said, her eyes narrowing, looking te the door te see if anyone was going te appear, then leaning inta me, giving me all her attention.

'Well,' I said, sitting back in me armchair, making meself comfortable and covering me knees, 'the Sisters were going te telephone the Reverend Mother!'

'What?' She nearly lost her mind. 'What were they doing?' she asked, gasping, hardly able te get a breath.

I took in a deep breath, staring back at her, shaking me head thinking of the shocking behaviour of the lot of them, then let it out slowly through me nose, hearing the sound of it, and took in another breath while she waited, holding hers and trying te be patient. 'They were gadding about, Sister, with men!'

'Gadding about?'

'Yes!' Using the word she always uses. 'Chasing men! A big gang of them came around the club te mess with the girls, and the girls were hanging outa them and . . . that's all I can say, Sister! The Legion of Mary Sisters were in fear; they said that something dreadful might happen te the girls' virtue. There was mention of what happened te Maria Goretti, the saint who was murdered!'

Sister Eleanor's eyes were turning in her head as she listened, and the colour of her face went from red te purple te grey, and she was up on her feet and opening the door and saying, 'Come quickly, Martha. We must find them.' Then she lifted up her rosary beads and started te pray. 'Oh, Divine Jesus, protect them and keep them from all harm,' she prayed, turning her head te the stars.

I trotted beside her, delighted te be walking in the dark with her all te meself, having her give me all the attention. 'We will walk down to the gate to see if there is any sign of them,' she said, looking inta the distance, hoping against hope they would appear.

I knew the gobshites were all well and fine – it's hard te kill a bad thing – but Sister Eleanor worries and fusses about nothing. 'No! Not a sign of them,' she said, looking down along the high wall of the convent, trying te picture them walking back from the village. 'Come on! We will have to go back to the convent. If only they had come back with you.'

'Yes,' I sighed, staring at her in the dark, making the same face as her.

We shook our heads up and down, then she started te lose the rag again. 'When they come back, I will have something to say to them!' she vowed, grinding her teeth and shaking her head, working herself inta a fit. Then she marched off, heading back te the convent, leaving me looking at thin air.

'Wait, Sister Eleanor, take it easy,' I shouted in a whisper, not wanting her te start getting so annoyed she'd end up giving out te me, and that would be the end of all the attention I'm getting.

We sat back down in the comfort of the chairs and the warm room, with me giving an exact picture of what went on in the club, with me the only one of the convent girls saying the rosary, the others all enjoying themselves no end outside on the street. Sister Eleanor sat listening te every word, narrowing her eyes when we got te the juicy bit where Dilly Nugent was hanging outa the fella with the long greasy hair. 'And he was very, very common, Sister! Very rough altogether! It was shocking te watch their behaviour. And I thought it was a very bad example te me, as I am younger than them and was banned for a whole year for less! But I couldn't possibly tell ye what else they were doing with the fellas, because, well, it wasn't very nice at all. I don't think they will be welcome in the club again, because the Legion of Mary were terribly shocked! They never saw the like of it in their life from the previous generation of convent girls, that's what they said. So I can't say any more, Sister! They would know it was me . . . and, it's not for me te say, Sister. Ye better ask them. No! I better keep outa it,' I said, looking at her, me face as shocked as hers.

We heard footsteps, then laughing. Sister Eleanor was on her feet, dropping her sewing, and she whipped open the door before they got near it.

'Sister Eleanor! Oh gawd, wait until you hear what that Martha Long one did. It was a scream! We never laughed so much!'

'How dare you come back here at this time?'

'Wha . . .'

'Get in!' barked Sister Eleanor.

'What are you talking about? We just got off the bus now!'

'Yes! And why were you not back with this child? She's been sitting here with me for the last hour and a half!'

They looked at me, confused, trying te make out what the nun was talking about. Then it hit them. 'Oh, yeah! Wait till we tell you what she did running for the bus!'

'Yes! She got the bus, you lot didn't, and I'm left sitting here in the cold late at night when I could be in my bed. But no! You choose to come waltzing back in here just when it suits you lot! Now, get up to your beds at once! And there will be no more gallivanting for any of you for some time to come. You are all grounded!'

'What? You can't do that! We did nothing! What did we do?'

'I am not going to argue with you! Now please get moving at once, or if you try my patience for one more time you will all sorely regret it!'

'We didn't miss the bus!' they all screamed, trying te figure out what was really happening and looking at me te see if I could throw any light on all the confusion.

I stood with me arms folded and me eyebrows raised, waiting

like Sister Eleanor for the explanation as te why they were not on the bus with me.

'Tell her, Martha Long! Did you tell her you ran for the bus?'

'Of course I did,' I said, in a quiet whisper, sounding like Sister Eleanor. 'I warned you girls the bus was coming, remember?'

'Yeah, but . . .'

'Yes! She certainly did!' barked Sister Eleanor. 'And you lot should have done the same. If that child could catch the bus, then why were you not on it?'

'But how could we?' they said, giving out, muttering, looking at each other, wondering where they went wrong.

'That bloody Long is a noticebox!' Dilly Nugent shouted, glaring at me, seeing me sitting here with Sister Eleanor, in the goody-goody books, and her not being able te figure out how it all went wrong.

'Yeah,' they all bleated, sounding like sheep. 'She got here first te get all the attention.'

'How dare you?' barked Sister Eleanor, giving them a clatter.

'Aaah! I hate you! I hate this place! Bloody rotten dirty filthy noticebox Long!' screamed Nugent, rubbing her ear.

'Gawd, Ellie! You're an awful bully,' wailed Blondie, moving herself quick outa harm's way, giving a nervous-dog look outa the corner of her eye.

'How dare you treat me with such disrespect? You girls are going to be severely punished for this. Now get moving,' and she started heaving them up the passage, clattering them when she could land her hand, and I kept nose in the air, trailing behind Sister as she looked around at me shocked, muttering, 'The audacity of these girls! The cheek of them to behave in this fashion!'

'Tut, tut! Shocking, Sister!' I agreed, shaking me head sadly, with me goody-goody face on.

'You're a big old noticebox,' screamed Dilly, looking back at me, rubbing her back where she got another clatter.

I raised me eyebrows, crossing me eyes and sticking out me tongue.

'Look at what she's doing, Sister Eleanor!' screamed Nugent, going red in the face with the rage on her. 'She's making faces behind your back.'

'I most certainly am not!' I breathed, outa breath at the idea of doing such a thing, listening te meself sounding exactly like Sister Eleanor.

'That is enough auld guff out of you,' barked Sister Eleanor, herding them along the passage, mumbling she should be in her bed, and wrapping her hands under her cloak, looking frostbitten. 'I will attend to you girls in the morning.'

Yeah, and I have more surprises up me sleeve for you lot! Ye're not going te know what hit ye's! I told meself.

'Out! And you and you,' Sister Eleanor snorted, herding the lot of them outa the refectory, grabbing the eggs off them. 'You are not getting that for your breakfast,' she said, grabbing Dilly Nugent's eggcup with the egg sitting in it.

'What? What's going on? Leave me alone,' screamed Nugent, as Eleanor grabbed her and pushed her inta Blondie, grabbing the rest of them.

'I am now taking action for last night's capers. You are all out of the group,' she snorted, putting a snout on her, making her nose go longer and her eyes look like a bloodhound, red and sad. Then she was back, shutting the door on the screams, leaving them te look in the glass panels on the side passage trying te scream in at her. The sound was deadened with the thick walls and we could only see their mouths going up and down, and their faces looking like mustard and mortal sin, as Sister Eleanor calls it. They saw me looking out at them, eating me egg slowly, and sucking on me cheeks, and giving them an awful look, raising me eyebrows and looking away, finding them not quite up te me standards.

'Blah, blah . . . goin to get this, Long!' I heard as they waved their fists at me.

I gave a quick cross-eyed look, flicking me head around, saying, 'Sister, they're threatening te throttle me! Do ye hear them?' I said, pointing at them, letting them see I was reporting them.

They stopped belly-aching for a minute, not believing their eyes. I was actually on the nun's side! Fraternising with the nuns! The enemy! In broad daylight and in front of everyone! That can't happen. If ye do cosy up te the nuns, it has te be in total secret!

'Sister, what did I do that was so wrong? The girls are out for me guts! Did I do the wrong thing? Why are they threatening me?'

'Who's threatening you?'

'They are! Did ye not hear them?' I said, pointing me finger at them, watching their faces hang down te their belly buttons wondering what I was saying about them. And seeing their mouths in action again, glaring at each other, twisting their mouths and squinting their eyes and pointing back at me.

Sister Eleanor flew out at them, pushing them up the passage, telling them they would be punished even more severely. 'I will go straight to the convent and bring the Reverend Mother here at once if you don't move up that passage, and if I hear a whisper out of any of you about that child in there you will all have me to reckon with.'

'What happened?' everyone shouted, looking over at me.

I shrugged me shoulders.

'Go on! Tell us! What did they do?' asked a big one, Johanna Henley, her brown eyes flashing with the excitement of getting te hear something terrible.

'Honestly, Johanna, I wish I knew what was going on. They went te the club . . .'

'Yeah, go on! Tell us!' then the big ones were over in a flash, leaning on me chair, pushing each other outa the way, trying te get a good spot te read me face.

'Well, the bus came. I got on it . . . and they didn't. So Eleanor went mad and now they're all in the doghouse! And they blame me.'

'For what?'

'Ask them!' I said, looking as puzzled as them.

'There must be more than that,' mumbled the head girl, Clarissa Seabert, sucking on her thumb, thinking about it.

The big ones all grouped around her, asking, 'What do you think they were up to, Clarissa?'

I watched, seeing her look back at me, thinking. She's very, very brainy, the only one who could go on te the university if she wanted te. I shook me head at her, making meself look thoughtful. 'Don't know what's going on, Clarissa,' I said, chewing on me bread, trying te make it out. 'Talk to them!'

'Yeah! Don't worry about that. We will!' said Johanna Henley, making it sound like a threat, disappointed she was no wiser.

I wandered down te the back door, knowing it would be locked this hour of the night, but hoping it might be open, even though it was pitch-black out, eight o'clock on a January night. I still wanted te ramble outside and get a bit of fresh air after working all day in the convent. I tried the handle. Locked. I looked down the empty dark passage, feeling empty meself. Work, bed. Nothing in between. I would love te have a bit of a laugh, someone te have a laugh with. But there's no one here I'd bother me arse with. They go around in gangs, keeping te themself, and their idea of fun is te laugh at people. They all have their own cronies. Anyway! They don't interest me. I'm the street kid te them and they're the culchie gobshites te me. Still, there is the brainy one who goes te the secondary school, Ruthie, but she's probably doing her homework. Wonder if there's anyone in the other groups? Nah, too young.

I wandered back down the passage, seeing the light on in our refectory. Then stopped just before I got there, hearing voices. I stopped te listen when I heard the whiny moaney voice of Dilly Nugent. 'Yeah, and I'll bring me bell-bottoms. One of you can hide them under the trees on the avenue.'

'Good idea, and I'll wear my trousers as well,' shouted Blondie in a whisper.

'Now, have we got that? You all know the plan, yeah? After lights out, we . . .'

'OK! We know what to do,' breathed Nugent, moving her chair, getting ready te leave. 'Come on! We'll miss the start of *The Virginian*.'

'No, Ellie said we're punished. We can't go into the television room to watch it.'

'Huh! That one is not going to stop me! We'll sneak in after she switches the television on and make sure she's gone to the convent first. Hannah! You keep watch. Hide around the corner in the toilets.'

'No! What if she catches me? Then I'll be in worse trouble!'

'Don't be so stupid, you gom! You're entitled to go to the toilet, aren't you?'

'Yeah, suppose so,' dopey Hannah said, afraid of her life of upsetting back-of-a-bus-face Nugent.

'Right, Dilly! You go ahead with yer plans, and I'm off te make short work of them,' I muttered. Shit! They're coming! I ducked around the corner, waiting behind the pillar until they came outa the refectory, then dived across inta the laundry passage, closing the door quietly behind me. I heard their footsteps heading up the passage making for the television room, counted te twenty, then another ten for good measure, and put me head up and down the passage. Nobody around! Right!

I made me way slowly up the passage and stood on the stairs, watching Hannah making her way down te the toilets while the others sat in the playroom waiting. With not even the radio te listen te, because they were banned from that, too!

Yep! I'm having a great time! I sniggered te meself, remembering how they got me inta trouble any which way they could, treating me like a leper. Fuckers! See how ye like getting a taste of yer own medicine. Ha! Ye's won't get the better of me! I'm going te enjoy meself no end!

I waited until I heard the rustle of habit and the jangling of rosary beads and flew around the corner, hiding in the cloakroom toilet. When I heard Eleanor flying down the passage with a herd of young ones roaring and hanging outa her, I crept back, waiting and watching, putting me head around the corner. Then I heard the music for *The Virginian* and flew back te me toilet, letting her pass. When she went through the door, heading down the convent passage, I flew out again, listening.

'Dilly! Girls!'

'What? Is she gone?'

'Yeah! Come on, quick! It's starting!'

I heard them flying up the passage and took off like the wind, racing for the convent, trying te catch Sister Eleanor before she buried herself in the chapel. I tore along the chapel passage on tiptoes, used te flying along that way without making a sound, and caught her just as the chapel door hissed closed. I grabbed the door, seeing her genuflect, making for her prie-dieu.

'Sister Eleanor!' I tiptoed in, letting her see me, and she creased her face inta a cry, moaning, 'What is it? Oh, Jesus, Mary and Joseph give me patience!' she muttered, looking up at the ceiling before genuflecting and coming out.

'I think ye should know, Sister Eleanor, Dilly and her lot are gone in te watch *The Virginian*. They think it is a great laugh ye punished them and have no idea you are wasting yer time!'

'WHAT? Do you mean to tell me they are disobeying my strict instructions to them they are not allowed to watch television?'

'Yes, Sister! They're down there right now having the time of their life. It's even more enjoyable te them because they're punished.'

'Get out of my way!' She grabbed up her habit with both fists and took off like a bat flying outa hell, with me flying behind her!

I parted company with her when we hit the passage, and I took off inta me toilet, waiting for the explosion.

'Get up to that dormitory!'

'Gawd! I hate you!'

Slap! 'Don't you dare speak to me like that!'

'YOU THINK YE'RE GOD!'

That's Dilly! I thought, cocking me ear te the door, having the best time of me life!

'You are all banned from watching television for the next month! Up those stairs.'

'GERROFF!'

Slap, wallop! 'Don't you dare shout at me!'

'How did you know we were watching the television in the first place?' screamed Dilly. 'You must have your spies out!'

'Yeah! She has her spies watching us!' shouted Blondie.

'Yeah! You can't stand us, you can't! You really hate us!' screeched Hannah.

'Don't push me, you bully!' – Dilly! Ha!

'Get up those stairs to the dormitory this minute, or I am off to get the Reverend Mother!'

'I don't care!'

Slap, wallop! 'AAAHHH!'

The noise died down as they hit the dormitory. Right, Dilly! I'm saving the best bit for later! Yep! There sure is more than one way te skin a cat, Dilly Nugent!

I wandered outa the playroom, looking for something interesting, or someone! The eejits in there were having a party, slapping each other around on the sofa. I turned up te the stairs and stopped on the landing, hearing voices coming from the toilet, and I could smell smoke. I looked down, seeing it wisp out from under the door and listened. DILLY AND HER GANG! Gawd! This is too much te miss! Thank gawd I gave up the smoking for the last six months. Once Sister Eleanor stopped belting me, and threatening me, and of course blaming me for starting the whole lot of them on the smokes. 'You are the ringleader!' she was screeching at me.

'No! They were smoking leaves from the trees rolled up and

setting fire te it. I was only smoking the real thing. So ye can't say it was all my fault!'

I started on Jackser's Woodbine butts that he used te leave on the mantlepiece. I would wait for him te go up and have his hard-earned rest during the day and light the butt from the fire and blow it up the chimney. I thought it would make me grow up faster! He used te think he was going mad! 'Where's me fuckin butt I left lyin there on the bleedin mantelpiece?' he used te roar at me, then blame the ma, who never put a Woodbine or a drop of alcohol te her lips in her life!

'I didn't touch yer fuckin Woodbines!' me ma screamed back at him.

Then his eyes peeled te Charlie, standin shakin in the short trousers hangin down like curtains, lettin his little matchstick legs stick out.

'No one touched yer butts, Jackser! Remember? Ye smoked it just before ye went up for yer rest!' I reminded him.

'Fuck me! I was sure I'd left a butt sittin on tha mantlepiece!'

Yeah, it was hard going. I was making meself sick as a parrot! But it didn't take me long te get used te them. Then when I got here I used te squeeze meself out through the big letterbox up at the front door and drop head-first, always managing te land on me hands and roll onta me back. Tricks I learned managing te avoid getting a mashing from Jackser's hobnailed boots! There's some good te be had in everything! Yeah, so when Sister Eleanor took me te one side and told me in a very kind and gentle way she was worried the house would go up in fire, and if I set an example, the rest would follow – well, I don't know about them following my example, but I gave up the Woodbines te please her. Now Dilly is definitely not following my example!

Right! Where's Sister Eleanor? . . . I flew like a blue-arse fly, making straight for the convent, tiptoeing like a ballerina along the chapel passage, feeling like air in me excitement te bend Sister's ear with the terrible news.

I flew back with Sister flying behind me. 'Can ye smell it, Sister?' I breathed, whispering in shocked tones before we hit the children's landing. I whipped open the door for her, letting her fly through, and pointed te the toilet before whipping meself down the stairs and making for me hideaway.

'Come out of there at once!'

Silence.

'Who is in there, please?'

Silence.

'Dilly Nugent! I know you are in there! Come out at once!'

Silence.

I crept up, seeing the smoke pouring out from under the door and seeing Sister Eleanor with her face turning purple.

'That is it! I am giving you one minute to come out. If you refuse, then I am going to the convent to get the Reverend Mother!'

Silence.

'That is it!' Then she took off heading for the convent.

I flew inta the playroom. 'Girls! Trouble! Quick!' I shouted te the shocked three young ones trying te strangle each other on the couch.

'What? What's happening?' Olivia Ryan puffed, lifting her head, loosening her grip on Vanessa Andrewson's neck.

'I just heard Sister Eleanor is gone over te the convent te get the Reverend Mother because there's girls smoking in the toilet!'

'Who?'

'Dunno.'

'Gawd! Quick! Let's go!' She was off the couch, slapping Andrewson in the kisser with her feet, and Sylvia Peters toppled head-first te the floor.

'Wait! Wait for me!' they shouted, trying te get themselves moving.

I was up on the landing with the other ones tearing up behind me. Now we can all gawk without me coming under suspicion!

'Who is in there? Sister Eleanor is gone for the Reverend Mother. Quick, come out!'

'Wait! Don't go out there,' whispered Nugent.

'Oh gawd! What am I going to do?' they moaned.

'Is she out there?' asked Dilly through the keyhole.

'No! Come on, girls!'

'No! Are ye sure?'

'No, wait! Someone's coming.'

'Oooh, aaahh! Is it the Reverend Mother?'

We said nothing, waiting for the convent passage door te open. Then the Reverend Mother peeled in with Sister Eleanor creeping in behind her all red-faced.

'Is the Reverend Mother coming?' squeaked Dilly Nugent through the keyhole.

I looked at the Mother's eyes bulging behind her milk-bottle glasses, and wriggling her head, trying te loosen the collar wrapped around her neck, then she exploded. 'COME OUT OF THERE AT ONCE!'

'Who's that?' squeaked Dilly.

'How dare you? This is the Reverend Mother.'

The door opened without another word and they all crept out with their heads hanging te their belly buttons.

'Line up there, please.' She pointed te the wall under the window. 'Sister, would you take these girls away, please.'

We crept off, heading down the stairs, taking our time and looking back, not wanting te miss a thing.

'Go to your playroom, please,' Sister Eleanor said, herding us down te the playroom.

'I need te go te the toilet, Sister,' I said, pushing past her.

'Get into that playroom,' she said.

'But I'm jigging te go,' I said, wrapping me legs around each other.

'Get into the playroom now! Or you will all be punished!'

'What about me?' I shouted te the door shutting in me face.

They all milled around the door, trying te hear the ructions upstairs.

'Shush!' I turned the handle very quietly. 'We'll sneak out and listen at the bottom of the stairs.'

'Yeah!' they tittered, watching the door opening quietly.

I put me head out the door and waved te the others. 'Come on! Quick. Shush! Don't make a sound.'

We crept along the passage, hearing the Reverend Mother tell them, 'There will be major consequences for your actions. I intend dealing with this serious matter by . . .'

'GET BACK INTO THAT PLAYROOM. YOU ARE ALL VERY BOLD FOR DISOBEYING ME!' Sister Eleanor whispered in a roar, running at us.

Aaah! We got such a fright, not expecting her te put her head around the stairs, and took off back te the playroom, not wanting te be in trouble like the Nugent one.

I roared laughing, and the others got an awful fright. 'Jaysus! That was great gas,' I laughed, thinking I'm not finished with Nugent yet! This is going te be the worst week of her life.

'Gawd! They could all be sent to the reformatory in the country,' said Olivia Ryan. 'That's what happened to loads of the girls who gave trouble.'

'Yeah, I know,' I said, thinking of the Reverend Mother sending me inta the Department of Education, trying te get them te send me away. She never got over the shock of being stuck with me and would still love te see the back of me. But I put a spoke in her wheel by playing them at their own game. Yeah! I work like a demon, go te Mass every morning, always be polite te them and helpful, and try te keep outa trouble. That is difficult, especially with the likes of the Dilly one and her ilk! But I'm going te grind her down! I waited long enough, getting hell on earth from the nuns and the kids. Now I'm the greatest thing since sliced pan with Mother Pius. I keep outa the way with the kids and put fuck-face Nugent in her place. She thinks she can bully everyone and is the leader of the gang . . . me arse! That one has been fucking around with me long enough, trying te get the better of me. So now it's war! Right! Just wait until Tuesday, Dilly dear, more shocks in store for you! Ha! Nobody gets the better of me!

'No! I am allowing no one out to the club tonight,' Sister Eleanor said te Loretta, stretching her face in disgust at even the mention of it.

'Why? Ah, fuck you!' muttered Loretta, making her way out the refectory door, not giving a damn if Sister Eleanor heard her or not. She was not really interested in Sister Eleanor anyway, because she got on very well with Sister Mercy in the kitchen, God help us!

It takes all sorts te make a world, I thought te meself, heading out the back door before they locked it. I flew off past the convent, hoping Matron Millington or one of the nuns wasn't looking out the window. I could always say I was looking for one of the nuns te give her a message. In the dark? Out in the grounds? Well, I'll think of something if I'm caught. Now! Where did the fuckers hide them trousers? I looked carefully around the bushes in the first oak tree. Then moved back, seeing a bit of grey sticking out. Ha! Here we are, four pairs of trousers, and all definitely forbidden. Oh, poor Dilly! You are all going te get it this time.

I put them back in their hiding place and took off flying past the convent and in the back door, looking for Sister Eleanor. Nope! Not in the refectory. I took off down the passage and inta our playroom.

'Sister! The priest was saying we should be learning about the facts of life and learning all about boys.'

'Who said that?' asked Sister Eleanor, getting all het-up and red in the face at the mention of the word, the facts of life!

'Well, we should, shouldn't we?' said Vanessa Andrewson, knowing full well, with the others all tittering around her, she was embarrassing poor aul Eleanor.

Sister Eleanor chewed on the needle she held between her

teeth and dropped her head inta the sewing machine, pedalling
like mad, making the needle fly across the white line.

'Yeah, the priest at the tech school talks to us about all sorts
of things.'

'Is that right now?' she said, keeping her head down, chewing
like mad on the needle. 'And what sort of things would he talk
about?'

'Oh, what the fellas might get up to,' Andrewson said, waving
her arms in the air, enjoying herself no end, shocking the life
outa Sister Eleanor.

'WHAT? What did you say?' Eleanor spluttered, nearly
swallowing the needle and losing her place, making a crooked
line in the sheet, her foot slipping off the pedal. 'Oh, really!'
she said. 'Now look what I have just done,' crying at the sewing
machine and scratching under her veil, trying te get at her hair
under the white linen bonnet, forgetting we were watching.

'Do you shave your head, Sister Eleanor?' said Olivia Ryan,
changing the subject.

'What?' roared Sister Eleanor, not really listening, looking very
distracted, wondering if she should rip the stitches out.

'Sister Eleanor!' I said.

'Yes, what?'

'You are wanted.'

'Where? Who wants me?'

'You better go, Sister, it's urgent.'

'Who?'

'Come on, Sister!'

'Is it the phone this hour of the night? Sure, the phone is
switched off!'

I kept walking and she followed me, not really with it, thinking
about the mess she made with the sheet.

'Sister, I have something terribly important te tell you,' I said.

'What? What do you want to say to me? Is someone in the
convent asking for me?'

'No, Sister. It's Dilly Nugent and the others again! They are going te get themself inta terrible trouble,' I said, looking at her straight in the eyes.

'Oh divine Mother of Jesus,' she said, putting her hand over her mouth and grabbing me, pushing me down te the cloakroom for a bit more privacy.

'Yes,' I said, swallowing me spit, taking me time, coughing and wanting te clear me throat.

'Out with it,' she punched me in the arm, getting herself all worked up with the fright of the mention of the name Dilly Nugent.

'Well, I heard them discussing in the refectory a few nights ago . . .'

'Yes! Go on!'

'Well, I heard them mention . . .'

'Get on with it!'

'Yes! I'm getting there, give me time! It was a terrible shock te me, ye know, when I heard what they were up te!' I snorted, full of indignation at having me story interrupted every few seconds.

'Well? Yes?'

I looked at her, hating when people say that, it ruins me concentration.

'They plan te do a bunk tonight,' I said, losing me place in the whole sorry mess.

'What do you mean?'

'Oh, right! Well, if you let me start at the beginning, I will be able te tell you the full story.'

'Jesus give me patience with these children,' she said, dropping her head in her hands then looking up at the ceiling like one of them saints getting themselves crucified.

'Well . . .' I said.

'Martha, if you say that word one more time . . . Will you please just get to the point!'

'Yeah, OK. They're planning te scarper out the dormitory window when the lights are out. After you go te bed. And shinny down the drainpipe and land on the television room roof, and shinny down the drainpipe on that one. And collect their TROUSERS hidden behind the trees on the avenue, and meet the fellas they met outside the Legion a Mary club the last night they went. And it's not the altar boys this time, it's the ratbags from the city centre with the long greasy hair,' I said, all in one breath.

Sister Eleanor stopped breathing. Her face was turning purple and her eyes were swimming in shock. 'Come on, I'll show you,' I said, 'where they have their trousers hidden behind the trees.'

'Jesus wept!' she said when she got her voice back. Then took off like someone had set fire te her arse.

'Where are you going, Sister?' I roared.

'Come with me,' she shouted, heading for the convent.

'But what about going out the back way, the back door?' I shouted.

'No! If they see you, they will know you were spying on them.'

'I was?' I said, getting a shock. I knew I was keeping an eye on them . . . but now I'm a spy! It doesn't sound nice coming outa her mouth! Makes me feel a bit . . .

'Come on! Show me where you found these trousers,' she said.

We dashed down the convent stairs, me marvelling at how fast she could run, even with the long habit tripping her up. No bother! She whipped it up, showing black cotton ankles and sensible laced-up leather shoes. We flew out the back convent door and shot past the convent kitchen. And I whizzed past her, not wanting te be outrun in the race te get our hands on the evidence. I left behind a black-and-white blur with hands holding up the habit and landed at the tree, scratching around in the bush, and lifted up the trousers, waving them at Sister Eleanor.

'So,' she said, 'it's true! They were planning to escape down the drainpipes and take off into the city to meet God knows who! Where on earth were they going to get the money for the bus fare?' she asked me, not able to take the whole thing in.

'Ah, they have money left from the Christmas, Sister. They didn't hand it all up for you te mind.'

'That's true,' she said, thinking about it. 'Well, this is the last they will see of these,' she said, shaking the trousers at me. 'Now, I am going to confront them,' she said, marching back up the avenue.

Oh, Dilly Dilly gum drops! You'll be fifty before you see the light of day, I cackled te meself.

I sat in me little waiting room, listening for the door or phone te ring, and read all about being a nun in an enclosed order and what you should do. I looked at the cover – fading brown leather – with the pages going yellow and ready te fall te pieces. Jaysus! It was written hundreds of years ago, I thought, examining the date when it was published. I borrowed it outa the nun's library. Well, they would say robbed or stole, but I'll put it back. Me robbing days are well gone.

I coughed and shook meself, getting ready, settling meself down for a good read. These days I'm mad about religion. Especially now as I'm thinking of joining the nuns and becoming a nun meself. I don't suppose they'd take me here; they know me too well. And I haven't got the education, but I'm getting there. I looked at the name of the book, *The Imitation of Christ*. It's written in very old-fashioned language. But I'll work it out.

'A nun must sleep with her arms folded in a cross lying on her chest,' it said. I tried te picture that. Hm! I think I could manage that with a bit of practice.

'The nun must keep custody of the eyes at all times, lest it lead one into the ways of sin.' Custody! Ahh! Don't be looking at yourself in the mirror! Right!

'A nun must wear a grey linen shift when taking a bath, lest the sight lead one into impure thoughts.' Right! No looking at yourself naked. Or ye might start mauling yourself. Got that.

'A nun must flagellate one's body with a birch made from rushes. But only under the direction of the Spiritual Director or the Mother Abbess! In case it cause one to lose their soul to the devil by indulging in ecstasy.' I looked at the picture of the nun, her back dripping in blood, her eyes twisted te heaven looking like she was there already. Hm! Don't like the sound of that. I could give meself little taps of the whip, I suppose, if I had te. Maybe I could ask Sister Eleanor about this. On the other hand, she'll only fuss about me borrowing the book from the nuns' library. No! Definitely not her. Right! Work that one out later!

On the other hand, this book is very old; maybe they don't do this sort of thing any more. Yeah! I can't imagine Sister Eleanor having a go at herself with one a them things. No, this is very old-fashioned; they definitely don't go in for that stuff any more. Jaysus! I'm glad a that. But what about me not having gone te school? I wonder if they would still take me. I could enter when I'm sixteen.

I had the picture of meself going around in a black habit. I hope I grow a lot taller; I'm still a bit small. But then so is Duck Egg. She looks tiny, wandering around in the black habit. I could be like Sister Eleanor. Praying all the time, flying down te look after the children: I'd like that. Yeah! Looking after children, I understand them, and they listen te me. I don't have te shout at them like some people. Small children know when ye like them. They just want ye te talk te them, and if ye are kind they will be very obliging and do what ye ask. I noticed that in the nursery. They only dig in their heels if ye roar at them. And the older ones go behind yer back and do what they like anyway, just for the devilment, because they want te get the better of ye. But if ye're kind, and ye put them on their trust, then, yeah, they want te please ye.

I suppose we are still like that. I would do anything for Sister Eleanor, providing she is nice te me, but if she acts like she doesn't like me, and has no time for me, then she gets the full lash. I had the picture of her once when she put me outa the group, and when she came in the morning te call us up for breakfast I lay on in the bed and she went mad, slapping the arse off me for all she was worth. It didn't work, and I lay on me side, not moving an inch. She grabbed the bedclothes and went off taking them with her, leaving me lying on the spring without even the mattress. I stayed put, freezing with the cold and shivering on the spring, with everyone looking and laughing, but I wouldn't give in. She came back for one more try, slapping away at me until the hand nearly fell offa her. Then the Reverend Mother arrived down, and I sat up and glared at her. 'Stand out, please.'

I stood by the side of the bed, not giving a fart about her. I felt cold inside, because they treated me like dirt, and the kids thought I was a great joke. They would call me names and hit me, then stand back and watch the fight. I got tired of that, and wanted Sister Eleanor te like me, but she didn't. She blamed me for all the trouble with the kids and me always fighting, and, anyway, they were expecting trouble from me right from the beginning, so it was a merry-go-round of me defending meself against the kids and fighting the nuns who had no time for me. That made me feel very lonely and someone who didn't belong. Like a leper. Yeah! Like the street kid who was dirt and a nuisance te everyone. Something that should be put down. I didn't know what te do. But when I stared inta that Reverend Mother's eyes, and saw the glint, her sizing me up and down, her mind flying, delighted te get her hands on me, I knew she thought I was only dirt. The holy nun was no different from anyone else. I saw no sign of the good God in them eyes.

'Are you not happy here?' she asked me, like she couldn't care less but was only getting around te saying what she really meant.

I stared at her, saying nothing.

'Maybe you would be better suited to a convent in the country. You were never suited to this convent.'

'I'm very happy here, Mother,' I said, seeing where she was leading. Down te a fucking reformatory, and now I had given her the excuse she needed.

'Yes, well, we shall have to see,' she said, looking at me with that glint again, saying, 'Get dressed, please, and if you give Sister Eleanor more trouble we will not be having this conversation. You will be leaving us a lot sooner.'

So I looked around, thinking. Then I saw the nun's pet, creeping past like a little mouse. Hoping te get by without the cat noticing, giving me a sideways look like she would hate te be like me.

'Good girl! How are you getting on in secondary school?' asked the Reverend Mother, standing out on the landing talking te her.

'Oh, very well, Mother!' I heard her gasp. 'I love it!'

'Yes, of course you would. A clever child like you would have no trouble with your studies,' I heard her say.

Right! I know exactly what I'm going te do. Mousey has given me an idea. I was outa the bed at the crack of dawn and flying down te the chapel for Mass, leaving the rest of the creeps sleeping the sleep of the dead, while I shuffled in, hearing the rustle of habits and the yawns stop halfway in shock while I pushed Mousey up in the bench te make room for me. She had the whole chapel te herself and sat herself right on the edge. I wanted te make us a matching pair. The two goody-goodies! She was raging, moving herself miles away from me down te the far end of the bench, letting the nuns know, watching from the back in their prie-dieux, she was certainly not associated with the likes of me!

So here I am, now thinking of becoming a nun. I could go on the missions. Just like in the film *The Nun's Story*. Dressed in a white habit, with little black babies swarming all around me, and me carrying one in each arm, and getting the rest of them te follow me, hanging on te me habit like some of them do here with Sister Eleanor. She moans all the time, but she really likes being a nun, rushing up te get her prayers and singing the office. I sit listening te them sometimes at night when I have te work late, and hear them chanting the vespers. I know it off by heart. So that's a start.

'What are you up to, Martha?'

'Aah! Ye gave me an awful fright, Matron!' I roared, looking up at her creeping inta the room. For some reason, she always creeps on her toes; I suppose it's because of living with the nuns so long, you always have te be quiet, not disturb them in their prayers.

'What's that ye're reading?' she said, squinting down at me book. 'Where did you get that?'

'From the convent library,' I whispered.

'Oohh! Don't let them catch you with that. They'll have your guts for garters. What are ye reading that old tripe for?'

'Ah well, I don't know, it's about nuns.'

'So, don't you see enough of them without having to read about them as well?' she laughed.

'Yeah, but maybe I might be interested in finding out all about them.'

'Why? Aah, would you go on outa that.' She nudged me, digging me with her elbow. 'I hope you're not thinking of joining them, are you?'

'Well . . .'

'Aah, you wouldn't last two minutes with the like a them. They would drive ye crazy! Put that nonsense outa your head. You're full a life. Go out into the world and enjoy yourself. Are you listening to me?' she said, belting me arm.

'Yeah!' I was thinking about what she just said. 'But what has being full of life got te do with being a nun? Does it mean I couldn't become a nun if I wanted te?'

'That's not the point. You would end up in the funny farm after spending a bit a time with them aul nuns. They drive each other crazy. Back-biting about each other, ignoring one another. No, no! It's not the life for you, Martha. You were never meant to live this kind of life. Now, promise me you will put it out of your head. Will you promise me that?' she said, bending down and looking inta me eyes.

'I still don't understand,' I said, shaking me head. 'What about Sister Eleanor? All the kids love her, and she's a great nun!'

'Ahh, she's different. Her father is a big shot in the medical world. Sure, she even has two sisters surgeons, and a brother a top medical professor in one of the big hospitals in London, and the rest of them are all doctors, too, even her mother was a doctor. They live in a big mansion down in the heart of the country. No, she's one of the few who was cut out to be a nun. But the rest of them! Listen, Martha. I have lived with these nuns now for more years than I can count. They go very peculiar after a while. That is, if they're not peculiar to begin with! It's the life they lead. Shut up in here, nowhere for them to escape. Living with each other day after day, looking at the same faces, they end up losing their health a lot of them. No! Say nothing to anyone, and don't go telling that chaplain! God knows where it might lead you. Even the young ones who come and try it out have a hard time getting back to themselves. So make plans that get you as far away from these people as you can get. No good would come of it. You must mark my words. If I had my time over again, I would never darken their doorstep,' she said, looking faraway, the light going outa her tired eyes.

Poor Matron! It looks like she has wasted her life, she thinks. I don't want that te happen te me. 'Maybe you're right, Matron,' I said slowly, thinking about it.

'I am,' she said. 'A lovely young girl like you should grab everything life has to offer you.'

'Why did you stay, Matron?' I asked her quietly, moving over te the windowsill and sitting down beside her.

'I wish to God I knew!' she said, dropping her shoulders, giving a big sigh. 'To be honest, I came in for a rest. I had seen too much, and I thought working here for a while would give me a breathing space. It took me a long time to lick my wounds.'

I could see the pain in her eyes; it still hurts, whatever she went through, even after all this time. That must be over forty years. I stayed quiet, listening te her.

'Life was short, so cheap! Out there it meant nothing. It was kill or be killed! The men suffered! Oh, many is the dark night I sat in this place picturing those young men; like the walking dead they were, Martha,' she said, looking at me. 'Life meant nothing. I suppose to be truthful to myself, I gave up on life after that. I stayed on here, dead inside myself. Going through the motions, happy enough with the routine and order, that's really what kept me going. The quiet routine, nothing to disturb the weak balance of my mind. The aul nuns and their crabby ways didn't bother me. I hardly noticed them half of the time; I was so locked up in my own world. Some of them acted like they had the world on their shoulders, and that would make me laugh. The contrast of how they lived their lives and what went on in the real world, or what happened in Belgium, anyway, was beyond most people. You couldn't talk to anyone; they didn't want to know, and they wouldn't have understood anyway. There was a lot of suffering and poverty in them days, Martha. A lot of things have changed for the better with the social welfare and housing. Most of the slums, the aul tenement houses are demolished. Yeah, things have changed all right. For a lot of people, anyway. But underneath, nothing changes. I see the helpless children coming in here, some of them half dead.'

'Yeah,' I murmured, remembering some of them. 'Matron, do you remember the little baby girl who went straight inta hospital when Doctor Blightman took one look at her? She never came back.'

'No, she died in the children's hospital,' the Matron said, shaking her head, thinking about it.

There were other children, too. Scabs in their shaved heads, skin and bone, brought straight from the city centre. The other kids staring at them like they were outa a zoo. Laughing at the idea of the little girls, two sisters they were. 'Do we have te share them sausages or do we do wha wit them?' they asked the other kids. I knew straight away what they were going through. Somehow it was like looking at meself at their age, and I knew then what I must have looked like. They didn't stay here no more than a few nights. Then they were gone again. 'Yeah, I know what you are talking about, Matron,' I said.

'So that's the way it goes,' she said, shaking her head slowly, thinking back on her life. 'So here I am. I wake up one day and

find I'm nearly at the end of my days. It was short yet very long,'
she said, miles away in herself.

I sat looking at her sitting on the deep windowsill, her white
frilly linen cap sitting on top of her head, with the grey wisps
of hair hanging out around her face, and I knew she tied it up
in a bun on top; her white face falling in folds hanging under
her cheeks, and her faded-blue eyes with veins in the whites,
still lit up with the kind of life ye only see in a very young child
who gets the idea of doing something great gas but very bold.
She has more life in her eyes than a lot of the kids here have,
and the nuns never had it. Most of the time their eyes are like
stone. Dead!

We sat in silence, her swinging her legs with the thick woollen
stockings falling down in rolls inta her black-laced soft-leather
high-heel boots. With her long, white, heavy linen uniform
covering her legs, and letting her white wrinkly hands rest in
her lap while she stared at them.

I lifted me head slowly, resting me eyes on the bare trees, with
the fruit rotting on the wet grass and everything dead now in the
orchard, having had their time, and waiting for the spring te come
and the new life will start over again. I suppose that's somehow
like life. Matron Mona has had her time, and it starts all over
again with a new generation. I'm one of the lucky ones who was
born and have a chance te have a go at making something outa
me life, I thought, looking back te Matron Mona, who lifted her
head, giving me a smile – full of contentment the two of us. Like
there was no age difference between us. She understands me and
I understand her, and we are easy in each other's company. She's
me one real friend here.

CHAPTER 20

I sat with me legs dangling over the edge of the armchair, taking it easy after a day of scrubbing and polishing, leaving the convent shining and the floor looking like glass. The nuns might, with a bit of luck, slip and land on their arse. I was fed up having them walk on me newly scrubbed stairs, then having te run back up and wipe their muddy shoeprints after they come in from their praying along the wet paths on the Cloistered Walk. All this so they could give themselves an airing, then creep past me, whispering, 'Oh, the weather is beautiful and crisp. I enjoyed that. Goodness! Look at the shine off that floor, Sister,' te the one making her way up behind her, stepping onta the wet floor and missing the bar of Sunlight soap – too bad! Then the two of them standing on me polished floor, looking like overgrown bats, saying, 'Tut, tut, she's a marvellous girl,' moving over, dragging the mud across the floor, and leaning down the stairs te tell me, 'You're a grand girl; sorry, dear, to disturb the hard work,' then lifting their habits and running off, leaving me te run back up the stairs and wipe off the mudprints sitting on me lovely white rubber lino and across me newly polished floor. I take great pride in doing a good job. But one of these days . . .

The door flew open and I dropped me legs, expecting a roaring match from Sister Eleanor, screaming, 'Get your legs off the side of my armchairs at once! How dare you treat my chairs with such disrespect?' Flying herself in all directions, sending us landing on the floor, getting her long navy-blue knickers hanging down te her knees in a twist. When the shagging springs of the chairs, sitting exposed, send ye flying inta the air with a ping up yer arse, the pain burns yer arse for hours afterwards. That's if ye forget yerself and throw yer full weight inta it, not making sure te sit yerself down easy. An she thinks they're lovely, wanting ye te treat them like priceless silk!

Tubby Jeffries put her nose in, looking around te see who was here. She looked at Sarah Manson, sprawled in the other armchair, chewing on her long rats' tails she calls hair, then landed her face back te me.

'Here! Do you want this *Bunty*, Martha?'

I looked at it dangling in her hand, reaching over te me. 'Eh, dunno. No, not really,' I said, not in the mood for the *Bunty*. I'd prefer a magazine with the problem pages. Forget it! Ellie whips them faster than we can get them!

'I want it!' roared Manson, flinging her rats' tails behind her back and reaching out, snatching it. Then the door closed, leaving me staring at Manson with my comic.

'Here! I want it after all,' I said, grabbing it back, seeing the value of it because she wanted it.

'Give that back here!' Manson roared, jumping te her feet.

'No! It's mine!'

'She gave it to me!' screamed Manson, jumping up and down, getting all excited.

'Well, she offered it te me first.'

'Give me back that fucking comic,' she roared, making a run at me.

I laughed, tearing out the door with yer woman tearing down the passage after me.

'Give that back to me, Long! I'm going to fucking kill you!'

'Temper, temper!' I laughed, enjoying the chase down the passage. I looked back, seeing her tearing after me, grinding her teeth, looking like she meant business, grabbing air with her hands out, like she already had me in her paws.

I tore off down the back passage and headed inta the kitchen. I switched the light on and made a run for the other side of the kitchen table, hanging on te it, hopping from one foot te the other, laughing and watching her come flying in the door and stopping te gauge the distance between us. I laughed, watching her bang the door slowly shut with her foot, never taking her eyes off me.

'Jaysus, Manson, ye're acting like someone outa the bleeding cowboy fillums!' I laughed, thinking this is great gas.

'You're not getting out of here alive,' she said, staring at me like someone sleepwalking. 'I want that comic, hand it over.' She spoke slowly, putting out her hand.

I started te get hysterical, thinking she's very determined te get the comic back, and I collapsed meself on the table, laughing at the whole idea of it. Yer woman thinks she's a fucking cowboy or something. She's acting like the tough guy outa the O.K. Corral. All she's short of is spitting out a bit of chewing tobacca. 'Nope! You is not goin teh get my here comic,' I said, sounding like something outa a Western fillum meself, and holding it up for her te look at, screaming me head laughing.

'Fuck you, Long! You are going to regret this.' She suddenly sprang at the table, opening the drawers and spilling all Sister Mercy's cutlery onta the floor, and picked up a huge carving knife, lifting it above her head, saying, 'Are you going to give that back?'

'No!' I leapt from one foot te the other, watching her eyes glinting with madness, having seen that look before. Fuck! She's outa her mind. 'Stop, ye silly cow! This is no longer a joking matter!' I screamed.

'No! You're right there!' She lifted the knife over her shoulder, flicking it back, staring at me for a split second, then aimed it straight for me head. I ducked, grabbing the chair, and came up holding it, and flung it across the table straight at her, going for another knife, hearing the old clock that sat up on the wall since the bloody nuns arrived here hundreds a years ago smash.

Fuck! I raced for the door, trying te get it open, and Manson grabbed me, wrapping her arms around mine and pinning me. I swung around, knocking her outa the way, and headed for the scullery. She tore after me and I stood with me back against the sink, hoping te knock her off balance and escape out the door.

'Bitch!' she screamed, sounding like a banshee, then threw herself at me, sending me flying against the big machine for peeling the potatoes and knocking against the switch, and the machine started grinding away like mad with nothing in it. I held her arms, trying te pin them down, and she used her feet, pushing against the floor, trying te bear down her weight on me, and heaved and pushed until she had me head hanging over the potato peeler.

'Stop, ye mad fucking bitch!'

Then she pushed her hand down on me head, bearing all her weight on it, trying te get me head inside the peeler. I could hear us grunting and her giving a little squeak of laugh, determined te do whatever it took te get what she wanted. Fuck! Help! I'm going te get me head mashed! This is not about a comic; this is about who is going te back down. Or maybe fucking not! This mad cow won't stop until me head topples inta the basin. All peeled and mashed, ready for tomorrow's dinner.

'Aah! This is not funny, Manson! Ye'll have me head in the potato peeler. For the love of Jaysus, stop!'

'Yeah! I'm going to fucking shred you!' she grunted, heaving herself more against me.

'No, ye're' . . . grunt . . . 'fuckin not!'

'Hah!' . . . grunt . . . 'Long! You're mincemeat.'

'Ah!' . . . grunt . . . I pushed back with me arse and pushed until I could get a grip on the floor, and lifted me foot, slamming it against the press and sending the two of us flying across the room, landing against a metal rack holding all Sister Mercy's metal heavy pots. The whole lot came tumbling down on top of us as I tried te crawl away, managing te get a grip on a pot just as Manson sent me flying with a kick up the arse and grabbed hold of a big pot and flung it at me. I ducked sideways, putting the pot out in front of me, and it banged away from me, and I sent my pot flying at her and ducked down for another one. The pots started flying in all directions, and she took a flying leap at me, and we locked on each other again, rolling around the floor.

We didn't hear the door open until Sister Mercy stood over us, screaming, 'Stop dis! What in the name of all dat is holy is going on here?' She was too shocked te say anything else, and just stood looking at the two of us and sweeping her head around the kitchen that looked like it had been hit with a bomb!

'We heard you up in the chapel,' she said, white as a sheet, her eyes staring outa her head.

I let go me fingers, uncurling them from Manson's hair, and she stopped trying te throttle me with her hand wound tightly around the neck of me jumper.

Mercy suddenly came te her senses and ran at us screaming, 'Get up! Get up! You pack of savages!'

I dived outa the way, hopping te me feet and making past her out the door. She grabbed a hold of Manson, shouting, 'Pick up all dem pots! Me kitchen! Oh my God,' she said, turning herself around, seeing the clock hanging by its springs. 'Jesus! Me clock.' Manson got an unmerciful clatter. 'You stupid clown,' she screamed. 'Where's dat other one? Long! Martha Long,' I heard her screams after me as I flew up the passage, wanting te make as much distance from all the madness as I could manage in the shortest time.

I shot along the convent passage, feeling me heart going like the clappers, the sweat pouring outa me. I landed meself in the chair of me little waiting room, sitting in the dark, not wanting te draw attention te meself by putting on the light.

Me chest heaved up and down as I stared out the window inta the dark orchard, trying te make sense of what happened. She was trying te annihilate me! Dear God! How did all that happen? And I wasn't expecting it! I didn't even see it coming. Jaysus! That look she had in her eyes when she cornered me in the kitchen, just before she started throwing them knives at me! That look of madness, I've seen it so often in Jackser, with that twisted smile. There's no sign of human flesh and blood behind them eyes, and the smile is enjoyment of what they are going te do te ye. Like ye are a bluebottle that has been tormenting them, and they finally made up their mind te get ye and put a stop te yer gallop for good. Standing and watching and judging yer movements, and calculating the effort they are going te have te put in te kill ye, just before they pounce.

I don't understand. Generally she is very quiet. Well, sort of. She doesn't bother about anyone and doesn't chase Sister Eleanor looking for attention. It's like she has no feelings; she doesn't care about anyone and doesn't need anyone te care about her. She just seems te get on with her own business, and yet come te think about it, she always seems te be watching people, taking everything in, but keeping her distance. She takes great enjoyment when someone gets inta trouble or accidentally hurts themself, then she laughs her head off, screaming like a fucking banshee. I shook me head, trying te get rid of the picture of her, not understanding how I never saw that before. She was so like Jackser with that look in her eye. I couldn't let go in that kitchen. If I had lost me grip on her, or she'd managed te get the upper hand on me . . . God knows what might have happened. Fuck! Life can be very treacherous! Ye never know when trouble's going te strike. Yeah! The only time ye can be sure, Martha, is when ye let your guard down. When ye are least expecting it.

CHAPTER 21

'Quickly, Martha, we are being flooded!' Sister Eleanor panted, rushing inta the playroom and dropping her hands on her knees, trying te get a breath. 'Get down to the kitchen passage and help. Hurry!' she flapped, dragging me te me feet and looking around te see who else she could get her hands on.

'Hurry! Run!' she panicked, shouting te the ones flying out the door, going in the opposite direction te where the flooding was. 'No, not that way, girls, down here,' she shouted 'To the kitchen passage,' she pointed, looking back, seeing them all running te get away from her. 'Stop this minute, girls. I forbid you to run off!' she roared, turning and making a run at them. But she was talking te the air. They disappeared down the end of the passage and around the corner. 'Oh, they are very bold,' she moaned, turning her head te me and screwing up her face like she was going te cry. 'Now, would you credit that? I ask them to do something for me and they have all suddenly found something to keep them busy. Such mean girls. No sense of generosity whatsoever.'

'No,' I agreed, thinking I hope she doesn't expect me te clear it all on me own. 'Where is the flood, Sister?'

'Yes, come on,' she said, remembering she still had me, and her face lit up with that happy thought.

We rushed down through the passages, seeing the water floating around the stone passage at the top of the back kitchen door. People were slopping through the water in the dull light with buckets and mops, trying te make out if they were getting the better of it and looking te see if the level was going down. I could smell the damp and see the grey mist from the water floating around in the air.

Sister Mercy was bent in two over a bucket, squeezing out a mop, and turned her red face in our direction, trying te stand herself up straight. 'Oh, come on, come on. Good girl' she said te me, happy with a bit of help and forgetting all about me previous run-in with her over getting her kitchen demolished. Thank God I never heard another word about that.

'Here, take dis mop and try te dry up the floor. Sister, is dere any more children about?'

'Oh, I'm trying to round them up, Sister Mercy, but they all seemed to have vanished!'

'Vanished, me eye,' snorted Sister Mercy, kicking out her sopping boots, trying te shake the water outa them, like a dog shaking its leg after a good piss.

I stared at her fat legs covered in black tights with her habit pinned up around her waist showing nearly up te the calf of her legs.

'We'd better go, I suppose,' muttered Sister Eleanor te Mercy in a nervous whisper, feeling embarrassed because Mercy knew the girls were making a fool of her.

'Yes, Sister, we'd better get going up to the chapel; we'll be late for prayers,' mumbled Mercy, looking back at Loretta and me, saying, 'The girls will manage now. I think it's under control,' throwing her eye along the passage at the inches of water lapping around our feet.

I grabbed the mop, swirling it around in the water and squeezing it out in the bucket. 'How did all this water get in here, Loretta?'

'How do you think? It came rushing in the back door when the storm started.'

'Yeah, but the drain must be blocked outside,' I said, looking at the sacks all piled against it.

'Yeah,' she grunted, bending down te squeeze out the mop.

'You're welcome to go outside in that torrential rain and take a look,' she laughed.

'Jaysus! That's some storm,' I said, listening te the rumble of the thunder, then an unmerciful explosion, sounding like a bomb had landed on the convent. I could see yellow flashes coming in through the keyhole, and it made me nervous. 'Jaysus! It really is getting bad, Loretta, do ye hear that rain? I can see the lightning through the keyhole. Do ye think we might be struck by lightning, Loretta, standing in this water?'

'I don't know,' she said, standing up and looking at the thick heavy door. 'If we are, we won't know anything about it,' she laughed. 'But I wouldn't worry about it, Long, it's hard to kill a bad thing.'

We pushed the mop through the water and squeezed, and bent and mopped and squeezed, and straightened and dragged the heavy tin bucket down te the kitchen and emptied it. Until me back seized up and we collapsed our backs against the wall, seeing the shiny wet on the stone floor. But the lapping water was now gone, down the sink and back inta the drains, and making its way down the Liffey and back out te sea, waiting te be sucked up again by the sky and start the whole thing all over again. I learned that stuff in one of the other girl's geography books, deciding te find out what geography was all about.

I snorted in me breath, feeling me chest lighten with the air flying out again, and said, 'Will we get going again, Loretta?'

'Yeah! Ellie is going to have a hard time getting me out of the bed in the morning; you can all go and whistle for your breakfast,' she said, throwing her back off the wall and making a move for the mop and bucket.

The convent door at the end of the passage opened and a pile of nuns came rushing down. 'Oh, you got it cleared, girls,' the Reverend Mother said, smiling at us and daintily stepping through the damp floor, making sure the hem of her habit didn't touch the ground.

'Oh, I see you have my girl here, Sister Eleanor,' sang Mother

Pius, laying her hand on me shoulder and inspecting the floor.

'Yes, Mother,' whispered Sister Eleanor, looking nervously at me, wondering if Ma Pius might have a go at her over the lazy good-for-nothing girls in her group who never seem te do anything around the house.

'Can we open this door now, Sister Mercy?' asked the Reverend Mother, swinging her head around and wrapping her arms inside her cloak.

'We could, Mother! But the rain . . .'

'Hm! Perhaps you are right. Best leave it to morning. Then we can get Mr Riddle to look at it. It is probably the drains, Sister, they must be blocked with leaves. Yes, well,' she said, swinging her head te look at Loretta and me, then down at the state of us, covered in wet dirty water, our hair plastered te our heads from the sweat. 'Well done, girls. I am very pleased you managed to get it under control!'

'Yes, of course. With Martha here, you can always rely on a job well done,' said Ma Pius, laying her hand on me head, smiling and giving me her blessing.

'My Loretta is a wonderful worker,' croaked Mercy, shaking her head at Loretta, getting very annoyed no one mentioned her, so in turn was insulting Mercy.

'Yes, well done, girls,' Ma Pius said, sweeping past me, holding up her habit, with the rest of them following. I tried te get outa the way, and stand back te let them pass, but I lost me balance, putting out me hand, stretching it against the wall, and me fingers shot up in the air and I felt a crack, and an unmerciful pain shot through me arm. 'Aah!' I muttered te meself, grabbing me arm and holding me hand. The pain was red-hot, and I held on waiting for it te pass. It didn't. The pain just kept going on, and I shook me arm trying te ease it.

'Come on, girls, leave it now,' said Sister Eleanor, putting her hand on our backs and heading us off. 'It's time you went to bed. Thank you so much for all your help. You were both very good.'

'Sister! Me hand is paining me.'

'What?'

'I hit it against the wall,' I said, lifting it up te show her.

'Come on,' she said, looking and seeing nothing. 'It will be fine. You both need to go to bed. Here! Let us put these buckets back.'

I held onta me arm, not moving, letting her fuss and grab the buckets, taking off for the kitchen with them.

'Gawd! That Ma Pius one thinks the sun shines out of your arse, Long,' Loretta said, looking very annoyed at me.

'Yeah, and Mercy thinks the sun shines outa yours. So there's a pair of them in it.'

'Still and all, I'd prefer to have Mercy any day. I get to eat all the goodies that you lot don't even see.'

I wasn't in the mood te argue, but I still said, 'Yeah, but Ma Pius controls the money, and she's close te the Reverend Mother.'

'Huh! You're welcome to her. That one talks like she has a mouthful of marbles.'

'Yeah, well, ye can always get yer hands on a bit a grub, but it's not easy te get anywhere unless ye know the right people,' I snorted. 'She has gotten me outa many a trouble! In this life, Loretta, it's not what you know but who you know gets you around. I learned that a long time ago,' I said, thinking how everyone leaves me alone; even the Reverend Mother backs off, though she can't stand the sight of me.

'Yeah, well, you have very grand ideas about yourself, Long. You talk like you'd swallowed the dictionary. It's all because you're an awful noticebox,' she sneered, laughing at me.

Say what ye like, Loretta, I don't care, I thought, keeping me ideas te meself about wanting te get on in life. Anyway, me bleeding hand is killing me.

'Come on, let's get moving before they find something else for us te do.'

'They can go and have a good shite for themselves,' Loretta snorted, heading up the passage.

I made me way down along the passage while she headed up

te the dormitory. I pushed open the door of the nursery and crept in, seeing the nightlight on, and made for me bed in the corner. Thank God they're all asleep. I looked over at the little ones sleeping soundly, and went over, trying te lift little Arthur's head back inta the bed; he was hanging out. My right hand was killing me with the pain; it wasn't easing, just getting worse. I went over and sat down on the side of me own bed and looked at me hand. The fingers are curling up and I can't straighten it out.

'Are you all right?' Sister Eleanor whispered, tiptoeing inta the room and looking around at all the little ones snoring softly. 'Get into bed now like a good girl,' she said, looking at me holding me hand.

'I can't sleep with the pain of this,' I puffed, holding out me hand.

'Let me see,' she said, staring at it. 'What can I do, Martha? It will be grand in the morning. Go on, get into bed and try to get some sleep.' Then she was gone, listening te me keening softly with the pain.

I tried te undress with me left hand and I couldn't get the wet frock over me head. I felt like roaring me head crying, with being tired and wet and the pain in me hand. But I just struggled, wrestling with the frock, using me right hand limply, trying te hold one side and pull with the other. I got inta me nightdress and under the covers when Sister Eleanor came rushing back with a roll a plaster. 'Here! Put that on,' she said, looking at me hand. 'Which finger is it?'

'No! That won't do any good, Sister. It's not bleeding. It's just paining me.'

'Come on, it might help.'

'There! It's that finger, the one next te me little finger.'

She lifted it, making me sob out a cry, the pain was so bad when she moved it.

I curled up on me left side, nursing me right hand in me lap, and tried te forget the splitting pain, and dozed off te sleep.

I woke up with Sister Eleanor shaking me and lifting me hand.

It was swollen very badly, looking all purple and curled inta a fist, looking three times its normal size. 'Oh, you will have to go to hospital with this,' she said, saying quickly, 'I have to take that plaster off.'

'No! Ye can't, Sister. Ye can't! The pain will kill me.'

'I have to, Martha,' she said, looking at me with a very shifty look on her face.

'No! I'm not letting anyone touch me hand,' I said, meaning her.

She was out the door and back in a flash with a pair of scissors, and taking me hand trying te lift the fingers, with me screaming and she trying te cut away at the plaster. I gritted me teeth and let her get it over with, thinking she must not want the hospital te see she put a bleeding plaster on for a pain in the hand. Fuck her! It really hurts, and why was she bloody messing? I suppose it was me own fault wanting her te do something, and she thought she was helping me.

'After breakfast, Miss will take you down to the hospital, so get ready, pet,' she said.

We got off the bus and walked inta the hospital, sitting on the wooden bench just outside the door of the Casualty department. 'Now, you sit here for a second while I go and knock on the door,' Miss said, making for the open door inta the clinic.

She gave a little tap on the door and the nurse turned around, looking at her while rolling a bandage on a man's leg. 'Be with you in a minute,' she shouted. 'Nurse Roche!'

'Yes?' a fair-haired nurse said, looking around from stacking shelves with boxes a stuff.

'Patient waiting for you.'

'Yes, what's the problem?' she said, looking at Miss, standing and smiling at her, coughing and blinking, her mouth working up and down trying te get herself talking. The nurse looked over at me, holding me bad hand in me other hand resting on me lap.

'This is Martha. She had an accident with her hand.'

'Ohh, that's looks bad,' she said, lifting it and gently examining it. 'Come along in and we'll get the doctor to look at that. Sit down there,' she said, putting me sitting up on the high bed with the white sheet covering the brown rubber on the mattress.

Miss stood beside me and we waited, staring over at the other man getting his leg dressed. 'He has ulcers on his leg, the poor man,' whispered Miss te me.

He watched the nurse very carefully wrapping yards of bandage the length of his leg, then looked over at us, smiling. 'Tha'll keep me goin for a while,' he croaked in a hoarse voice, sounding like he had been roaring for a long time with the pain of it. 'The pain does be somethin shockin,' he said, gettin outa breath with the thought of it.

'Oh, there's nothing worse,' the nurse said in a loud voice, giving him plenty a sympathy.

'Old age is a terrible thing,' he said, shaking his head, looking very sorrowful. '

No, there's nothing worse,' the nurse said, holding the leg with one hand, then grabbing the scissors and dropping his leg on the stool, and the man let out a roar. 'Oh, sorry, pet! Sorry! Did I hurt you at all, you poor thing?' she said, lifting the leg and rubbing his foot, the only part ye could get at.

'Ah, it's all right,' he smiled, looking very brave. 'Sure, if I'm not used te it be now!'

'Oh, you're a great old soldier, so you are; there's no doubt about that!' she said, looking at the two of us, and landing her eyes at the Miss, who coughed and blinked and shook her face and smiled, agreeing with the nurse, who dropped her scissors te pull at the cap on her head and take out the white hairclips, then hold them between her teeth and fix her long hair trailing out from beneath her cap, and pin it up again, fixing the cap straight on her head, then went back te the business of fixing the man up. 'Now, all done,' she said, standing herself straight up.

The doors swung open and a doctor came flying inta the room, skating te a stop in the middle of the floor and swinging his brown floppy hair around, landing his face on me. 'So, what have we here?' he shouted, lifting up me hand. He whistled out through his teeth, 'My, my! That's a nasty one. How did you do that?' he said, looking down at me and holding me hand gently.

'I banged it against the wall,' I said.

His face changed inta a frown, and he said, 'When did this happen?'

'Last night,' I said, looking at him turning his head and getting very annoyed.

'Why did you not bring this child in when it happened?' he roared at Miss, glaring at her, watching her trying te think.

'She's a convent child, doctor. I'm the staff there. Sister told me to take her down this morning,' she trailed off, looking down at me hand then back up te the doctor.

'That is downright negligence. Look at it! She should have been brought here sooner. It will have to be X-rayed. But I can see straight away there is a break in that hand. We need to see how bad it is.' He shook his head, looking very annoyed. 'You know we won't be able to put that in plaster of Paris! That is a terrible state of affairs. It should be bound in plaster of Paris! Now all we can do is wrap it. It is too badly swollen!' Then he marched off, shaking his head in annoyance.

I felt sorry for the poor Miss, standing there wringing her hands, not knowing what te say or do. It's not her fault, I felt like saying, feeling very annoyed with the nuns and very sorry for meself, and feeling sick with the bloody pain. But I decided it would be best te keep me mouth shut. I might do more harm than good. I smiled up at Miss, saying, 'Ah, don't worry, Miss, sure it's not your fault.'

She nodded te me, looking very worried, but saying nothing either.

'Nurse! Take this child down to X-ray.'

'Right, doctor. What's your name, pet?' the blonde nurse said, smiling at me, taking me arm and bringing me along a corridor and inta a big room with machines all over the place. 'Now, love! Just try to keep your fingers out like that,' she said, picking me fingers out one by one and stretching them.

'No, no! I can't,' I said, staring at me hand, like a big claw, trying te keep me fingers from curling inta a fist again.

'I won't be long,' she shouted, leaving me hand on a table underneath a big machine, while she ran te another one, shouting, 'Good girl, just one more, we won't be a second, hold it!'

'No! Sorry, aaah! Me hand!' I cried, lifting me hand and crying with the pain. I felt worn out and couldn't take any more of it.

'Aaah! We'll have to leave it. I won't be able to do any more with it. It's too badly swollen', she said, lifting me hand and taking me outa the room. 'I got enough for the doctor to look at. You were wonderful,' she said te me, stroking me back and handing me over te the nurse waiting outside the door. 'It's too badly bruised and swollen,' she said te the nurse. 'Hang on and I'll get you the X-rays,' and she was gone, then back in a minute, handing over the X-rays, and we made our way back te the clinic.

The doctor put them up on the wall and switched on a light and examined them, saying, 'Yes, she has chipped a piece of bone at the top of the finger close to the knuckle. There's nothing we can do now,' he said, shaking his head, holding the X-ray in his hand. 'It should, as I have said, be put into plaster of Paris. But now all we can do is put it in a splint and give support, using a sling around her neck. You are going to be in pain for quite a while until it starts to heal,' he said, looking down at me.

I shook me head, feeling sick from the pain. All I wanted te do was lie down and get a good sleep and have no pain.

We left the hospital and stood at the bus stop waiting for a bus te come. I looked down at me hand, completely covered in a white bandage with a splint underneath te keep the fingers together. And kept me arm still, wrapped inside a white sling. It had been agony when the nurse was trying te put the splint on, and the doctor gave me a tablet for the pain. But it wasn't doing me any good. At least I have it wrapped now, and if I keep it very still the pain only whines, not screams.

'Stand back from the edge,' Miss said, pulling the sleeves of me green school coat and pointing at the running water flowing along the side of the road, with sweet papers and rubbish all getting carried along rushing for a shore that wasn't blocked. I stood back, staring down the road inta the distance, seeing no sign of the bus. The cold wind and damp was running up me legs, making the hem of me coat whip around me, cutting the legs off me.

'Brrr!' Miss shivered, dropping her neck inside her coat and tying the scarf around her head and clapping her feet together. 'That wind would cut you in two,' she said, looking frostbitten, her nose drippin with snots.

'Yeah,' I mumbled hoarsely, looking around at the canvas shade hanging over the vegetables sitting in their boxes on the table outside the shop across the road from us. The wind is so vicious, it was threatening te lift the poles clean outa the wall and tear the canvas cover te shreds. I watched as it yanked and pulled, making the canvas lift and slap back down again.

A woman wearing a scarf and a hat on her head, holding tight te her shopping bag on her arm, and her purse held tight between her two hands, stopped te get a look at the vegetables, then thought better of it when the canvas gave an almighty bang and the pole came swinging outa the wall. She jumped back with the shock, looking up at it, shaking her head and probably wondering why she hadn't been killed. Then she moved herself off slowly, giving a last look back, and took off down the road.

The owner came out wearing a long dirty blue apron and looked after her, rushing herself down the road, nearly tripping over her long black coat that was miles too big for her. Then swung his head up at his shade, looking like he was thinking it was all the woman's fault. I wanted te laugh, but there was no laugh in me, I just thought about it, feeling the pain going all around me as if it wasn't just me hand.

Then I peeled me eyes on a man struggling like his life depended on it. I watched until the man came puffing past us on his bicycle, pedalling away like mad for all he was worth, but going nowhere in a hurry. He had his head down and his legs pumping like pistons on the pedals, determined he was going te get where he wanted te go on the bike, even if it killed him. We could hear him snorting and breathing, pressing his knees down for all he was worth, then giving a look up te see how far he got, but he was being blown backwards. The storm was too strong te best, and he finally gave up and threw his leg over the bar and landed himself on the footpath, lifting the bike and slamming it down again, muttering, 'The curse a Jaysus on tha wind,' looking back at the Miss. She smiled and squinted, and he put his head inta the wind again and took off pushing the bike, keeping his head down, his long brown gabardine coat flapping out behind him.

'Did you ever see anything like this storm?' said the Miss, looking shocked at the idea anything could be so bad. 'Where's that bus?' she said, trying te see over me head. But she was too small, and jumped out, leaning te one side te see if there was anything that looked like a bus coming in our direction.

There wasn't a sinner te be seen on the streets. Only the sight of a mangy aul dog chasing and barking its head off, trying te catch a paper bag flying through the air. When it landed, he dived on it, stamping his paw down over the greaseproof paper for wrapping bread and nosed out a half-eaten sandwich, wolfing it down, getting the lot inta his mouth and heaving his neck up and down trying te swallow it in one go. He finished that, lifting his paw and letting the paper take off in the wind again, and moseyed over te sniff under the vegetable table, then stopped te lift his leg and piss on the bag of potatoes sitting at the leg of the table. Satisfied he was done, he cocked his two back legs one at a time, giving them a good shake te get rid of the piss, and took off again, lifting his head and sniffing the wind, hoping for another good landing of grub. The canvas was left hanging from one pole, swinging around te slap itself against the brick wall and back again, knocking the onions outa the box and rolling them onta the road. The man had given up and rushed himself back inside, deciding the weather was too treacherous te have a go at trying te fix it.

CHAPTER 22

'Well, back at last,' said Miss, opening the back door and rushing in. 'Oh, brrr! Am I glad to be in out of that!' she said, rubbing her hands and opening the staffroom door te see if there was anyone in there. 'We'll go and find Sister, tell her we are back and let her know what the hospital said. Then I can go and have a nice pot of tea to warm myself. Come on. She may be around the house.'

I followed her up the passage and we bumped inta Sister Eleanor coming off the convent landing on the way down the stairs. 'You are back, Miss. How did the child get on?' she said, looking at me bandaged arm.

'She has a fracture, Sister, a chip of bone broke off,' she said, taking me arm te show Sister Eleanor.

'Oh, I knew as soon as I saw it this morning, you poor creature.'

'Yes, it will be six weeks at least before she can take that off. That's how long it is going to take for the bone to heal. The doctor said a chip is worse than a break.'

'Oh no! Does that mean you will not be able to work in the convent?' Sister Eleanor moaned, looking at me, her face turning red with the annoyance of what this means, and putting her hand te her mouth. 'What are we going to do about the convent?' she said, getting very distracted and moving off, muttering te herself.

'Right so, Sister. I'll be off now and get a hot cup of tea for myself,' said Miss, taking off down the corridor.

'Oh, thank you, Miss,' Sister Eleanor said, changing her mind about wandering inta the cloakroom and making off down the passage behind the Miss.

I watched them go, wondering what I was supposed te do. 'What about the pain in me arm?' I muttered te meself, knowing I was talking te the fresh air and that was the end of that. I can do what I like; she has no time for me now I can't work. Fucker! I hate nuns! I hate this place. I wandered up the passage feeling cold and tired and sick and in pain, but I didn't know what I wanted or what anyone could do. I opened the door inta the playroom and looked in seeing the emptiness, feeling the cold. It's never warm in here. That aul storage heater isn't worth a curse. We sit up on top of it te get the heat, and she comes in and roars at us te get off. I sat meself down in the armchair and waited, looking around at the wooden partition in the middle of the room and Sister Eleanor's floor-to-ceiling old pitch-pine press that she keeps all her sweets in.

The time passed and nothing happened. I just sat feeling the nausea in me chest and the pain throbbing in me arm, feeling cold and stiff and not thinking and not expecting anything, just waiting for the time te pass, then something will change. But I can do nothing about anything, just sit and wait and feel the pain and me senses completely numb. Then I had a thought, something good I can do for meself. Tell Sister Eleanor I am not sleeping in the nursery any more. I am going back up te me own dormitory and sleeping in me own bed, and she can find someone else te mind the babies at night.

I heard footsteps outside and the door opened. I lifted me head, seeing the Reverend Mother coming in the door. 'What is this?' she said, looking very annoyed and marching over te take in me arm all bandaged and in a white sling. I could smell the disinfectant off the bandage when I moved me arm, reminding me of the hospital. I lifted meself outa the armchair slowly and stood on me feet. Ye have te stand up when she's speaking te ye.

'You can't use that arm?' she barked at me, looking shocked and pointing te me arm.

'No, Mother, it's fractured.'

'How did that happen?'

'I fell against the wall in the kitchen passage when I was mopping up the flooding last night.'

'Oh, really! This is too much,' she said, shaking heself and wrapping her hands under her cloak. 'What about your work? The convent?' she said, glaring at me.

I said nothing, just stared back at her, knowing she knows the answer as well as I do.

'So what am I going to do about the convent?' she asked me again, hoping this time the right answer might appear by magic.

Ah, feck off, I thought te meself. She's acting as if this is all my fault. Like I did it on purpose. I watched her turn away like she had no further use for me and I'm outa her head already. I might as well not be here at all.

'Really,' she muttered, opening the door and talking te herself, 'this is too bad.' Then she was gone, banging the door after her, leaving me standing here wondering why she didn't even ask me was I all right.

So, that's the way it is. I'm only a grand girl and a very hard worker so long as I am useful te them. Now I can't do anything, they don't want te know me. They haven't even bothered their arse te ask me am I in pain. Would I like a cup of tea? Or what about if I give you an aspirin for the pain and put you to bed with a hot water bottle, and you can have the transistor radio to keep you company? I knew it! I fucking knew it! Sister Eleanor wouldn't treat any of the others like this. When they're sick, she fusses over them like mad. No! I'm not here long enough for them te treat me as one of their own. I'm nobody, only somebody when I have something te give. They're just like Jackser and the ma. I sat meself down on the sofa and started te cry with the pain and the shivering feeling inside me. Me head was hot and the rest of me was ice-cold. The painkiller they gave me in the hospital was wearing off, and it felt like someone was sawing off me hand and arm. And I wanted someone te come and mind me, just someone te care, treat me as if I matter te them just for meself, not for giving them things or working hard for them. No! When I get outa here, no one is ever going te get the best outa me for nothing. Fuck them, I sniffed, looking at the sleeve of me cardigan, wondering if I should wipe me snots in it. I did, thinking I have no hankie.

CHAPTER 23

Right, finished at last. I blew the damp hair sticking te the side of me face, and peeled meself up off me knees, standing up straight, and stretched. Getting the tangles outa me muscles. Another week over, getting me closer te the door and on me way out inta the world.

I wonder what kind of a job I'm going te get. The girls like me usually end up as domestics, working in houses, cleaning and looking after children, while the mother goes off te get her hair and nails done. No! I'm definitely not ending up as a skivvy, having te live in the house and being at the beck and call of some aul one and aul fella. That's what the girls who have already left complain about when they come back for a while between jobs, after getting themselves fired. Or leaving and ending up with nowhere te go and no money in their pocket.

Anyway, this is back-breaking work. Down on yer hands and knees scrubbing and polishing. There must be something else I can do. I'm going te have te work on finding a way outa this. The real problem is young ones like me don't earn enough, say, working in a factory. I wouldn't earn enough money te get meself a bedsitter, pay the rent, electricity, food and probably bus fare. Never mind about clothes or having a bit te spend on meself. Fuck it! That's why we end up working as mothers' helps. There's really nothing else. But there must be a way outa that. I promised meself that when them fuckers in the refectory laughed at me when I was washing up after them and sweeping the floor. I saw the picture again of them saying, 'We are all going to get good jobs when we finish our education. Unlike some, who will end up in the back of some restaurant, in the kitchen, pot walloping!' That fuck-face Hatchet-face, with the long stringy hair and beady eyes, threw her ugly mug over at me, squinting and sniffing and giving me the evil eye. It was her saying that started the rest of them off. So any time they wanted te get the better of me, they would chant that. That's when I clamped me mouth shut tight, saying te meself, never! Whatever I do, I will rise te the top by working hard, and one day you fuckers will be looking up te me, polishing me shoes. Fuck youse all and yer educations, I will educate meself.

After that, I started te teach meself te speak properly. The first thing people will judge ye with is their eyes, how ye look. Then hear exactly who and what ye are by the way ye speak. I have been listening te Ma Pius. They can laugh at the way she speaks, sounding very grand. But that suits me, and now they are laughing at the way I speak. Fuck them. I will always know more about the world and its ways than they will. They are going te have te learn the hard way, God help them. Are they in for a nasty shock!

I stooped down te pick up the bar of soap and scrubbing brush, putting them outa harm's way in case some aul nun slips and breaks her neck, and I'd have te limp through the rest of me life with the picture of her splattered on the ground dead as a dodo, and me only claim te fame was, 'Lookit! There goes yer woman tha kilt tha poor unfortunate nun! Yeah! Lookit the state a her! She looks haunted and hunted. They say she did it on purpose! And they only let her outa the lunatic asylum a year ago. She must be nearly hittin fifty if she's a day! And lookit all the hair growin on her chin! They must a been feedin her them hormones we hear about! Jaysus! Don't let her see ye lookin, she might come after us!'

I laughed out loud at the picture of it, just as the Reverend

Mother's head appeared around the banisters. 'Are you there, Martha?'

I picked up the bucket of dirty water, making me way up the lovely clean stairs, saying, 'Yes, Mother! I'm coming.' Jaysus, she'll think I'm queer in the head if she saw me laughing te meself. I stopped on the little landing next te the nuns' toilet and dropped the bucket, waiting te hear what she wanted.

'Listen! Would you ever go outside to the poor man's hut and tell those children to please leave the grounds.'

'Which children, Mother?'

'The two girls who came up earlier for the tea. They are rambling around the grounds and goodness knows what mischief they may get up to. Will you go straight away?' she said, looking at me watching me bucket.

'Right! Do you want me to empty this dirty water now, or shall I leave it here?' I said in me best Ma Pius voice.

'Oh, for goodness' sake, use your intelligence. Empty the bucket of course.' She rushed off shaking her head, not understanding how she manages te put up with someone as thick as me!

'Tut, tut,' I clucked under me breath. 'Yer yoke is a heavy one, Mother!' Ha! I got that one from reading all the religious books in the library! They ran outa decent ones, so I had te read something. 'Right, Mother! I'm just slopping out now,' I shouted. 'Then I shall fly to the hall door and tell those brats to move off!'

'What?' she said, coming back, sensing a note of cheek in my tone.

'I'm saying, Mother, I will get rid of this dirty water, then get rid of those bold brats.'

'Yes! That's what I said. So why are you repeating after me?'

'Sorry, Mother! I just wanted to be sure that's what ye meant.'

She went off slowly, trying te figure out if I really am thick as two short planks or just being downright cheeky! I dumped the water inta the toilet and rinsed it out, banging and slapping it against the toilet bowl and making an awful racket! I could hear her clucking outside the chapel and knew she was running her fingers around the edges of the skirting board and along the windowsills, te make sure I had dusted. I shot up the stairs, seeing her doing just that, and flew past on me way out the front door, shouting, 'I'm on me way out now, Mother, te get rid of them pests!'

'Come back here, you!' she screamed.

I came te a skidding halt and turned, making me way back inta the passage. 'Yes, Mother?'

'Look, what is all this nonsense you repeating yourself after me and shouting around the convent like this? Really!'

'Oh, sorry, Mother. If ye tell me . . . Oh, right! I understand now! Whatever ye say te me, I am te keep quiet and not repeat it!'

'Yes,' she said slowly, trying te figure me out. 'I don't know what has come over you these last couple of months. That accident must have caused more than just damage to your hand,' she said, dismissing me with a wave of her wrist.

Touché, Mother! Touché, as the French would say. Ye got me back on that one. Next round te me!

I flew out the door, seeing the same two young ones who had been throwing their eye at the cow, wanting te rob the milk, the last time they showed up here. They are about ten and sixteen years old now, I thought, watching them making for the nuns' private garden, where they hang out all their privates. Knickers and vests and stuff like that. Fuck! They are probably after the stuff on the line!

I slowed down, taking me time getting there. Let them have a few pairs of knickers; they can give them te their ma. They certainly wouldn't fit them! I strolled in, opening me Woodbine packet and pulled out a full cigarette. Pity I had te go back on these, I sighed, slipping the cigarette back inta the pocket of me work smock. 'Hello, girls. What are ye's up te?' I said, bouncing in and catching them swinging outa the knickers on the line. I knew that's just what they would be up te.

'Oh, hello, Miss! We weren't doin nothin wrong, were we, Biddy?'

'No! We was just havin a look,' the little one said, throwing her hair the colour of hay outa her eyes te get a better look at me.

I saw her pass the navy-blue knickers wrapped up in a ball behind her back, and the other one moved in close and shoved it under her coat. 'Come on. Let's go, girls. These nuns wouldn't think twice about calling the coppers if they catch ye robbing anything.'

'Wha? Honest te God, on me granny's grave would I tell ye a word of a lie!' she said, shoving the stuff further up under the coat and catching it under her arm.

I laughed. 'Are they a pair of nun's knickers ye have there, shoved under yer coat?' I pointed.

'Wha? No, Miss! Honest te God, we took nothin. Did we, Biddy?'

'No, honest te God! We didn't touch nothin,' lisped the little one.

'Nothin at all!' repeated the big one, her eyes staring outa her head, swearing her life away. 'But would ye have any aul clothes ye don't want?'

'Well, the only old clothes I have,' I said slowly, looking down at meself, 'I'm wearing them!'

'Oh!' she said, looking at me grey woollen skirt that had seen better days, then down at me brown shoes that someone had left behind in the 1950s. They probably looked lovely when they were in the fashion, but now the heels were bokety, going down on one side, making me walk as if I had bad hips. But that's all I could find in the shoe room. Anything good was gone before it hit the floor.

'Oh,' she said again, looking down the length of me and feeling sorry for me. 'Are ye an orphan, then? Are there many orphan childre livin in this place?' she said, looking around at the big buildings.

'Oh, a good number,' I said, looking at her feeling very sad at the thought of all the orphans locked up here.

'Tha's terrible,' she said. 'Innit, Biddy?'

'Yeah, terrible!' Biddy said, nodding her head up and down, looking like she was going te cry.

'An have ye no mammy an daddy?' the big one asked in a very sorrowful voice.

'Ah, I have a ma, all right. But listen, don't waste yer time worrying about the kids here; sure, they don't know they are born with the life they have. They are better fed than you!'

'Still and all,' she said, 'not havin a mammy and daddy, especially a mammy. I wouldn't want te be in their shoes. Would we, Biddy?'

'No, I wouldn't!' Biddy said, staring at me like I'm the most interesting thing she ever saw in her life. Every time I opened me mouth, she stared from me face then dropped her head down te me toes again, trying te get a good picture of what an orphan looks like.

'I'd go mad if anythin happened te me mammy, wouldn't we, Biddy?'

'Yeah, we'd go mad!'

'Right! We better get moving, before someone comes in and asks questions about why ye are in here.'

'Right so, Miss! Come on, Biddy, let's get moving.'

Then they took off, heading down the avenue, and I felt a sadness inside me. They remind me so much of meself not too long ago. I felt sorry for them, having te scratch around for something te eat, always on the lookout for trouble. The poor things felt sorry for me! They have more of a bit of humanity in their little finger than some of the nuns and kids in this place. They would rob the eyes outa yer head, but they would share their last crust of bread with ye.

Somehow, I take more te people like them than I do te the likes of the people living here, or most of the so-called respectable people. They may not have much, but they love their ma. So she must be good te them. And they are right. Having food in yer belly and a roof over yer head is not enough. I used te think that's all I needed te make me happy, and te get away from Jackser, of course. That still is the best thing that ever happened te me. But there are other things too. Like belonging te someone. I was very quick te say I had a ma. But I don't really, not in the way she thinks. Her ma probably has a bit more sense than mine ever did. I never felt like me ma's child. She was always looking for me te take care of her. So she never got te be me ma, and I never got te be her child; that was the way with me and the ma. Yeah! It was always me looking after her.

These days I want someone te look after me, make a fuss of me, love me. I never thought about that until I came here. It never occurred te me that there was such a thing. I never looked for it. I never even heard the word mentioned; there was no such thing. I suppose I had more important things te worry about, like trying te stay alive. It's true what they say. The more ye get the more ye want. I don't understand that. It's what stops us from being happy, I suppose.

I watched the girls hurrying off down the avenue. I suppose they must have thought of somewhere else they could go for a feed and hopefully get something te bring back te their ma and feed the other kids. God! Am I glad I am outa all that. Thank you, God for looking after me. I sure am lucky.

The air suddenly turned cooler and the sun had dipped in. I felt a drop of rain landing on me and looked up at the sky. Jaysus! It's turning pitch black. I heard Neddy the donkey roaring his head off in the distance. He's probably raging the two girls ignored him. Then there was an unmerciful clap of thunder. It boomed just over me head, and the sky suddenly fell apart without warning, dropping its heavy load of clouds, soaking me te the skin in seconds. Neddy screamed his head off, and the cows joined in the roaring, and it sounded like the end of the world. With the bleeding thunder drowning out the lot of them, making me feel God was having a party all for himself, playing bowls up in his heaven. Me eyes peeled over te the playing-fields toilet. Then whipping over te the back door. Which is quickest? Toilet! I need a smoke.

I had a quick look around. Nobody about. Good! I tore over and rushed inside, slipping the cigarette outa me pocket. I looked at it sitting in me hand as it collapsed inta a mess of soggy tobacco. Ah, fuck. What an awful waste. Water dropped from me head, landing on me nose, and sat there wobbling while I thought what te do about me smoke. I shook me head, seeing sparks of rainwater flying around me, and threw the tobacco down the toilet, flushing the chain in case Sister Eleanor comes across it, then opened me packet, checking how many I had left. Seven. The packet was damp and I gently took out one, trying te light a match. Fuck! They're damp, too. I managed te get it lighting after nearly wasting the whole box of matches, putting it close te the cigarette te dry it out, then lit up and sucked in a great gulp of hot burning tobacco, making me feel I was sitting next te God, happy as Larry.

Ah, this is the life, I shivered, looking out at the pouring rain and enjoying having the open air te meself, with not a soul in sight. Gawd! It's great having a smoke, and even better because it's not allowed. I better keep these hidden. If Sister Eleanor gets her hands on them, that will be the end of me smokes. And as for me! I won't hear the end of it for many a day te come. And she won't speak te me for a bloody month. Gawd! She's an awful woman for holding a grudge. And she sulks like mad. Sometimes I think she's very childish. Jaysus! Come te that, all them bleeding nuns are very childish in their own way. It comes of not having te worry about putting the bread on the table or worrying about having a roof over their heads. Everything is laid on for them. All they have te do is do what they are told and obey the rules. No! That's not for me. I don't like rules. I get a terrible urge te break them, just because ye're not supposed te do that. I have always been like that, even as a little kid. I suppose that's the childish side of me. I certainly don't take orders from anyone. Nope! So that gets me inta a lot of trouble.

I sighed happily, hopping up and down, enjoying me sense of freedom. Then held me breath, listening. The silence was deeper now. Jaysus! How long have I been out here? Ah, help, Mammy! They will kill me. They're probably looking for me right now, from one end of the convent te the other. Oohh! I better get back. I was whining and keening te meself, listening te me sobs rattling outa me chest as I ran. What will I say? Oooh, think of something quick in case they catch ye! Got it! I had te fly after them young ones who held up the nuns' knickers – no, undergarments – after whipping them off the line, and ran off with them saying we were not getting them back. I chased them, Mother, all the way te the village. But they hopped on the bus, and I had te walk all the way back in the rain, getting meself soaked!

Yeah! She thinks I'm thick anyway, so she should believe I'm capable of anything . . .

'Eh, then I stood for a few minutes outa the rain, Mother, under a tree and not getting much shelter, Mother! Look at the state of me, Mother! I'm soaked te the skin,' I said, holding out me smock and flicking me rats' tails up at her. 'Then I didn't realise the time passing,' I sniffed, looking up at her, making meself sound like I'm crying, and dripping wet all over me shiny polished chapel passage.

'You expect me to believe that?' she roared, steam coming outa her nose, her big goitre eyes going red with the rage. 'So while you have been gadding about, goodness knows where,' she snorted, flinging her veil back and stamping her foot, 'the phone has been hopping off the hook, and Mother Pius and I spent precious time searching for you! How dare you vanish and abandon your post?' she screamed, nearly spitting all over me, her face turning purple now, and sounding like she was going te explode. 'I expect in the next couple of months you will be coming to me looking for a reference. Well, madam, I shall certainly not be recommending you for any job if you do not pull your socks up and become more responsible. I most certainly could not recommend you to any employer with your present record. No!' she said, giving her neck an unmerciful jerk, the collar getting tighter as her eyes got redder, and her purple face turning black, then flinging her veil back with a flying flip of the back of her hand. I could see the knobby pin fly off the top of her head, sending the veil hanging te one side. 'Get out of my sight!' she snorted, wrestling the veil back in its place, and her mouth flew up and down with funny sounds coming out like she was trying te stop herself from cursing.

'Right, Mother,' I said, backing away from her.

'And Sister Eleanor will have something to say to you when she meets you. So do not dare leave your waiting room!' she screamed, losing the rag with the veil and me and the whole job of being a Reverend Mother.

Ah, yakety yak, Mother! Stick yer reference up yer arse. I'll make me own way without any help from you. So go and fuck yerself!

Oh hell, Sister Eleanor! I forgot about her. She only has te come near me and she'll know exactly what I was up te. She'll smell the smoke off me and launch herself inta a mad frenzy trying te find the cigarettes. She wouldn't even think twice of grabbing the knickers offa me, knowing where we hide our smokes. Oh, gawd. Where will I hide them? The chapel! They wouldn't think of looking in there. No! I wouldn't be able te get them back. There's always some aul nun in there day or night wearing their knees out praying. Fuck, think. I shot inta the linen room and hid them under the bottom sheet in the press. It will dry them out anyway. Then I wandered back up, gently opening the chapel door, seeing the Reverend Mother on her knees, praying for patience and understanding with poor aul me! Sniff! I could easily have been chasing after them kids te get the nuns' knickers back. How does she know I wasn't? Now I will have te listen te Sister Eleanor roaring and screaming and gnashing her teeth because I got her inta trouble with the Reverend Mother! Well, the two of us! Then she'll start beating her chest with her fist, vowing

she will never speak te me again and threatening me with blue
murder and not speaking te me for the next two months.

Hm! I had an idea. I crept up te the phone, in case Ma Pius
sprang outa her office, and leaned in, grabbing the telephone book.
Then crept past the chapel in an awful hurry, making straight for
me own private little room.

I closed the book shut, saying the telephone number te meself,
then crept past the chapel again, creeping and creaking along the
passage on me tiptoes in case Ma Pius caught me. Then landed
the phone book back in the little box and made me way te Ma
Pius's office. What will I say if she's there? Right! I'll ask her
if the Reverend Mother is around, because I have an important
matter te discuss with her.

If she asks, I'll tell her the same story about the knickers
and say I wanted te know if I should report the theft te Sister
Mary Innocent in the laundry. Yeah! Sounds mad. She'll lose her
patience with me, but I'll get away with it. I gave a little tap at
her office and listened. Not a sound. Then a harder tap just in
case. No! She's not there, good. I let out me breath and made
back in for the telephone and lifted the receiver and dialled the
number I memorised. Then waited, holding me breath.

'Gardai! Sergeant Michael Tom Tosh here.'

'Yesss!' I drawled out through me nose. 'This is Miss Lillybeth
Puckingham, spelled with a P. I live in Puckingham Manor,
directly across from the convent.'

'Yes, Miss Buckingham,' he said, smartening himself up and
giving a cough, all attention. 'How can I help you, madam? What
is the trouble?'

'The trouble?' I shrieked. 'Those dreadful nuns are leaving that
poor unfortunate donkey out in the middle of a field, allowing
it to face the awful weather we have been having . . . Goodness,
it has been awful, don't you think? I mean, do you think we will
be having a summer?'

'Well . . .' he said.

'Anyway!' I roared. 'To get back to the matter at hand. About that poor neglected donkey! It is simply frightful,' I gasped, 'listening to it crying night and day, all alone and getting soaking wet. It is simply pitiful. I want you to drop whatever you are doing – it can't be more important than that poor donkey's welfare – go up and speak to that dreadful Reverend Mother and tell her to take the donkey in for shelter at once!'

There was silence while he thought about this.

'Hello, Sergeant? Are you still there?' I screeched, sounding like Ma Pius when she's searching for me.

'Oh, oh, I am listening. Yes! I will get someone onto that straight away.'

'What? No, Sergeant! This is too important to leave to one of your subordinates.' I thought of that at the last minute. 'Please go up yourself at once! At once! Or I shall take this matter to my cousin, the President of Ireland! Mr De Valera himself!' I snorted. 'Do I make myself clear?'

'Oh, oh, yes! Very clear, Miss, eh, Buckingham.'

'Puckingham!' I screeched. 'Puckingham!'

'Yes, sorry about that. No, no! Don't you worry. I am on me way as soon as I put this phone down.'

'Excellent! I shall look forward to seeing results, then. Goodbye.' Then I slammed down the phone and beetled back te me little room, waiting for the door te ring.

I better say nothing or he might recognise me. I sat waiting and nothing happened. No sign of him, not even a phone call. I got up and started te mooch around the chapel passage, looking up at the bell, dying te ring it. No! But I will, just before I am ready te leave this place for good.

The doorbell rang just as Ma Pius came down the stairs. Me heart leapt with the shock, and Ma Pius stood on the passage, waiting te see who was at the door. I moved quickly past her, seeing her staring out, and opened the door.

'Hello!' roared a big aul fella wearing a copper's uniform and taking his hat off and lifting his big size-twenty boot and landing it on the hall mat. 'Is the Reverend Mother about?'

I dropped me head, making meself look dopey, and kept me mouth shut, muttering, 'Ye can folley me, sir!' showing him inta the little parlour, because the big one is only for priests and women in fur coats that arrive in big cars. I was just closing the door on him still talking te me when Ma Pius pushed past me, saying, 'What is this all about? Thank you, Martha. I will deal with this.'

I crept off on me tiptoes, then stopped te listen. Sister Benedict came swinging along in an awful hurry from the chapel passage and stopped in front of me, looking at the front door, and shouted outa breath, 'Was that a policeman I saw coming up the avenue?'

'Yes, Sister.'

'What did he want?'

'I don't know,' I mumbled, mooching closer te her, not wanting me voice te be recognised. 'Mother Pius is in the parlour with him,' I gasped, in a whisper.

'I hope that's not trouble he's bringing to the door,' roared Sister Benedict, looking at the parlour door, dying te know what was going on.

'Yes, Sister,' I muttered, taking meself off and rushing down te me little room.

I heard the chapel door open and someone came out, then Sister Benedict roaring, 'Reverend Mother! There is a policeman in the parlour, and Mother Pius is speaking to him right now. Do you think there is something wrong?'

I heard the Reverend Mother muttering in a whisper, then the rustle of rosary beads and habit as she flew inta the parlour. Jaysus! I'm dying te know what they're saying. Pity I can't make meself invisible. I'd love te go back up there and find out! But not on yer nelly, Martha. Sit here and mind yer own business! I might get te hear the gossip later. And Neddy might get something outa it, too.

CHAPTER 24

I know now what I want te do. I have been talking te some of the girls who know about the ones who went off te do children's nursing. They won't take me there because I have no education. Anyway, it is run by an order of nuns that is very strict. I don't fancy that. I couldn't bear the idea of having te live with nuns. No, definitely not! I want te get away from them. I have had enough of nuns te last me a lifetime.

I sucked on the biro, staring at the new sheet of writing paper Ma Pius gave me te write the letter te Clover House for Little Children. Matron Millington told me about it, saying there was no harm in writing: 'Sure, they might even give you a chance by considering ye! There's nothing gained by nothing ventured, Martha. So go on!' She nudged me with her elbow. 'Write to them; you'll find the address in the phone book. Anyway, they're not nuns! That place is run by the Protestants,' she whispered, nudging me with her elbow and looking around te see if anyone heard us.

'Right!' I said, dashing up te ask Ma Pius for a sheet of notepaper and the lend of a biro pen.

'Please do not lose that pen and bring it straight back as soon as you are finished with it,' she said, handing it te me and looking after it as if it was made of gold.

'Thank you, Sister, I will take great care of it,' I gushed, making off with me stuff, dying te get the letter written.

'Dear Sir or Madam, I am mad about kids' . . . Rubbish! Jaysus! What will I write? I never wrote a letter in me life!

Two hours later, I carefully put the sheet of paper in the envelope and licked it closed. I looked at what was left of Sister Ma Pius's notepad. Two sheets outa a nearly new pad! I had te keep running up and down te her asking for another sheet of writing paper, until she lost the rag and threw me the notepad. Me eyes flew over the wads of paper rolled up in a ball and scattered around the room. Jaysus! It's not easy writing a letter. But I got it done. Now all I have te do is post it and hope I hear back from them.

I picked up all the rubbish on the floor and headed off te Ma Pius with what was left of her notepad and looked at the pen. Fuck! The end of it was chewed down te nothing! She'll go mad. 'These pens cost one shilling and sixpence!' she'll probably roar. Or whatever they cost! Ah, take it outa me five-shillings-a-week wages, I'm going te tell her. That will shut her up! No! On the other hand, she's not getting a penny of my money. Let her have her moan; I can always think of something else te entertain me while she drones away.

Yakety yak! . . . 'And you have no sense of responsibility!'

'No, Mother Pius.'

'What? You agree with me?'

'Eh . . . no! Yes!' I tried te wake meself outa the doze.

'And you expect me to use this?' she said, holding up the half-chewed pen, looking at it.

'Yes, Mother Pius,' I droned, still miles away, picturing meself in a white nurse's uniform, with loads of little children hanging outa me.

'SO WHAT AM I SUPPOSED TO DO WITH IT?' she roared, waking me up.

'Oh, eh . . .' I said, shaking me head, clearing me eyes, looking at it. 'Oh, I will buy ye a new one,' I heard meself say.

'You do that,' she sniffed, satisfied! Then slammed her office door on me face.

Damn! Ye should have kept wide awake! What did ye go and say that for? I moaned, seeing meself being handed a few coppers for me wages this week, and Ma Pius telling me she took what was due te her and that's what's left outa it.

Oooh, how stupid can ye get? I thought, wanting te give meself a good kick up the arse as I headed off down te get me tea. Ye really are a silly bloody cow, Martha Long. Ah, fuck! Maybe she will forget. Yep! That's what I will do: I'll say nothing if she doesn't mention it.

This is definitely turning out te be a bad week for me. Yesterday I lost nine whole cigarettes te Sister Eleanor. Nearly a new packet! Jaysus! That was very unlucky. There I was, strolling arm in arm with Dilly Nugent, the pair of us after having a lovely smoke out in the playing-fields toilet, when Sister Eleanor comes flying outa nowhere, making straight for us. I only had time te hold me breath when she pounced like a cat, grabbing the box of cigarettes outa me pocket. I watched them fly through the air then vanish under her cloak, as she said, 'I am going to confiscate these,' giving me a vicious look of victory as she watched me eyes hang outa me head and me face drop in rage. She was gone before I could scream at her, telling her what I thought of her. Fuck. Now I will have te find a way of sneaking out after tea te get meself another packet down in the village.

The bell was ringing for the angelus as I passed the kitchen. Sister Mercy and Loretta were blessing themself as I stopped outside the door, sticking me tongue out at her and crossing me eyes, waving me shoulders around because she was stuffing herself with our sausages outa our pie dish. Loretta picked up two more sausages and stuck one in each nostril, letting them hang outa her nose, then crossed her eyes, shaking her face at me. Yuk! I stared in at her in disgust, while Mercy stood with her eyes closed, moaning out the prayers.

'Ah, Jaysus, look what she's doing now,' I muttered, watching her lick the sausages then drop them back, making a face at me.

I moved off, giving her a dirty look, seeing her face crack in a malicious grin, delighted with herself she had turned me off me tea. Fuck! I'm not eating them, I thought, rushing on, intending te get the ones at the bottom of the dish.

'Now and at the hour of our death, Amen,' Sister Eleanor cried, sounding like she was there already, giving us a mournful look because we were already dragging our chairs out te sit ourselves down.

'IN THE NAME OF THE FATHER,' she shouted, glaring at us te stand up again. 'And of the Son, and of the Holy Spirit, Amen. Really, girls,' she moaned, twisting her face and the rest of her, saying, 'You have no respect for our Lord. It would only cost you a few minutes of your time. Would you not even give our Lord God Almighty that little?'

She waited. No one was listening. Everyone was watching the pie dish flying in the door with Loretta slamming it down on the table. Sister Eleanor pounced on it before the sausages vanished. She flew around the tables, giving everyone two each, lifting them out with a fork, saying, 'They look lovely, girls, enjoy your tea now.'

I muttered, 'Give me the two at the bottom, Sister!' as she took the ones from the top. 'No! I want them from the bottom, Sister!'

'Ah, will you go on out of that for yourself,' she roared, flying off with the dish.

'No, please!' I said, going after her.

'Oh, go on, then. You would crucify Jesus on the cross,' she snorted.

Loretta marched over te her table, cackling at me, whispering, 'I think I have rabies!'

'Fuck off, Loretta.'

Sister Eleanor heard me and whipped her head around, looking shocked at the two of us.

'Tut, tut,' said Loretta, 'you need to mind your language, Long,' then sat herself down, laughing her head over at me.

'Fucking cow. I'm going te get ye back for this!' I mouthed at her behind Eleanor's back.

'Now! I have an announcement to make,' shouted Sister Eleanor, standing in the middle of the refectory while we all shovelled down the bread and sausages. Nobody was listening, so she clapped her hands and shouted, 'Please pay attention, girls. This is very important. Reverend Mother has decided to give you all a present!'

A present! Everyone whipped their heads around, giving her their full attention.

'Yeah, Sister! Go on, we are all listening, tell us!' everyone shouted up at her while she stood still, waiting for us te shut up.

'The Reverend Mother went personally into Clerys store on O'Connell Street and ordered especially for each and every one of you a new set of dishes. They are now sitting in front of you.' We all looked at our new cups and plates, not really noticing them until she opened her mouth.

'Is that it?' we moaned.

'Yes! You all have a set each, because Mother has decided you are all old enough now to take care of them. You don't need to be eating off plastic.'

'Ah, goney! I thought we were going to get something good!' people complained up at her.

'Now! When you are washing them,' she continued on with her sermon, taking no notice of the moaners, 'you must take great care not to break any. Then they will be carefully stacked on this table.'

'Oooh, they're awful looking! Green! Could she not have picked a nicer colour?' people were saying.

'She probably got them cheap,' someone whispered.

'Please pay attention,' Sister Eleanor roared, clapping her hands. 'If any one of you dare break a dish, you will have me to reckon with!' she shouted, getting red in the face at the ingratitude of the lot of us. 'Do you all hear me?' she roared. 'I do not want to hear you have broken any of these dishes,' she warned, pointing her finger at all our dishes. Then she was gone. Flying out the door over te the convent.

I raced back up the avenue, hiding the new ten-packet of cigarettes in the band of me skirt. I stopped at the tree, just before dipping across and running along the hedge, then got down on me hands and knees, crawling under the nuns' refectory, listening te them chattering and munching away on their tea. I held me breath, waiting for any sign of footsteps, or some aul nun breathing out the window, getting a look at me crawling underneath. Then I took off again, crawling like mad now past the convent kitchen window and up on me feet running in the side door. Made it! I flew through the door and up the kitchen passage, making for the back door and out for me smoke.

Ah, happiness is in a Woodbine! I thought, taking a deep puff of tobacco inta me lungs.

'Caught you!' screamed a young one from the middle group coming outa the toilet.

'Aaah!' I screamed, throwing the cigarette inta the air with the fright I got. 'Jaysus! Don't do that, ye little runt! Ye nearly sent me inta an early grave!' I roared, jumping on me cigarette and taking a deep puff.

'I'm telling Sister Eleanor on you,' she shouted, running off and daring me.

'Wait until I get ye!' I roared, knowing she would tell.

'Ha, ha! You can't catch me.'

'No! Come back, I want te talk te ye,' I shouted, pulled between getting me hands on her and smoking what's left of me cigarette.

'If you can catch me, I won't tell,' she shouted, hopping up and down from one leg te the other.

'Right! Ye're on,' I shouted. 'Give me a minute te finish this.'

I threw the butt down the toilet, flushing it, and took off after her. She tore in through the back door, her slinky blonde hair flapping around her head, and her legs going like propellers. She weaved in and out, flying from one side of the wide passage te the other. Then took off inta our refectory.

'Got ye!' I said, closing the door behind me and stalking her like a snake.

'No chance,' she laughed, making for the long table with the new dishes stacked. I raced around the table and she appeared on the other side, grinning and watching me like a hawk, her hands gripping the edge of the table, hopping from one foot te the other. I watched her, rocking me body left and right, judging which way she would run. I went right, she went right, me reaching me hand out te grab her and catching the sleeve of me jumper in the stacked cups, then we both stopped dead at the sound of china crashing te the ground.

'Ohhhh! You broke a cup!' said Gail, as we both stood staring down at the shattered cup sitting on the floor.

'Oh my God! Listen, say nothing,' I said, grabbing the dustpan and handbrush, sweeping the lot up and flying out te the bin with it.

She followed me out saying, 'What are we going to do? You broke the cup.'

'Yes, I did. And you were in our refectory; that is strictly outa bounds. Ye know we can't go inta each other's groups.'

'Yeah, I know,' she said, her eyes staring outa her head in fright, the colour gone from her face.

'It's best we say nothing. Are we agreed?'

'Yeah,' she said, shaking her head up and down, only too delighted te forget about it.

'Sister, there's one cup missing! I have no cup!'

'What?' Sister Eleanor roared, her mouth all swollen after just arriving back from the dentist. 'Count them!' she roared, going around the table counting every one of them.

Uh oh! Here we go! Me heart was pounding at the thought

of what she was going te do te me when she finds out one of her cups is broken and we only had them a day.

'No! It is definitely missing,' she nearly cried, looking mystified around at the lot of us, trying te pin down the culprit. 'I am going to get to the end of this!' she fumed, snorting her way out the door on her way over te the convent. 'I will be back and I intend to search this house from top to bottom until I get to the end of this.'

I watched her go, knowing she meant every word of it. She never lets anything go. Oh, bloody hell! What do I do now? I am definitely not owning up. I would never hear the end of it. I only hope Gail keeps her mouth shut.

'Oh gawd! I would hate to be in the shoes of whoever broke that cup!'

'Yeah, Sister Eleanor will kill them.'

'Imagine breaking Sister Eleanor's new china when she just got it,' gossiped the three eejits washing up at the sink, shivering with the excitement of knowing someone was going te be in big trouble and it wasn't them.

I whipped meself outa the refectory and tore out te the playing-fields toilet for a smoke. Before I went up in smoke meself, when Sister Eleanor finds out it was me.

I was making me way back when Sister Eleanor came tearing out the back door with a load of helpers looking for the missing evidence. 'Come with me, Martha,' she snorted, 'I am determined to find this missing cup. I know it's broken and someone has hidden it.'

'Right, Sister,' I said, not believing my bad misfortune at getting roped in te help her te find the culprit. Me! Meself!

She looked under the hedge in the nuns' private garden, ignoring the knickers hanging on the line. 'Come on,' she said te us, taking off on her mission again, her eyes swinging in all directions, looking te see the most likely spot for hiding a broken cup.

We shot back in the door again, and the others took off

shouting, 'We have to run, Sister! *The Virginian* is starting.' That just left her and me. She flew past the dustbin, not thinking someone would be stupid enough te hide it in the obvious place, then stopped suddenly, as I was letting me breath out with relief, and stooped down, whipping off the dustbin lid and rooting around, coming up with the broken remains of the cup. She held it in her hand for a minute, staring at it, not believing her eyes. 'Now!' she said, still bending over the dustbin. 'Now!' she said, shaking the evidence at me, her eyes glittering with the victory of winning half of the battle. 'Would you credit that? Broken! In the dustbin!'

'Tut, tut, shocking,' I said, shaking me head in disbelief.

'Right! Come with me. I will not rest until the culprit is caught.' Then she whipped herself off down te the television room and raced in the door, flying up te the stage and switching off the battered old television while a hundred pair of eyes all gaped up at her in terrible shock.

I made a run for it, straight back down the passage, hearing a voice scream after me, 'Come back here, you! I want to talk to you.'

I looked back, seeing Gail standing with her hands on her hips staring, her eyes blazing down at me and her mouth shut so tight it was tipping her nose.

Ah, damn! Bloody hell! I came up slowly, hearing her say, 'You have to admit it was you! We are all being punished over what you did.'

I could hear the screams in the television room, as Sister Eleanor tried te shout over them that there would be no television until the person who broke this cup was caught.

'Tell! Own up, or I will,' she said, gritting her teeth.

'OK,' I said. 'It's gone too far. Now everyone is involved.'

She ran back inta the room, roaring, 'Sister Eleanor! Martha Long has something to tell you.'

'What is it?' said Sister Eleanor flying past me, muttering te herself, 'I am going to get to the end of this!'

'Sister!'

She ignored me, flying inta our sitting room te switch off the radio on our group.

'Sister!' I roared, racing after her.

'What? What is it?' she said, looking distracted.

'It was me that broke the cup.'

'I am going to switch . . . WHAT? . . . What did you say?'

'Sorry, Sister,' I said, feeling foolish. 'It was me that broke yer cup and put it in the dustbin.'

She let the door go shut, coming slowly over te me with her eyes hanging down te her belly button and her mouth dropped open in shock. 'But . . . But! How can that be? You were helping me to look for the . . . I don't believe it!'

'Yes, it was me,' I said, examining me brown shoes with holes nearly appearing in the toes.

'I am shocked,' she whispered, looking around her, shaking her head, not understanding how someone could be so deceitful. Then she took off, leaving me standing there, wishing she had thrown the lot at me. Or at least shouted the head off me. But this . . . I knew I had forfeited something precious. Her trust. I felt very cowardly and don't like the feeling at all. It wasn't worth it. I had given away a very important, precious bit of meself, and for nothing. No! I won't put meself in that position again. It's more important te be able te hold my head up high. That's what really matters in the long run. Never again. My word will be my bond.

CHAPTER 25

'Happy Birthday to you! Happy Birthday to you! Happy birthday, dear Martha! Happy birthday to you. Three Cheers! Hip hip hurrah!'

'Now, Martha,' Sister Eleanor smiled, bending down te give me her present. 'You are sixteen today,' she said, putting her hand on me shoulder.

'Yeah, thanks, Sister,' I smiled, feeling shy and delighted with all fuss. I looked up at her, saying, Thank you for the present,' as I opened it slowly, with everyone shouting, 'Hurry up! Open it. We want to see what you got.'

'A book! That's not much of a present,' some of them whined, snorting with disappointment.

'*Great Expectations* by Charles Dickens. Oh, lovely, Sister,' I said, delighted.

'Ah, ye can't be serious?' cried Dilly Nugent, leaning over me shoulder.

'What's wrong with that?' screeched Sister Eleanor.

'A book!' they all moaned.

'Take no notice of them, Sister,' I laughed. 'It's just what I wanted.'

'Yeah, she would, what a gom!'

'Stop this behaviour at once! Or you won't get any of these sweets I brought you,' sniffed Sister Eleanor, holding on tight te the tin of sweets, cradling them under her arms like a newborn baby.

'Ah, we didn't mean it, Sister. Go on. Don't mind them,' roared Dilly Nugent, throwing her arms around the refectory, taking in the lot of them.

'Look who's talking!' shouted people standing behind me and roaring inta me ear.

'Open your other present,' shouted Loretta, lifting up me present all gift-wrapped in fancy paper.

'Give that back!' I roared, taking it off her.

'Yeah, keep your maulers off!' roared Dilly, putting her hand on me shoulder and whispering, 'Hurry! Open it up and let's all see what you got. Is that the one you got from Ma Pius?'

'Yeah!' I said, hearing Sister Eleanor roar in me other ear, 'Mother Pius! Don't dare call her that. She is your superior!'

'Yeah, yeah! Open up the present, because we are all going to go mental with the waiting.'

I took off the lovely red ribbon slowly, dying te know what she bought me, not believing this was happening te me. Me day had come at last! I'm now free te go where I like! I am going te be leaving here any day now. God! What a thought.

'Go on! Blow out the candle and make a wish!' shouted Sister Mercy, wanting me te taste the lovely cake she baked for me. I stared at it. A queen cake with a cherry on top and one candle. I laughed, knowing it was the thought that counts. She would have te make a huge cake if it was going te be shared with the whole group. I blew out the candle and paused for a second. God! Help me on me way and keep me ma and the children from all harm. And look after Charlie. That's all I ask. Then me eyes lit on the present, and I opened it, taking out a beautiful white frilly babydoll slip and matching knickers.

'Oooooh! They're gorgeous!' everyone gasped, while Dilly grabbed them, holding them up in the air te get a better look.

'Gawd! You would never know she would think of buying something as lovely as that,' whispered the girls.

'Thanks, Dilly,' I said, taking it off her and feeling the softness and looking at how lovely it was. I never saw anything as beautiful as these, never mind owned them. I quickly wrapped them back in the lovely wrapping paper te keep them safe, and everyone started shouting, 'Come on, Sister Eleanor! Give us out the sweets.'

'You are not getting them all!' she said, carefully counting out four sweets for each person.

'Ah, gawd! How mean can ye get?' the moans went up.

'Well, if you are not happy . . .' cried Sister Eleanor, upset because her generosity was not being appreciated. 'I will put them back in the box, and you can go without any.'

'Martha, I am going to take you into town and buy you your going-away clothes,' panted the Reverend Mother, watching my face flash from delight at the mention of buying clothes te shock at the mention of her taking me! Ah, hell! I thought, wondering if that was good or bad.

'We will go into that new shop they have opened in Clerys. It is a shop especially for teenagers,' she beamed, getting all excited and staring at me, waiting for my reaction. Teenagers! A shop special for them. That's me! They are now calling people like us teenagers! That's a new word.

'Yes!' she said, seeing me trying te work it out. 'It's called a boutique! Wouldn't you like that?' she said, all delighted and excited.

'Oh, yes! I would love that Mother!' I said, shaking me head up and down, the excitement beginning te hit me.

'We will go in on Saturday, wouldn't that be very nice?'

'Oh, yes!' I puffed, getting outa breath, never hearing the like of it in me life.

'That's settled, then,' she said, waving her veil back on her shoulder and taking off quite happy with herself.

I flew down te me little room and danced up and down, me heart racing, not believing what she just said.

'AAHHH! A BOUTIQUE! Oh, you are really lucky! We got nothing like that when we turned sixteen,' screamed Dilly Nugent and her gang, listening te me as I was telling Loretta.

'Yeah, I heard about it. It's called The Rave. And it's only for teenagers. The aul ones can't go in. Listen, Martha! When you get there, grab the first thing that takes your eye. Don't let the Reverend Mother pick your clothes for you!' panted Dilly, breathing inta me face, looking shocked at the thought I might be done outa something good.

'Yeah!' everyone shouted. 'Grab the first thing and hang on to it. Make her buy it and don't listen to what she says. Yeah!' everyone was shouting, and me head was spinning trying te take in what everyone was saying. They all wanted te give me advice and get their tuppence ha'penny worth in.

'Right!' I shook me head. 'I'll pick me own stuff,' I said, thinking it was a good idea.

'It's best to be prepared. Otherwise you might end up getting nothing!' Dilly shouted, knowing all about these things.

Yeah, ye could be right, I thought. Nothing's ever that easy. There might be a catch!

'Yeah!' they agreed, satisfied they had taken the smile off me face, bringing me down te earth. But they are right all the same. It doesn't do te get yer hopes up.

We stepped off the bus on O'Connell Street and walked miles up te the traffic lights at the Nelson's Pillar and waited for the lights te change. I would have been across the road now and in the shop if I had been on me own. But I stood next te the Reverend Mother, standing in her long coat habit that buttoned from her black boots up te her chin, and waited patiently te cross the road, while people stood back, giving us plenty of space, outa respect for the holy nun.

'Come along, now,' she said, holding on te her leather bag with the money in it, I hoped! Or maybe she will put it on their account. Ma Pius says they have an account there. I'm feeling hot and bothered with all the excitement and the waiting, and now we just stepped inta the shop. Me eyes flew around the store, not seeing anything but shapes, I was that worn out.

'Come along,' she said, following some sign up above she spotted and I didn't.

We arrived on the next floor and headed over te a little area carpeted off with flashing different-coloured balls and lights and racks holding lines of bright clothes in every colour under the sun. I was blinded for a minute, making after her, trying te feast me eyes on one thing.

'What do you think?' she said, holding up a long black maxi coat, something like the one she was wearing.

'Eh . . .' Me head flew around the racks, getting dizzy from the balls changing colour, and suddenly me eyes rested on a rack of coats. I made straight for them, lifting up the first one I laid hands on.

Oooh, it's a Bonnie and Clyde coat! A trench coat in an off-white colour, with a wraparound belt and a split at the back, and duffel buttons, with wide lapels, and . . . Oh my gawd! I always wanted something like this. Even the spies used te wear them. The men went mad after the women wearing one of these in the fillums.

I whipped off me aul green one, letting it fall on the carpet, and tried it on. 'What do ye think, Mother?' I said, straightening meself up and fastening the belt.

'It's a bit tight,' she said, not looking very impressed.

I looked at the sleeves; they are a bit short for me all right. But . . .

'Would you not like to try something else?' she asked me, looking around.

'No, no!' I said, grabbing the coat off me and wrapping it tightly around me arm. 'I'll take this,' I said, me stomach lurching with nerves in case she wouldn't buy it. I really, desperately, wanted this coat. I have dreamed about wearing something like this. All them spy films . . . and especially Bonnie and Clyde! Oh, God! Make sure she buys it for me.

'Are you sure?' she said, seeing me carry the coat wrapped tightly around me arm.

'Oh, yes, Mother! This is fine.'

'Would you not try on a bigger size?'

I didn't hear her. All I could hear was, 'Hang on to the coat! Hang on to the coat for dear life. Let that down and you won't see the like of it again!'

'It's grand, Mother,' I smiled, feeling weak from the agony of it all.

'Right! Let us find you a dress,' she said, not looking too sure. Then lifting her head te swing around the boutique with all the flashing colours and lights. We walked on, sinking down inta the deep carpet, with the lights swimming around and around, throwing different-coloured shapes on te the carpet and around the walls, making me eyes cross and me head spin, taking in too much and not seeing anything at all.

We made our way over te the rack of dresses, and me eye lit on a red one with a snow-white linen collar. I grabbed it, holding it up against meself. 'This is the one I want, Mother!' I gasped, nearly suffocating from the shock of it all, not really understanding what is happening te me.

'Are you sure?' she said, looking down at me and creasing her eyebrows, her eyes staring outa her head, wondering how I could know what I wanted in such a flash.

'Oh, yes! It's really lovely,' I panted.

'But what size is it? What size are you?'

I didn't know! 'Oh, it's my size, Mother,' I said holding it against me again and looking down, seeing it just above me knees. Not too short, I thought, hoping she wouldn't make me get something longer. It would hang down under the coat! Gawd! No! I'm not having that. 'It fits me perfectly,' I said, seeing her staring, looking from the size of me te the size of the frock.

'OK! If that's what you want,' she sighed, giving in. 'Come now and we'll find you a nice pair of shoes.'

Oh, this is too much, I thought, me heart lepping in me chest, wondering if something is going te go wrong and I'll end up with having te put the lot of the stuff back. We made for the shoe rack, me following behind. She was always one step ahead of me, because I couldn't see properly, with me head swimming around at all the stuff.

'Now! What do you think of these?' she said, picking up a pair of black walking shoes with laces. I flicked me eyes over them, not giving them the time of day, grabbing up instead a shiny black patent pair with wedge heels and tried them on.

'They fit me perfectly,' I said, throwing out me foot for the two of us te get a good look.

'Hm! They are nice,' she said, smiling for the first time.

'Do ye like them, Mother?' I said, getting very excited.

'Yes! They look lovely on you,' she said. 'Right! I think we have everything,' she said, her eyes sweeping around the floor.

'Eh, what about me hat, Mother?'

'Hat? Oh, no! You won't be needing a hat,' she laughed. 'Sure, people don't wear hats any more.'

'Yes they do! Everyone wears a hat now. Look!' I showed her the hats sitting on racks on the wall. 'Caps, Mother!'

'Oh, they are nonsense. Sure, you surely wouldn't wear something like that!' she laughed. 'They are like something our farmer would wear,' she said, 'only they are in different colours. They are only old caps, like something a man would wear,' she said, laughing, staring at me then looking back at them.

'You are right, Mother. I wouldn't wear one of them. What I want is a Bonnie and Clyde hat.'

'A what?' she said, her mouth dropping open, trying te figure out what that was.

'Like this one!' I said, grabbing a black soft-wool French beret off the wall and slapping it on me head and pulling it down one side and over me right eye. 'It will go with my coat,' I said, rushing over te get a look in the mirror. 'Ooooh! It looks smashing on me,' I gasped, seeing Marlene Dietrich standing under her lamppost, singing with her, 'Oh! I ham sooo beauti ful. Kum! And grov el at my feet, you sil ley, boys,' voice on her, staring out at ye with her smouldering eyes, driving all the fellas mad. Well, I'm not there yet! But . . . I stared at me hat sitting on top of me coppery shoulder-length hair resting on me shoulders, and leaned in closer te get a better look at me grey eyes dancing outa me white face, and gave meself a huge smile, admiring me snow-white teeth. Yeah! I need te work on smouldering me eyes, then I'll be any man's fancy when I start wearing me new rig-out! Me heart gave a leap, thinking of all me new style. Gawd! I am definitely going te look like something that stepped outa the fillums. Ooooh! Wait until the others see me in my new get-up. They are going te be sick as a dog. Raging with the look of me! I can't wait te get back and show off everything.

I raced back te the Reverend Mother, who was staring at a pair of bell-bottom trousers in purple velvet. 'Goodness! Who would wear those?' she said. 'They look like something Groucho Marx would wear.'

'Yeah! They're awful,' I said, looking at them in disgust.

A young one pushed past and grabbed up a pair, screaming, 'Ohhh, look! Mammeeee! These are the ones I was telling you about! And look, they will go with this hat,' she squealed, grabbing a big felt hat and plopping it on her head, smothering her face.

'It looks like a sombrero!' the ma wailed. 'Like one a them Mexicans wear!'

'Yeah, Mammy! But it's all the fashion now!'

The Reverend Mother stared from one te the other, looking confused at the taste of the young one, and watching the mammy's face te see what she thought. The mammy raised her eyes te heaven and looked at the Reverend Mother, who gave a squeal of laughing outa her and pushed me on te get me moving, saying, 'Thank goodness we have that out of the way. Now! Where do we pay for them?' she said, still laughing.

I couldn't believe me eyes. She's laughing! I never remember ever seeing her laughing until yesterday, and that was not screaming laughing like she is now. We left the shop with me carrying a big brown carrier bag with two handles on it, and the

Reverend Mother carried a big blue stripy suitcase, specially for me when I'm leaving the convent.

'Martha! I received a phone call from the children's home where you applied for training. They have agreed to accept you. They will be expecting you to begin your training next Saturday. So you will be leaving us in two days. You will need a reference. Here is one I have written out for you. Always keep this for yourself. Do not hand it over to anybody. Make copies and give them one.'

'Yes, Mother! Thank you very much,' I said, taking the letter from her, listening te her say, 'I wish you all the very best, Martha. I know you will do well in whatever you choose to do.'

'Thank you, Mother!' I said, seeing her look like she wanted te cry. God! She must have liked me after all, I thought, feeling very sorry for all the terrible things I used te think about her. Funny! She never showed it.

I stood in me new frock and black patent shoes with new tights, and wearing me new trench coat. The Reverend Mother was right. I could have got a size bigger, I thought, looking at the sleeves. There would have been more room inside; this just fits me. Still, I look grand in it. And with me new Bonny and Clyde hat, I'm really up in the fashion.

'Now!' Sister Eleanor said, handing me a little holy picture with 'In memory of this day' and the day and month and year of me leaving inscribed on it. I don't need te be reminded. I will never forget this day. 'Goodbye, now! Be a good girl and keep out of trouble,' said Sister Eleanor, waving me off.

'Yes, Sister Eleanor,' I smiled, picking up me suitcase.

'Work hard! And keep practising your diction,' roared Mother Pius.

'Yes, Mother Pius.'

'Oh, so now she's off!' said the Reverend Mother, giving me a present of a pair of mother-of-pearl rosary beads wrapped in cotton wool in a white box. 'Don't forget to say your prayers,' she whispered.

'Yes, Mother,' I whispered, taking the box and putting it in me new handbag that Ma Pius gave me.

'Goodbye, Martha! You look after yourself,' whispered Matron Mona, grabbing both me hands and giving them a squeeze. 'It will not be the same without you,' she said, turning her back and walking off.

'Thanks, Matron Millington,' I said, staring after her, picking up me suitcase and heading out the door. She turned around and gave me a wave, then vanished back inta the convent. I won't forget you, Matron, I thought, waving at her back.

'Goodbye. Safe journey now!'

'Bye! And thank you all for everything,' I smiled, feeling sad and excited at the same time.

The door closed and I stood on the top step hearing shouting. I gave a look over te the playing fields. Some of the girls were over there and jumped up and down, giving me waves and shouting, 'Good luck, Martha! Have a great life!'

I gave a wave back, then stared for a second, looking at the paths shrouded in trees, seeing meself flying down the Cloistered Walk with the little gong in me hand, hurrying te catch up with the nuns walking in pairs, getting their prayers. Telling them outa breath, 'You are wanted on the telephone.' I seemed so young then. Fourteen! Now I am sixteen, all grown up and ready te face the world. I walked down the steps and took off heading down the avenue, then stopped at the gates for one long last look back at me childhood.

'Goodbye, Ma. Goodbye, Sisters, ye weren't the worst,' I whispered, tears streaming down me face. It wasn't so bad after all. Lonely! Yes, it was very lonely. I learned ye can have a full belly but yer heart can be very empty. The hunger te have a kind word or a gentle smile, or someone te put their arms around ye, can be far worse than an aching empty belly. But nothing so bad as what I was escaping from with Jackser. May ye die roaring, Jackser! For all yer badness. I knew that even when I first came through the gates with what seems now a lifetime ago. Remembering the first time, all of us sitting in the Black Maria and listening as it slowed down. Me heart nearly stopping with the fright, wondering what was happening. It was those gates we came through. I didn't know then what was waiting for me. I felt a life sentence ahead of me. I was frightened te death, not knowing what was going te happen, but wishing for this day te come. When I could walk out a free young woman and nobody could hold any control over me.

Well, here I am, and whatever happens from now on will be of my own making. This is the start of my very own life. I have waited sixteen years for this moment. Goodbye, childhood! It was a long aul hard struggle. Ye were never a child anyway. Ye just had te wait until the world gave ye permission te do what ye always did: run in the world on yer own, hunting and helping yerself and others te survive, especially the little ones. Now it's just you te take care of. The grown-up Martha.

If I ever want te meet ye again, little one, well, I only have te walk through these gates, and here ye'll be. Playing and fighting, laughing and crying, haunting and hunting, desperately hoping for love. Keeping the eyes peeled for Sister Eleanor. Trying desperately te find a little spot in this place where ye'll fit in, belong. Always hoping against hope someone would magically wrap their arms around ye, filling that empty cold feeling inside ye. Wanting te feel the warmth of a mother's arms wrapped around ye, smothering ye with her kisses and telling ye everything will be all right. She'll take care of ye. Oh, gawd almighty, ye craved that feeling of being safe and warm and loved, wiping away the years of pain and loneliness, that numbing sense of knowing no one wants ye. Ye have te buy their interest. Ye belong nowhere, te nobody. That pain! I could feel it now, clawing its way up te push out the happiness of leaving everything behind. God! I don't think it will ever leave me. Ye pinned all yer hopes on Sister Eleanor. That was a waste of tears and energy. She could never have done anything for ye. Anyway, the queue was too long and ye ran outa time. Ye were too late! She only gave love te the little ones. The babies. Pity it took me so long te work that out. I might have saved meself a lot more pain.

I picked up me suitcase and turned me back, walking off hearing the voice of the little Martha's ghost grow fainter with every step I took, taking me further away from her cries, and lifted my face inta the sharp October wind, letting it dry and ease the sores of that little one's wounds and carry her away te rest in some dark forgotten place where only I will know she ever existed. Even then, I must now pretend she never was. This is the only way I can live. I stared inta the distance, closing my eyes for a brief second, feeling a part of me close down. Then lifted my head hurrying off ready te face inta the unknown.